S0-BCT-704

Biology of Human Aging

Biology of Human Aging

Alexander P. Spence

SUNY College at Cortland

PRENTICE HALL ENGLEWOOD CLIFFS N.J. 07632

Library of Congress Cataloging-in-Publication Data

Spence, Alexander P., 1929-
  Biology of human aging.

  Includes bibliographies and index.
  1. Aging—Physiological aspects.   I. Title.
[DNLM: 1. Aging—physiology.   WT 104 S744b]
QP86.S64 1989   612'.67   88-15147

Cover design: Lundgren Graphics, Ltd.
Manufacturing buyer: Paula Massanero

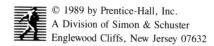 © 1989 by Prentice-Hall, Inc.
A Division of Simon & Schuster
Englewood Cliffs, New Jersey 07632

All rights reserved. No part of this book may be
reproduced, in any form or by any means,
without permission in writing from the publisher.

Printed in the United States of America

10 9 8 7 6 5 4 3 2

ISBN 0-13-079823-1
ISBN 0-13-080185-2 PBK

Prentice-Hall International (UK) Limited, London
Prentice-Hall of Australia Pty. Limited, Sydney
Prentice-Hall Canada Inc., Toronto
Prentice-Hall Hispanoamericana, S.A., Mexico
Prentice-Hall of India Private Limited, New Delhi
Prentice-Hall of Japan, Inc., Tokyo
Simon & Schuster Asia Pte. Ltd., Singapore
Editora Prentice-Hall do Brasil, Ltda., Rio de Janeiro

To my mother, Mildred Spence,
and my mother-in-law,
Charlotte Torrance, who serve
as examples of how
to grow old gracefully.

Contents

CONTENTS

Preface

Robert Browning presented an eloquent and upbeat view of aging when he said, "Grow old along with me! The best is yet to be, the last of life for which the first was made." This optimistic view seems to me indicative of the changing concept of aging that has slowly developed over the years. No longer is aging necessarily a stage of life to be dreaded. As a result of better medical care, improved diets, and more emphasis on continuing exercise, not only are more people living longer, they are enjoying better health than previous generations. Consequently, today's elderly are more active and provide more positive and forceful images in the final stage of their lives than did their parents.

Because of a growing population of persons over 65 years of age the care of the elderly has become a national priority, and gerontology a major field. There are many aspects of aging that must be addressed in order to provide complete gerontological care. One aspect is a better understanding of the physical and functional changes that can be expected to occur with aging. The importance of an understanding of the biology of aging has increased as it has become more apparent that some of the physical and functional decline which may commonly be attributed to aging is actually due more to disuse, and may be reversible if proper remedial actions are followed.

Accompanying the increased interest in aging, and particularly in age-related changes in the body, courses in the biology of human aging have become more prevalent and are often included in the core requirements of gerontology programs. Such courses are important not only to those who are preparing for a career in gerontology but also to those who have older persons in their families, and even to older persons themselves, as they provide a means of alleviating common misconceptions about the aging process.

This book is intended to meet the needs of such a diverse audience. Although it was written primarily for those preparing to work with elderly persons—whether as social workers, nurses, nurse's aids, rehabilitation therapists, or counselors—I would expect that it will also prove informative to those who would like to better understand the changes which are occurring in their own bodies. Some biology-of-aging books are too comprehensive for students who want only a general overview of the aging process, whereas others do not provide sufficient information for the reader to be able to understand the biological changes that must be discussed. I have attempted to follow a path midway between these two levels.

While writing the book I kept in mind that most readers would not have much depth, or, perhaps, even interest, in biology. Therefore, I have kept scientific terminology to a minimum, although it has not been possible to eliminate it entirely. Most scientific terminology is descriptive, and description becomes too cumbersome if some terms are not used. To make the book more readable for its intended audience, I have omitted specific citations within the text. Although such citations may provide useful information, they interfere with the flow of reading, and beginning students often find them so distracting that they lose the thought of the sentence. For those who wish to read in greater depth about the effects of aging on the body I have included a rather extensive bibliography containing general references and more specific references for each chapter.

The book begins with an introduction in which the need to study human aging is addressed and common terms related to aging are introduced. Following this is a consideration of the various theories that have been proposed to explain why the body ages. The survey of the actual aging effects on the body begins with a description of the effects of aging at the cellular level, followed by discussions of the aging changes in each body system. Each chapter begins with a brief review of the normal structure and function of the organs of the particular body system, followed by consideration of the more common age-related changes and dysfunctions in the system.

I appreciate the interest shown in this book by professors who teach biology of aging courses and the numerous suggestions they made for strengthening the book. I am especially indebted to the following persons for their reviews of the manuscript:

Paul Benko
Sonoma State University
Rohnert Park, California

James Siniscalchi
Jersey City State College
Jersey City, New Jersey

Newtol Press
University of Wisconsin
Milwaukee, Wisconsin

Dorothy Moses
University of Akron
Akron, Ohio

Elizabeth C. Hager
Trenton State College
Trenton, New Jersey

Of course, this book would not have been completed if it were not for the efforts of the many dedicated professionals at Prentice-Hall. I wish to express my sincere appreciation to them.

Alexander P. Spence

About the Author

Alexander Spence was born in St. Louis, Missouri in 1929. After serving four years in the U.S. Navy he attended Washington University in St. Louis and completed his bachelor's and master's degrees at the University of Missouri at Columbia. Following two years of graduate work in anatomy at the State University of New York Health Sciences Center in Syracuse he earned a Ph.D. degree from Cornell University.

Dr. Spence is a professor of biological sciences at the State University of New York College at Cortland, where he has taught courses in human anatomy and physiology, comparative anatomy, vertebrate embryology, and the biology of human aging for over 25 years. He is the author of *Basic Human Anatomy* and coauthor of *Human Anatomy and Physiology*.

In an effort to slow his own rate of aging, Dr. Spence relaxes by walking, bicycling, cross-country skiing, and sailing.

Introduction to Human Aging

Increase in the Number and Percentage of
Elderly Persons

General Effects of Aging

Common Terms Related to Aging

Rates of Aging

General Aging Changes in the Body

Body Structural Changes • *Body Compositional Changes*

Most of us have a natural curiosity about our body. We are interested in how we appear to others and are concerned when one or more of our bodily functions does not seem to be normal. This curiosity and concern often heightens as we grow older. With increased age we notice structural changes that gradually alter our appearance, and we may become aware for the first time of functional changes in a number of our organs. Aging is a complicated process involving all of the many subtle changes that occur in our body with the passage of time. These changes tend to decrease our ability to withstand stress, and death is the inevitable end result.

The study of the changes associated with aging has become an increasingly important and popular research area in recent years. To support this research, the amount of funds available from private, state, and federal sources has multiplied dramatically. And along with the increase in funds and research there has been a large increase in the number of scientific publications in the field. But the increased study of the bodily changes associated with aging has become most noticeable to the general public in the popular press. Articles concerning aging are common in newspapers and in many magazines. Even some television programs have begun to be slanted so that they attract an audience of older persons.

The scientific and the popular articles both vary considerably in the manner in which they consider aging, reflecting the many aspects of aging.

Some writers are interested in the social aspects of aging; others in the recreational, psychological, economic, or physical aspects. Accompanying the increased research activities on, and public awareness of, the aging process there has developed a need for more support-level persons with some knowledge of the biological changes associated with human aging. This book provides such a background.

In this book we are interested in the *biological* aspects of aging. We consider the changes that can occur in body structure—at both the microscopic and the macroscopic levels—as we get older, and the functional restrictions and impairments that are often associated with increasing age. These include bodily changes that do not adversely affect the health of the individual, as well as disease conditions that are typically associated with aging.

We restrict our considerations to the biology of *human* aging, but we should be aware that many significant studies on aging have been done with lower animals, and even some with plants. Humans and most mammals have life spans that are too long to make it practical to follow one particular group throughout an entire life span—from birth to death—although there are a few such studies in progress. One well known study of this type has been in progress since 1950 on about five thousand people in Framingham, Massachusetts. This research method is referred to as a *longitudinal study*. In contrast to humans, lower animals have much shorter life spans, making it easily possible to study numerous generations from birth to death. Many longitudinal studies that produced much data on aging have been done with rotifers, paramecia, and fruit flies, as well as with mice, which are relatively short-lived mammals. *Cross-sectional studies* are more commonly used in humans. In this technique the parameters to be studied are measured and compared for persons within various age groups, such as those from 20 to 30 years old, or from 40 to 60 years old.

Another reason for using lower animals for aging research is that it is advantageous for any study of aging to be performed on genetically uniform organisms. Humans are among the most hybridized species of animals, but it is easily possible to breed lower animals so that their genetic makeup is known and is consistent.

Still another advantage of using lower animals for aging research is that it is much easier to control their environment than it is to control every aspect of the environment of humans, and environmental conditions may greatly affect aging.

But we are primarily interested in the aging process as it occurs in humans, and we will consider the findings of studies using lower animals only insofar as they may relate to humans. We must remember, however, that it is risky to extrapolate findings from one phylum to another. Data obtained from studies on lower animals may or may not be applicable to humans.

Increase in the Number and Percentage of Elderly Persons

Perhaps the primary reason for the expanded attention that aging is receiving is the rapid increase in the number of persons aged 65 and over. For instance, a study done at Princeton University indicated that in 1980 in the United States, 65% of the 50-year-old women had living mothers, compared with only 37% in 1940. According to the Bureau of the Census, there are now more than 32,000 persons over 100 years of age in the United States.

Although it is not important for our purposes that we have precise figures on the number of persons over 65 years of age, it is vital to our understanding of the urgency of aging studies that we have an appreciation of how the ratio of the elderly to the total population is changing and is projected to continue to change. As Table 1-1 shows, between 1900 and 1970 the percentage of the population in the United States that was over 65 years old increased from 4.1% to 10% and is projected to approach

Table 1-1 Estimates and projections of the total population in the United States and the percentage of elderly, 1900–2030.

YEAR	TOTAL POPULATION	OVER 65	%
1900	75,600,000	3,100,000	4.1
1940	132,300,000	9,000,000	6.8
1960	181,000,000	16,600,000	9.2
1970	203,100,000	20,300,000	10.0
1980	228,000,000	25,600,000	11.2
2000*	268,500,000	34,900,000	13.0
2030*	304,700,000	64,600,000	21.2

* = projected

13% of the total population by the year 2000. In 1986 alone, about 2.1 million persons became 65 while only about 1.5 million persons 65 or older died, for a net increase of about 600,000 persons over 65. Also notice on the table the rapid increase in the older population between the years 2000 and 2030, when persons over 65 years of age are expected to comprise about 21% of the total population in the United States. This increase reflects the aging of those born during the 1960s, when birth rates were high. It should be pointed out that the projected continued increase in the percentage of elderly persons in the total population is due in part to lower birth rates up to the 1960s, which slowed the growth rate of the total population.

Not only has the number of elderly persons increased, but a higher percentage of people are living to be 80 and 90 years old. In fact, the fastest growing segment of the population in the United States is the group over 85 years old. In 1986 the 65 to 74 age group was more than 8 times larger than it was in 1900, the 75 to 84 age group was 12 times larger, while the group over 85 years old was 22 times larger than in 1900. In 1960 approximately 0.5% of the population in the United States were over 85 years old. By 1980 that percentage had about doubled, and the U.S. Bureau of the Census estimates that approximately 4.5% of the population will be 85 years old by the year 2040 (Figure 1-1). It is important to realize that this increase in the number of old people in the population has been due almost entirely to a reduction in the mortality of younger age groups. Although the average life expectancy in the United States increased from 47 years in 1900 to about 70 years in 1974, the maximum life span and the age at death that is characteristic for humans (75 to 80 years) have not been significantly altered. Rather, more people are living long enough to reach their full potential life span. This is especially true of women. In 1986 there were 17.4 million women over 65, compared to 11.8 million men. Thus, by 65 years of age the sex ratio is 147 women to 100 men. This ratio becomes even larger with increased age. In those 85 and over the ratio is 253 women to 100 men.

Although the significant increase that is occurring in the percentage of older people in our population is encouraging to persons approaching old age, it presents considerable problems for the younger members of our society. Older persons generally require increased levels of medical care, social services, and specialized recreational facilities, as today's elderly tend to be more active than those of past generations. They are not content to sit passively all day; rather, they want to interact with each other and with other segments of society. These services and activities require large sums of money. The burden of financially supporting this increasing

Fig. 1-1   Percentage of elderly in the U. S. population, by age group.

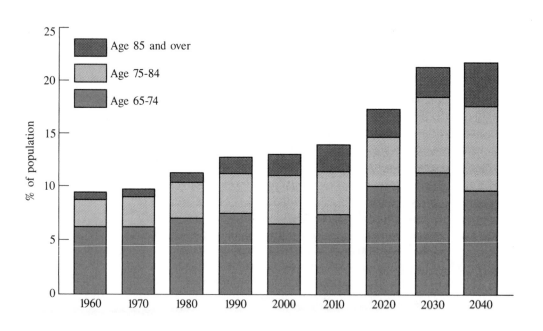

(Source: U.S. Bureau of the Census)

     Chapter 1   Introduction to Human Aging

number of senior citizens will largely be a problem the young must solve. The usual method of providing such financial support is increased taxation, and many older persons are on fixed incomes which are not high enough to make it possible for them to pay significantly higher taxes. Therefore, the younger members of our society can expect to have to pay a large share of any higher taxes.

General Effects of Aging

Aging is not something that happens only to old people. It is a continuing process that begins at conception and eventually ends with death. All of us are in various phases of aging. The effects of aging, however, tend to become more noticeable after about age 40. Old persons can be considered to be in the final phases of aging.

We will consider the specific effects of aging on each body system in the following chapters. However, there are a number of general effects that are fundamental to the aging process. For instance, there is a general tendency for aging to lower the capacity to function properly—at the cellular level as well as at the organ level (Table 1-2). Much of the lowered functional capacity is due to the tendency of structural elements within the body to deteriorate. Because of lowered functional capacity, older persons are not able to respond to various stimuli—either internal or external—as effectively as can younger persons. The reduced capacity to respond to a changing internal environment makes it increasingly difficult for older persons to maintain stable chemical and physical states within the body—that is, to maintain *homeostasis*. In the absence of homeostasis, dysfunction of the various organ systems is more likely to occur, and aging, therefore, increases the likelihood of death.

These general changes seem to paint a gloomy picture of old age. This is not necessarily accurate. In fact, old age can be a healthy, happy, and productive period of one's life. These positive aspects of aging become increasingly evident when one visits a retirement city, such as Sun City, Arizona, which the author recently visited. Sun City has a population of over 50,000 and a person must be over 50 years old in order to purchase a home and live there. A visitor cannot help but be impressed with how active the senior citizens that live there are and with the positive outlook they have. They accept the fact that death may occur most any time, but they certainly do not dwell on it; nor do they seem to dread it.

Table 1-2 Approximate declines in various human functional capacities with age, considering function at age 30 to be 100%.

	PERCENT OF FUNCTION REMAINING	
	60 YEARS	80 YEARS
Nerve conduction velocity	96	88
Basal metabolic rate	96	84
Standard cell water	94	81
Cardiac index	82	70
Glomerular filtration rate	96	61
Vital capacity	80	58
Renal plasma flow	89	51
Maximal breathing capacity	80	42

Common Terms Related to Aging

As is the case in any specialized study, the study of aging uses some terms that everyone may not be completely familiar with. We should understand the following terms as we study aging.

- *Aging* is the process of growing old, regardless of chronological age.

- *Senescence* is a term used to describe the group of deleterious effects that lead to a decrease in the efficient functioning of an organism with increasing age, and leads to an increased probability of death. Although *senescence* and *aging* both describe the same process, *senescence* tends to be the more restrictive of the two terms in that it is often used to refer to the state of old age characteristic of the late years of lifespan and infers pathological effects.

- *Senility* refers to the physical and mental deterioration often associated with old age.

- In an attempt to standardize terms, the World Health Organization classifies persons who are between 60 and 75 years of age as *elderly*. Those between 76 and 90 are classified as *old*, and those over 90 years of age are referred to as *very old*.

- *Gerontology* is the scientific study of the process of aging, and all aspects—biological, sociological, and historical— of the problems associated with aging.

- *Geriatrics* is the branch of medicine that treats the conditions and diseases associated with aging and old age.

- *Longevity* refers to the duration of life (i.e. life span) of an individual. There are two aspects of longevity that are often considered: mean longevity and maximum longevity.

  Mean longevity is the average longevity of a population. To determine the mean longevity, the ages of all the members of a population at death are added together and divided by the number of individuals in the population. This is often referred to as *life expectancy*. In humans, life expectancy has shown a continuous increase over the centuries, due primarily to better sanitation and medical care. For example, in 1776 the life expectancy in the United States was 35 years. By 1975 the life expectancy had increased to 72 years.

  Maximum longevity is the age at death of the longest-lived member of the population. In humans, which are the longest-lived species of mammals, maximum longevity is difficult to verify but is believed to be between 110 and 120 years.

- *Demography* is the statistical study of human populations collectively, including geographical changes and trends in births, marriages, diseases, and deaths. These data provide vital basic information in many aging studies.

Rates of Aging

Although people may be classified as elderly after 60 years of age, we should keep in mind that this age is selected for reasons other than biological reasons. All organs in an individual do not age at the same rate; and any specific organ does not necessarily age at the same rate in different individuals. Consequently, different individuals undergo aging at different rates. Some individuals may have symptoms that cause them to become aware of aging processes in their 40s, whereas others are still active and in good health in their 70s and do not feel old.

Because aging occurs at different rates in different individuals, the goal of most studies on aging is not so much to significantly *interfere* with the processes of senescence as it is to attempt to *understand* the processes in order that its diseases may be better treated and aging may become more pleasant. With the increased number of old persons in the population, age-linked diseases now account for over one-half of the major cases in most Western medical practices. For this reason it is urgent for physicians to better understand the scientific basis of geriatrics.

General Aging Changes in the Body

As we grow older we notice changes in our bodies that alert us to the fact that aging is occurring. We are not, as a rule, aware of the many cellular changes that are directly responsible for these alterations in structure and function. Rather, the signs of aging that are most obvious to the individual occur in the structure and composition of the body.

Body Structural Changes
Some studies which measure various parameters in different people included in the same group mainly because they are the same age (cross-sectional studies) indicate an apparent loss of height with aging, beginning at about age 30 and progressing at a very slow rate thereafter. In contrast, some longitudinal studies, in which data is obtained from the same individuals over a number of years, have shown a small increase in height beyond 30 years followed by a gradual decline in height beginning after 40 years of age. The loss of height, when it does begin, seems to be divided almost equally between trunk length and lower limb length. A shortening of the lower limbs often occurs before any loss of trunk length. Since the length of the bones in the lower limbs shows very little, if any, age-related change, the loss in lower limb length is thought to be mostly a result of age changes that occur in the joints and in the arches of the feet. The loss in trunk length is thought to be largely due to an increase in the normal anterior-posterior curvatures of the spinal column and some compression of the intervertebral disks, both of which commonly occur during aging.

Because of a gradual deterioration of muscles with age, including those of the shoulders, shoulder width decreases with age. In contrast, the diameter of the hips tends to increase with age, due largely to increased fat deposition in the region. With a loss of elasticity that occurs in the lungs during aging, breathing requires more effort. Consequently, the circumference of the thorax tends to increase with age.

Changes in body weight with aging tend to follow different patterns in men and women. Men generally increase in weight until their middle 50s and then gradually lose weight. Women tend to continue to gain weight until their 60s before beginning to lose weight, and the weight is lost at a slower rate than in men.

Body Compositional Changes

It is possible to obtain some indication of the composition of the body without the necessity of sampling body tissues. One noninvasive means of doing so is the measurement of total body water by administering an indicator compound which enters the body water and then determining the dilution of the indicator. This procedure provides an estimation of the amount of fat in the body, since fat contains very little water and thus affects the dilution of the indicator. Another noninvasive method of obtaining information concerning body composition is the measurement of the specific gravity of the body. This can be done by weighing an individual in air and then in water. Specific gravity measures the buoyancy of the body, which is indicative of the amount of fat in the body. Still another noninvasive method involves measuring the skin-fold thickness in specific areas of the body. This measurement provides an indication of the amount of subcutaneous fat present—that is, fat deposited just beneath the skin.

There is much individual variation in these parameters, but in a young male total body water that is 60% of body weight is considered to be average. In a young woman total body water of about 52% of body weight is considered average. With aging, total body water declines to about 54% in males and 46% in females. This reduction in the percentage of water in the body with aging is thought not to be primarily due to dehydration. Rather, elderly persons undergo a change in the ratio of lean to fat, thereby reducing the space available to accommodate body water.

Changes in the skin-fold thickness with age depend on where the measurement is taken. The thickness of the fold increases in some areas until rather late in life. This is the case in the abdominal wall. In other areas there is a gradual but steady decrease in skin-fold thickness with age. The skin-fold measurements of most areas in women tend to remain constant until about age 64. The results obtained by skin-fold measurement suggest that most of the extra adipose tissue that accumulates in elderly persons is laid down internally, within or around organs or in the mesenteries that attach the intestines to the body wall, rather than just beneath the skin.

There are two major compartments in the body where body water is stored; within the individual cells (*intracellular water*) and in the spaces between the cells (*extracellular water*). Intracellular water and extracellular water both decrease with age, but not equally. A greater amount of the reduction in fluid volume that occurs with age is due to water loss from the cells rather than from the extracellular spaces. That is, there appears to be a certain amount of cellular dehydration with aging, or else the loss of intracellular water may be an indicator of the loss in the total number of body cells that occurs with aging. Most organs show an age-related loss of mass, although most of the loss of lean body mass occurs in muscles.

Theories of Aging

Mechanisms of Aging

General Theories of Aging

Aging by Program • *Gene Theory* • *Gene Mutation Theory* • *Cross-Linkage Theory* • *Free Radical Theory* • *Cellular Garbage Theory* • *Accumulation-of-Errors Theory* • *Wear-and-Tear Theory* • *Autoimmune Theory*

Summary

There is no question that aging is characterized by a general reduction in functional capacities and by structural changes in the body. We are unable to perform most activities as well as we could in our earlier years, and things seem to go wrong in our bodies more often than they used to. The question that we would like to answer is, what causes the changes that are associated with aging? If the underlying cause of aging can be determined it might be possible to interfere with the process and thus extend human longevity. It is conceivable that this goal of increasing human life-span could be attained either by suppressing the causes of death in younger persons or by delaying the aging processes that make us more susceptible to disease and death as we grow older.

We mentioned earlier that significant progress has been made in reducing death in infants and children in developed countries. Consequently, more people are living longer and are reaching the age of death that is characteristic for humans (75 to 80 years). But little progress has been made in delaying the aging process. The age at death has not been altered appreciably. This is a goal of prime importance, and although it may never be attained, much of the research that is now in progress is attempting to obtain as much information as possible about the various aspects of the aging process in the hope that it might be possible to postpone it somewhat.

If there is to be any chance that the aging process can be postponed, we must first understand what *causes* aging. The cause of aging, of course, is not known. In fact, it is most likely that there is no *one* cause of aging. The data from many experiments using different approaches have provided enticing and encouraging information concerning the causes of aging. However, these results often lead in different directions. So that you will have an appreciation of the various directions taken by the research, we will consider some of the main theories of aging. As we do so you should keep in mind that although these are commonly referred to as theories, some are more hypotheses than theories. That is, they are based to some extent on common assumptions rather than being based entirely on a set of facts.

Mechanisms of Aging

In order to better understand the theories of aging we should first consider the mechanisms that may cause the changes associated with aging. Humans, like all mammals, are composed of three biological components: (1) They contain some types of cells that divide and produce new cells as long as the person is alive. This is true of most of the various types of body cells. (2) There are some types of body cells that, although they actively divide during embryonic development, are incapable of dividing following birth. These cells are referred to as *postmitotics*, indicating that they are no longer capable of undergoing mitosis. Nerve cells and muscle cells are postmitotic cells. (3) In addition to cells, the body also has a large component of noncellular material located between the cells. For this reason they are referred to as intercellular substances. A protein substance called *collagen* is one of the main intercellular substances. It provides support in the skin, bone, cartilage, tendons, and other tissues.

All three of these components are subject to physiological controls that function within the body. Consequently, there were several early hypotheses advanced that attempted to explain the mechanisms that produce aging changes based on the three components. One such hypothesis suggested that a person's vigor declines as a result of changes that occur in those cells which remain capable of multiplying. Another hypothesis proposed that a person becomes less vigorous with age as a result of the loss of, or injury to, cells that are no longer capable of multiplying—specifically, nerve cells and muscle cells. Yet another early hypothesis suggested that a person's vigor declines with age as a result of changes in the intercellular materials of the body—such as collagen.

These were early hypotheses and are now considered to be too simplistic. However, they made important contributions to the study of the mechanisms of aging. In fact, the ideas they advanced are still apparent in some modern aging research.

General Theories of Aging

If a proposed theory of aging is to be valid it must meet three broad criteria: (1) The aging changes that the theory addresses must occur commonly in all members of a given species. In our case, the changes must commonly occur with advancing age in all humans. (2) The process must be progressive with time. That is, the changes that result from the proposed process must become more obvious as the person grows older. (3) The process must produce changes that cause organ dysfunctions and that ultimately cause a particular body organ or system to fail. It will be useful if, as we describe some of the proposed theories of aging, you keep these criteria in mind. In that way you can form your own opinions as to how valid each theory might be.

Some of the theories that we will consider attempt to link aging with the death of increasing numbers of cells as they "wear out" from extended usage and prolonged exposure to various deleterious factors. Others suggest mechanical or chemical explanations for the cellular changes and the dysfunctions characteristic of aging. Still other theories suggest there is a self-poisoning that occurs at the cellular level which increases steadily with age, ultimately reaching levels that cause organs to dysfunction or to cease functioning. And some theories advance genetic mechanisms as the basis of aging changes, suggesting the changes result from mechanisms such as somatic mutations or the loss of biological information.

Having so many different theories that attempt to explain the mechanisms of aging can be confusing to those who want only a general overview of the biology of aging. It might help to consider that all the theories can be reasonably well placed into one of two general groups: (1) Those theories which suggest that aging results from some form of damage or wearing out. Perhaps an organ or a system of organs becomes worn or damaged. This could place additional stress on some other organ system which, in turn, stresses yet another system, and so forth. In this manner damage or excessive wear in one particular organ or system can cause a continuing downward spiral on body functioning, such as occurs during aging. (2) The other general group into which several of the theories can be placed suggests that aging is genetically programmed by some kind of neurological center which functions as a biological clock, measuring the time left until death. Some investigators place such an intrinsic aging chronometer in every cell. Others suggest there is one master controlling clock located in a single center. The site most often suggested for this control center is the brain.

Considering the theories of aging in any depth is beyond the scope of this book, but briefly reviewing some of the more popular theories will help you to understand the various changes commonly associated with aging. As we consider these theories you will notice that there is overlap between them, which is to be expected, as no single theory has been able to satisfactorily explain all of the possible causes of aging.

Aging by Program

Since aging begins at birth and each species seems to have its own average longevity, there are strong arguments supporting the suggestion that aging is in some manner programmed into each species. The site most often suggested for a localized aging chronometer (i.e. timekeeper) is in a region called the *hypothalamus* in the base of the brain. The hypothalamus contains centers which control the production of growth hormone by the pituitary gland, as well as the development and activities of the gonads, the thyroid, and the adrenal glands.

Information originating from this aging chronometer could be carried to cells throughout the body by neurons and hormones. As the organism grows older, its ability to transmit information by either of these means may decline. Nerve conduction rates may decrease, the structure and amounts of the hormones produced may be affected, and the receptors for either the nerve impulses or the hormones may become less capable of reacting appropriately to the incoming impulse or molecular message. These changes could alter the functioning of body cells in various ways, and it is conceivable that changes typical of aging could occur.

It has been suggested that there may be a gradual programmed elevation of the minimal level (i.e. threshold level) of sensitivity of the hypothalamus to the normal feedback suppression that it receives from various endocrine glands and by which the hypothalamus is normally able to maintain the metabolic stability of the body. This would affect the reactivity of the hypothalamus, which could, in turn, bring about some of the aforementioned changes.

Some studies suggest that the thymus, which is a lymphoid gland located beneath the sternum, might also be involved in some manner in the programmed regulation of aging. The gland atrophies at about the onset of adolescence, and the implication is that aging occurs more readily in the absence of the thymus gland.

Some research data that support programmed aging do not suggest a central nervous system (i.e. hypothalamus) control site. When normal human cells were cultured in the laboratory it was found that they underwent a finite number of divisions, and then they died. The number of divisions the cells were capable of was constant for each type of cell being cultured. When human fibroblast cells were taken from embryos they would divide about fifty times; if taken from adults the fibroblasts would divide only about twenty times. This would suggest that cell death is an inherent property of the cells themselves, rather than being controlled by the hypothalamus or some other center that acts as an aging chronometer.

One interpretation of these data is that in the body normal cells are also capable of approximately the same number of divisions as observed in cultured cells, and there is an inverse relationship between the age of a human cell donor and the dividing capacity of cells when cultured. That is, when older cells are cultured they will undergo fewer divisions than will embryonic cells. This supports the concept that each cell has the capacity to divide only a certain number of times, and that older cells have already "used up" some of their divisions by the time they are cultured. However, it should be emphasized that these results are obtained only when normal cells are cultured. In contrast, cancer cells can be cultured indefinitely. This is also true of eggs and sperm, which are very specialized cells.

Another interpretation that could explain a programmed longevity is that perhaps only in early life do the genes produce messenger RNA (mRNA), transfer RNA (tRNA), ribosomal RNA (rRNA), and enzymes. These are products that are vital to cellular functions. As cells grow old these substances would ultimately be used up, and if they could not be replenished the cells would cease functioning. The amounts of these substances within each type of cell could specifically limit the number of divisions that that cell type was capable of.

But an important question that needs answering is, how can there be life-long division of many types of cells in the body if each cell type is capable of only a limited number of cell divisions? One suggestion is that there are several generations of dormant "renewal cells" in each tissue that begin dividing at different times. These renewal cells are, in effect,

Chapter 2 Theories of Aging

reserve embryonic cells. Only when all of these reserve cells have been used will the tissue begin to show aging changes.

The general consensus concerning aging by program seems to be that it is unlikely that aging results from the loss of the capacity to divide by one or more important cell populations. It is considered to be more probable that, although normal cells may have only a finite capacity for replication, this limit, which can be demonstrated in tissue cultures, is rarely, if ever, reached in the body. Rather, it is suggested that other functional losses that occur in cells produce physiological dysfunctions in the cells which cause aging changes before they reach their finite limits to divide.

Gene Theory

The *gene theory* also states that aging is programmed but suggests that the programming is due to one or more harmful genes within each organism which become active only late in life and alter the physiology of the organism in ways which result in its death. Or perhaps there are genes which direct many cellular activities during the early years that become altered in later years, thus altering their function. In their altered state, the genes may be responsible for the functional decline and structural changes associated with aging.

The gene theory suggests that human life-span is an inherited trait, and there are a number of studies of twins that provide support for this suggestion. Several twin studies have shown that there is considerable similarity in age at death of pairs of monozygous (single egg) twins, whereas this similarity is not apparent in the case of dizygous (two eggs) twins or in other siblings who are not twins.

Gene Mutation Theory

It is well accepted that mutations occur in the genes of cells composing the various tissues during life, and the mutations alter the functioning of the cells—generally to the detriment of the cells. The *gene mutation theory* suggests that the accumulation of cells with altered structure and function which results from these mutations may lead, with the passage of time, to malfunctions and eventually death. Radiation is known to cause mutations and shorten life span. Therefore, it has been suggested that natural radiation might cause some acceleration of the aging process. Much of the evidence for this theory comes from studies which showed that liver cells from older mice have greater numbers of genetic mutations than do similar cells of younger mice. Furthermore, it was shown that liver cells from a strain of mice having a short life span consistently show a higher incidence of mutations than do comparable cells from a strain of mice with a longer life span.

Genes are composed largely of compounds called nucleotides which are joined together to form a double-stranded molecule called deoxyribonucleic acid (DNA). When considering any theory that suggests aging is due to damage to genes it should be kept in mind that cells possess a number of mechanisms by which damaged DNA can be repaired. Basically, repair is accomplished by enzymes within the cell cutting out the damaged region of the gene and adding back a new set of nucleotides, utilizing the undamaged DNA strand as a template. The gene mutation theory assumes that with the passage of time gene-repair mechanisms within each cell become less efficient and some mutations remain uncorrected, thereby causing structural and functional aging changes.

Cross-linkage Theory

When proteins are denatured they are irreversibly altered. For example, when an egg is cooked its proteins are denatured and its physical state is changed permanently. Proteins are composed of smaller molecules called peptides, and denaturation is caused by the formation of cross-links between the strands of peptides. The cross-links cause changes in the structure and function of the proteins. Many of the cross-links are in the form of chemical bonds that develop between hydrogen atoms in the peptides.

The *cross-linkage theory* proposes that with age and the formation of new cross-links, some proteins in cells are irreversibly altered structurally. This, in turn, alters the functioning of the proteins and ultimately causes the failure of the cells, and the tissues and organs which the cells form.

The proteins most often mentioned as being affected by cross-linking are enzymes and collagen. *Enzymes* are proteins that are responsible for many processes in the body. They are referred to as organic catalysts because they accelerate the rate of chemical reactions—such as those involved in digestion, metabolism, and many other physiological activities of the body. *Collagen* is a metabolically inert supportive tissue that is located between cells. It is composed of fibers of protein embedded in an intercellular matrix. Both the fibers and the matrix undergo molecular changes with age. Collagen is very common in the body, forming the structural framework of most organs, lining blood vessels, and holding cells together. In fact, collagen makes up about 30% of all proteins in the body. When the structure of collagen is altered, the structure of the organ in which it is located is also affected and this, in turn, alters the function of the organ. For instance, a change in the structure of collagen is largely responsible for the loss of elasticity in blood vessels which often occurs with aging. An interesting aspect of collagen's role on aging is that there seems to be an increase in the deposition of collagen with aging, often producing such an excess of fibers that the condition is referred to as fibrosis.

Collagen is an important component in several types of connective tissue located throughout the body. When specific cells and tissues are injured and die, they are often replaced with connective tissue cells, which lack the functional capacities of the original cells or tissues. So the accumulation of collagen with aging is felt to occur at the expense of the functional tissues of an organ. It can also interfere with the supply of oxygen and nutrients to the cells of the organ and may affect the organ in other ways. For example, with age the elastic fibers which are normally prevalent in the skin gradually degenerate and are replaced by collagen fibers. These fibers are less flexible than elastic fibers, and therefore the elasticity of the skin tends to decrease with age.

There are also molecular changes that often occur with age in the matrix surrounding collagen fibers. In general, these changes cause the matrix to be less permeable than it was. Because of this, capillaries, which contain considerable matrix and collagen in their walls, tend to become less permeable, thereby slowing transport of gases, nutrients, and wastes across their walls and greatly affecting metabolism. When this reduction of permeability occurs in the capillaries of the kidneys, it reduces the filtration rate across the capillary walls and can significantly impair kidney function.

This theory also suggests that some essential molecules other than proteins may become cross-linked with age, including DNA. If DNA becomes cross-linked, its ability to direct protein synthesis may be adversely affected. This could have serious results, including disruption of normal immunological responses by the body.

Cross-linking of proteins has also been shown to be one of the reasons that diabetics commonly have hardened and clogged arteries, reduced kidney function, and stiff joints. Diabetics are particularly susceptible to excessive cross-linkage of collagen because, even with daily insulin injections, they often have abnormally high levels of sugar in their blood—and sugar is known to promote cross-linkage formation. Researchers have recently found a drug that prevents sugar from causing cross-links to form between collagen fibers. This drug has been effective in laboratory animals and will be tested in human diabetics. The hope is that if cross-linkage is a cause of aging, perhaps this drug could also be useful in the treatment of some of the disorders of aging in persons who are not diabetics.

Free Radical Theory

Free radicals are cellular chemicals containing an unpaired electron. They are formed as by-products of various normal cellular processes involving interactions with oxygen. They react chemically with other substances—especially with unsaturated fats—so quickly that they exist for only a very brief time, generally less than a second. Because the cell membrane contains sizeable amounts of fats it can react with free radicals and be altered by them. This alteration of the membrane structure may cause the cell membrane to become more permeable to some substances and allow them to pass more freely through the membrane. The membrane surrounding other structures within cells, such as mitochondria and lysosomes, also contain fats and are affected by free radicals. Free radicals can also cause mutations of chromosomes, thereby damaging the normal genetic machinery of the cells.

Whether they damage the cell membranes or the chromosomes, free radicals can alter the functioning of the cell. Therefore, the *free radical theory* suggests that there may be a gradual accumulation of free radicals in cells with time, and as they exceed threshold concentrations, they may contribute to changes commonly associated with aging.

What compounds the problems of accumulating free radicals is that they are self-propagating. When a free radical reacts with a molecule it often forms several new free radicals, each of which is also capable of producing new free radicals. If left unchecked, free radicals can increase dramatically in numbers. And as the numbers of free radicals increase, their potential to cause cellular damage also increases. The production of new free radicals can be inhibited by *antioxidants*, which are compounds that prevent oxidation from occurring. Vitamins C and E are antioxidants, and it has been suggested that they can extend a person's life span by reducing the amount of free radicals in that person's cells. This has yet to be proven. Another antioxidant (butylated hydroxytoluene) is a commonly used food preservative. It has been shown to significantly extend the life span when fed to mice, but it is uncertain whether it does so in humans.

Cellular Garbage Theory

As cells age they accumulate increased amounts of various substances within their cytoplasm. Many of these substances are by-products of normal cellular metabolism. Substances which are known to accumulate within cells with increasing age include free radicals, aldehydes, histones, and lipofuscins. These latter by-products, the *lipofuscins*, are yellow-brown pigments that are so common in many types of aging cells that they are often referred to as "age pigments." Lipofuscins are considered to be a sort of cellular garbage. They are chemically inert and consist of strongly cross-linked molecules that cannot be separated by enzyme action. The lipofuscins are stored in lysosome-like structures for the life of the cell.

The *cellular garbage theory* suggests that the gradual accumulation of inert substances such as the lipofuscins within cells interferes with the normal functioning of the cells, perhaps by causing displacement of other cytoplasmic components. Those substances that are considered to be cellular garbage but are not inert, such as free radicals and histones, are thought to interfere with normal cell functioning by causing deleterious and irreversible changes in certain cellular components. Thus, it is suggested that the accumulation of both inert and reactive substances can interfere with normal cell functioning and contribute to aging.

Accumulation-of-Errors Theory

The *accumulation-of-errors theory* suggests that cellular dysfunction, and ultimately cell death, could result from the accumulation of random errors in the mechanism by which new proteins are synthesized. Protein synthesis involves a complex series of sequential reactions, beginning with the cell's DNA being copied, and this copy, in the form of mRNA, then entering the cytoplasm from the nucleus. In the cytoplasm the mRNA directs the formation of specific proteins by certain cellular organelles (ribosomes).

Many of the proteins formed are enzymes that carry out their functions within the cells. Enzymes serve as catalysts, upon which all cellular activities depend. Therefore, any error in their formation can have significant effects on many cellular functions. Some enzymes assist in the synthesis of other proteins. If an error occurs in the structure of such an enzyme, the protein will not be formed precisely as it should have been and may not function precisely as it normally would. This could lead to an accumulation of errors in cellular proteins, and with time, normal protein synthesis may be affected to the extent that the cell is no longer able to function normally.

This theory, then, suggests that aging is caused by an accumulation of errors in protein synthesis with time. It is proposed that the errors would cause the production of faulty enzymes, which, in turn, would produce faulty proteins. This was an attractive theory; however, although experimental results suggest that enzymes may decrease in activity in older persons, it has not been possible to conclusively demonstrate any changes in enzyme structure in older cells that are due to faulty formation. The data indicate that proteins are synthesized properly in older cells, and any alternation in their structure occurs after they are formed. For this reason, some researchers no longer consider the accumulation-of-errors theory to have any validity.

Wear-and-Tear Theory

The *wear-and-tear theory* supports the concept that aging is a programmed process. It suggests that each animal, and perhaps each cell, has a specific amount of metabolic energy available to it, and the rate at which this energy is used determines the animal's length of life.

Experimental evidence for this theory was provided by demonstrating that rats kept in a cold environment and those that had their food consumption restricted both showed considerable increase in life span. In fact, reduction of caloric intake is the most effective known method for modifying the apparent rate of aging in rats. Rats on restricted diets have the appearance and behavior of younger animals. As yet, there is no conclusive evidence of similar results in humans.

In addition to the depletion of available energy, wear-and-tear theories generally include the effects of the accumulation of harmful by-products of metabolism and of faulty enzymes due to random errors as contributing to aging changes.

Autoimmune Theory

The immune system functions to protect an individual from invasion by foreign substances called *antigens*. If an antigen—which is often a protein—enters a person's body the immune system recognizes that protein as one that does not belong in the body and attempts to destroy it. It does so by producing specialized proteins called *antibodies* which act against that specific antigen and by activating phagocytic white blood cells that attack the foreign protein. In order to destroy only foreign proteins and not normal body proteins the immune system must be able to recognize the structures of all of the many proteins present in the body and suppress its tendency to form antibodies against these body proteins. *Autoimmune theories* propose that, with advancing age, the immune system is no longer able to faultlessly distinguish foreign proteins from the body's own proteins. As a consequence, antibodies against the body's own proteins may be formed in older persons. If this happens, the body's immune system will attack and destroy body cells.

Autoimmune theories of aging fall into two categories: those which suggest that, with age, new antigens appear, and those that suggest aging is accomplished by an increase in autoimmune reactions.

New Antigens. There are two sources suggested for the new antigens that may appear in later years. These antigens may result from mutations that cause the formation of altered RNA or DNA and, consequently, of altered proteins. The altered proteins would not be recognized by the body's immune system and would therefore act as new—and foreign—antigens. Another suggested source of new antigens is that perhaps some cells may be "hidden" in the body during embryonic development in such a way that the immune system does not have any contact with them during development. As a result, the immune system would not have its capacity to form antibodies against them suppressed and it would not recognize the proteins of these cells as being normally present in the body. If, at a later time, perhaps as a consequence of damage or disease, these cells (and their proteins), which had been inaccessible, were released into the circulatory system, the immune system would consider them to be foreign proteins and would produce antibodies to destroy them.

Increase in Autoimmune Reactions. According to those who support this view, autoimmune reactions increase progressively as a person ages because of changes that occur in antibody molecules. It has been shown that antibodies may be modified by combining with their specific antigens, by aggregating into a mass, or by being split into smaller components (polypeptides). It is suggested that after undergoing such modification the antibodies may acquire *antigenic* potential against the body and thus stimulate the body's immune system. It has also been suggested that the continuous circulation of antigen-antibody complexes that result from immune responses may affect various organs and tissues in such a manner as to produce the cumulative lesions characteristic of aging. Another possibility is that microorganisms that persist in the body for prolonged periods of time may possess antigens that cross-react, thereby inducing pathologic changes in normal tissues. It is also possible that drugs taken as medication may form complexes with body proteins, and these complexes may then be identified by the immune system as foreign substances. This would cause the formation of antibodies that would attack the complexes, resulting in destruction of normal body proteins.

Summary

After this brief overview of some theories of aging it should be clear to you that no one theory adequately explains the process of growing old.

Aging processes are better explained if a number of these theories are integrated.

For instance, those theories that suggest programmed control of aging can readily explain differences in the aging process in different species. The genetic makeup of a species determines the early development of an individual and will determine many factors, such as rate of growth and metabolism, that have a direct bearing on aging. On the other hand, the theories that suggest reasons for aging other than genetic makeup are useful in explaining why all members of the same species do not age in an identical manner. It may be that programmed aging directs the similar changes characteristic of all individuals with identical genetic makeup in their earlier years, but eventually bodily changes due to disease, the presence of excessive accumulations of substances in the cells, errors in protein synthesis, etc., may alter programmed aging. Since these factors can be expected to vary between individuals it is to be expected that individual aging will vary, even among members of the same species.

Cellular Aging

Cell Components

Validity of Cell-Culture Findings

Specific Cellular Changes during Aging

Summary

A central concept that is apparent in the theories of aging which we considered in Chapter 2 and that is a basic premise in much aging research is that many of the aspects of aging seen at the organ level are the results of changes that occur with age at the cellular level. For instance, the loss of immune competency with age is a result of changes that occur in certain types of immune system cells; and certain kinds of age-related senility have been shown to be caused by a reduction in the population of specific types of neurons in the brain.

Although it is difficult to trace one specific aspect of an organism's physiology to a particular cell type, in this chapter we will consider cellular changes that are known to occur with age and will, when possible, relate those changes with general physiological changes that are typical of aging. In order to consider the changes that are known to occur during cellular aging, we need to have an understanding of the normal structure and functioning of cells before they have aged.

Cell Components

Although individual cells are very small, they are, in fact, highly organized units and contain various types of tiny structures called *organ-*

elles, which carry out specific cellular functions (Figure 3-1). Cells also contain a number of chemical substances that are called *inclusions*. Glycogen granules and fat (lipid) droplets are common cellular inclusions.

Cellular functioning is controlled by a cellular component called the *nucleus*. The nucleus is surrounded by a semifluid substance called the *cytoplasm*, in which most of the cell organelles are located. The cytoplasm is surrounded by a membrane called the *plasma membrane* (or cell membrane), which forms the outer boundary of the cell. Membranes also surround the nucleus and several of the organelles. Membranes provide points of attachment for various cell components and act as barriers that regulate the movement of different materials into and out of cells, as well as into and out of those organelles that are surrounded by membranes. The membranes are selectively permeable, allowing some molecules to pass through them more easily than others.

Plasma Membrane

The *plasma membrane* is composed primarily of lipids. Various proteins are associated with the lipids, being either embedded in the lipid or bound loosely to the membrane surface (Figure 3-2). Some of the embedded proteins extend completely through the membrane, forming channels that connect the cytoplasm with the intercellular space between cells. Carbohydrates are often attached to the outer surface of the plasma membrane. All materials that enter or leave a cell must pass either through the plasma membrane or through the channels in the membrane. Therefore, the ease with which substances enter or leave cells depends largely on the permeability of the plasma membrane.

Nucleus

Most cells contain a single *nucleus*. However, there are some cells that contain more than one, and mature red blood cells do not contain a nucleus. Cells that lack a nucleus are incapable of forming proteins or undergoing cell division. The nucleus is separated from the rest of the cell by a nuclear membrane, which has numerous pores extending through it. The genetic material of the cell is located in the nucleus in the form of chromatin threads, which are composed of DNA combined with protein. The DNA of the genes contains coded messages that direct the synthesis of particular proteins by the cell. Most of the proteins formed act as enzymes or structural proteins.

With the exception of the reproductive cells, all cells contain a person's full genetic complement of DNA. However, all of the possible proteins the DNA can cause to be formed are not present at all times in

Fig. 3-1   An idealized animal cell showing various cytoplasmic organelles.

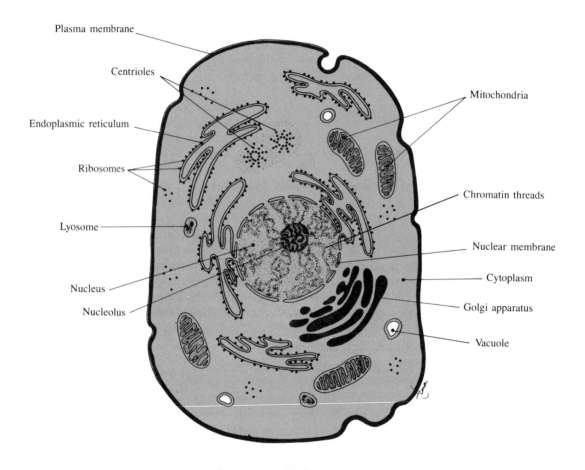

Plasma membrane

Centrioles

Endoplasmic reticulum

Ribosomes

Lyosome

Nucleus

Nucleolus

Mitochondria

Chromatin threads

Nuclear membrane

Cytoplasm

Golgi apparatus

Vacuole

From Rice, J.: Medical Terminology with Human Anatomy. *Norwalk, Ct., Appleton and Lange, 1986, p. 21; adapted from Evans, W.F.:* Anatomy and Physiology, *3rd Ed. Englewood Cliffs, N.J., Prentice Hall, p. 20.*

Chapter 3   Cellular Aging

Fig. 3-2   A proposed model of the structure of the plasma membrane.

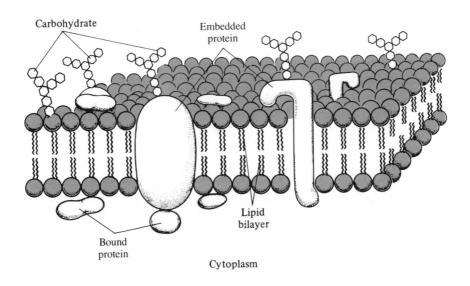

Carbohydrate

Embedded
protein

Bound
protein

Lipid
bilayer

Cytoplasm

From Barrett, J.M., et al.: Biology. *Englewood Cliffs, N.J., Prentice Hall, 1986, p. 119.*

Cell Components

all cells. Various control mechanisms regulate the production of proteins by cells, so a particular protein may be produced by one type of cell but not by another, even though both types of cells contain the same genetic information. This is important because a cell's functions depend largely on the proteins it produces. For example, if a cell is to carry out a specific sequence of reactions it must produce the particular enzymes that will cause those reactions. Thus, thyroid gland cells must produce the enzymes that will cause the various reactions necessary to synthesize thyroid hormones, and adrenal gland cells must produce the enzymes necessary to manufacture adrenal hormones. Because DNA provides the instructions for synthesizing particular proteins in each cell, it plays a central role in determining how each cell functions.

However, DNA is unable to pass through the nuclear membrane and enter the cytoplasm, which is where proteins are synthesized. To get around this problem, DNA transfers its instructions for synthesizing particular proteins to another nucleic acid, RNA, which can pass through the nuclear membrane. RNA, in turn, carries the instructions from DNA to organelles called *ribosomes* in the cytoplasm, which follow the instructions and synthesize proteins. The transferring of instructions from DNA to RNA is accomplished through a process called *transcription*, in which DNA serves as a template that directs the sequential linking together of molecules of RNA. Therefore, the RNA so formed carries the same information as the DNA. The RNA then undergoes further modifications which produce three types of RNA molecules—*messenger RNA* (mRNA), *transfer RNA* (tRNA), and *ribosomal RNA* (rRNA)—each with a different function.

Messenger RNA molecules are able to pass through the nuclear membrane and carry the instructions from nuclear DNA to the sites of protein synthesise in the cytoplasm. Each mRNA molecule contains a coded message from the DNA of the genes that specifies the exact sequence in which different free amino acids available in the cytoplasm are to be joined together in order to form a specific protein. Transfer RNA molecules combine with free amino acids in the cytoplasm and carry them to the sites where amino acids are incorporated into a specific protein (Figure 3-3). Each tRNA molecule carries a specific amino acid. Ribosomal RNA molecules join with proteins in the cytoplasm to form structures called ribosomes. Ribosomes are the organelles where proteins are actually synthesized in response to the instructions of DNA. This is accomplished when a ribosome travels along an mRNA molecule and "reads" its message. As it does so, the ribosome assembles the amino acids that are delivered to it by tRNA in the sequence directed by the mRNA.

Fig. 3-3   **The role of messenger RNA, transfer RNA, and ribosomes in protein synthesis.**

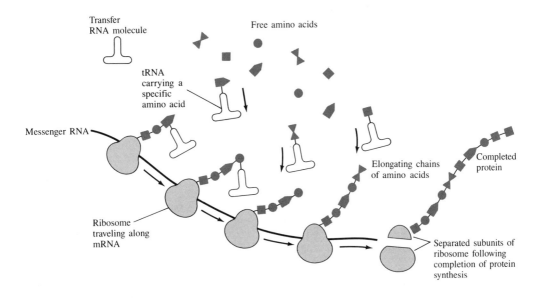

Since the mRNA is a copy of the nuclear DNA, the proteins produced are those coded for by the genes.

Endoplasmic Reticulum

The *endoplasmic reticulum* is a network of membranous tubules that form channels which extend throughout the cytoplasm of the cell. Enzymes located in the walls of the endoplasmic reticulum are involved in the synthesis of various substances, including fatty acids and steroids. Ribosomes are often attached to the walls of the reticulum, although many ribosomes are also found unattached in the cytoplasm.

Golgi Apparatus

The *Golgi apparatus* consists of a series of flattened membranous sacs located in the cytoplasm. The sacs contain enzymes which act on proteins and carbohydrates, joining them together to form glycoproteins, or adding fatty acids or other groups to proteins, for example. Eventually, the molecules formed in the Golgi apparatus become surrounded by a membrane as they pinch off from the sacs and form vesicles. The vesicles move to the surface of the cell, fuse with the plasma membrane, and release their contents to the exterior of the cell. The Golgi apparatus is particularly evident in cells that are manufacturing various secretions.

Lysosomes

Lysosomes are cytoplasmic organelles that appear granular when inactive but form into vesicles when active. They are surrounded by a membrane and contain strong digestive enzymes capable of breaking down such things as proteins, lipids, certain carbohydrates, DNA, and RNA. Lysosomes are particularly abundant in phagocytic cells, such as certain white blood cells, which are capable of digesting other cells or foreign particles. In this manner they assist in the removal of dead or dying cells and foreign materials from the body.

Mitochondria

Mitochondria are oval-shaped structures found in the cytoplasm. Like a number of other cytoplasmic organelles, they are bounded by a membrane. However, the mitochondrial membrane is a double membrane. The outer membrane is smooth and forms the boundary of the mitochondrion. The inner membrane has folds that extend into the central portion of the mitochondrion, which is filled with a semisolid matrix. Located on the inner membrane are enzymes capable of sequentially breaking down carbohydrates, fats, and proteins into energy, carbon dioxide, and water. Thus, mitochondria are vital to the generation of metabolic energy for cellular activities.

Mitochondria have their own supply of DNA and contain ribosomes, and are capable of self-duplication. As might be expected, cells that are active metabolically contain more mitochondria than less active cells.

Centrioles

Two cylinder-shaped structures called *centrioles* are also present in the cytoplasm. They are often located close to the nucleus, but may be found elsewhere within the cytoplasm. The centrioles are involved in cell division. They consist of parallel microtubules that are capable of self-duplication, and during cell division the centrioles divide, forming two pairs. As cell division proceeds, one pair of centrioles moves to each end of the cell. A network of microtubules called spindle fibers develops between the two pairs of centrioles. The spindle fibers are involved in the redistribution of chromosomes into the daughter cells that are formed by cell division.

Cytoskeleton

The cytoplasm of cells also contains a *cytoskeleton* consisting of a three-dimensional network of tiny fibrils (microfilaments) and tubules (microtubules). The components of the cytoskeleton maintain the shape and organization of the cell and are involved in the transport of substances within the cell, cell division, and in some cells, cellular movement.

Validity of Cell-Culture Findings

It is well accepted that at least some of the cells in an old organism must no longer function as effectively as they once did. Alterations of various cellular functions must occur at different rates, since not all functional capacities decline at the same rates during aging. What is not known is whether the changes seen in individual cells are the direct result of a programmed series of events that occur inside the cells, or whether they are indirect effects of random changes that occur outside the cells. Much of the information available concerning cellular aging has been obtained by growing cells in culture—that is, *in vitro*. What must be considered is, how valid are the data obtained by this method? Do they coincide closely enough with the growth patterns of cells in the body—that is, *in vivo*—to allow for the changes observed in culture to be expected to occur in the body?

There is evidence which suggests cells do behave similarly in both environments. For instance, it has been shown that normal cells, when cultured, will divide for various periods of time, but eventually they lose the capacity to divide. The period of time cells are capable of dividing varies with the type of tissue being cultured. At any point during their cultivation, cells can be frozen in liquid nitrogen, and when thawed they will begin to divide again. Significantly, in spite of having their mitotic activity halted by freezing and then being allowed to resume it by thawing, the total number of divisions the cells will undergo remains the same. This has been done with cells from embryos as well as adults. To determine whether this limitation of mitotic activity is caused by something in the culture medium, a mixture of "old" cells and "young" cells were cultured on the medium and then observed to see how long it took each type of cell to cease dividing and die. The results were compared with those obtained from control cultures consisting of unmixed old and young cells on the same medium. It was found that in the mixed cultures old cells stopped dividing after the same number of divisions as did control cultures only of old cells, and young cells in the mixed cultures stopped dividing after the same number of divisions as did controls consisting only of young cells. Thus, the medium must not be limiting the life span of the cells, since in the same medium, old cells stopped dividing, while young cells were still dividing vigorously. This indicates that cells from adult tissues have a shorter life span when cultured than those from fetuses, which would be expected to also be the case with cells in the body.

That body cells, like cultured cells, are intrinsically regulated and have only a limited capacity to divide has been indicated by transplanting normal cells from tissues of various ages into young hosts. The results obtained indicate that skin transplanted from young animals survives longer than skin from old animals. To further support this concept of intrinsic control of cellular aging, a number of researchers have studied cells from individuals with *progeria*. People suffering from progeria undergo changes that somewhat resemble accelerated aging. The condition generally begins during the first year of life, and the mean age at death is about 13 years. During that time they have a slower than normal growth rate and experience some loss and graying of hair, calcification of the skin and blood vessels may occur, and there are often skeletal deformities, including an expanded skull. Some (but not all) studies have reported that cells called fibroblasts obtained from patients with progeria have a shorter life span in culture than fibroblasts from normal persons of the same age. Therefore, it appears as if age-related changes in cells in the body may be reflected in the growth of cells in culture, and thus cultured cells can provide a valid comparison for *in vivo* cellular aging.

It is important to realize, however, that both *in vivo* and *in vitro* studies indicate that the capacity of a cell to undergo division generally exceeds the number of divisions the cells will undergo during a normal lifetime. Therefore, it is considered probable that any aging changes in the body that are affected by cell division are associated more with the *rate* of cell division than with the actual cessation of division. But it does appear as if there is a limit to the number of cell divisions possible by each cell. What could cause such a restriction? It has been suggested that a progressive imbalance in normal cellular components may limit cell division. For instance, it is possible that the formation of certain cellular organelles does not occur at the same rate as cell division, with the result that in succeeding generations of cells those organelles gradually become fewer in number and eventually are not present in high enough numbers to support cell division. Or organelles may be produced in progressively greater numbers during cell division until eventually this causes an imbalance that is lethal to the cell. There is evidence for such a mechanism in some fungi, where cellular senescence is associated with a proliferation of mitochondria that contain abnormal DNA. Although there is no evidence that this occurs in vertebrates, there is evidence that changes in certain nuclear DNA sequences occur with aging in some vertebrate cells, which raises the possibility that aging could be due to a failure of the cellular mechanisms that normally repair and maintain DNA.

Specific Cellular Changes During Aging

Cellular aging is generally thought to be influenced by complex cellular functions which cause changes in protein synthesis and turnover, and reduce the efficiency of DNA repair and the activity of enzymes. Although we would like to describe all the specific changes that occur within cells as they age, not enough is known concerning cellular aging to enable us to do that. But we can consider some of the more consistent changes that are observed within aging cells and attempt to relate them in some manner to the aging process.

Membrane Changes

The plasma membranes surrounding cells are very important because they regulate the transport of molecules into and out of cells. Thus, changes in the properties of plasma membranes can substantially affect cell metabolism.

Functional changes with age in plasma membranes, including alterations in the transport of ions, nutrients, amino acids, and proteins across the membrane, have been reported and are felt to play a key role in aging. There are a number of structural changes that could affect the permeability of the plasma membrane. One such change that has been reported is that cell membranes become less fluid in older animals.

Changes in the membranes surrounding certain cellular organelles are also thought to affect aging. In particular, changes in the membrane surrounding each mitochondrion are suspected of being responsible for an observed decline in the metabolic capacity of old mitochondria.

Nuclear Changes

The cellular apparatus which function in the synthesis of RNA from DNA and the synthesis of proteins are potentially unstable. Although the original changes affecting these apparatus would occur in the nucleus, the resulting cellular changes would be in the cytoplasm, where protein synthesis takes place. An increase of errors in protein synthesis would be expected to have a variety of secondary consequences, including the formation of faulty DNA, defects in the plasma membrane and in the membranes surrounding certain organelles that would affect transport across the membranes, and a progressive decline in the manufacture of mitochondria and other cellular organelles. It has been shown that during aging there is an increase in DNA damage, while the activities of the DNA repair processes decrease—both of which would tend to increase errors in protein synthesis.

The chromatin (DNA) of genes appears to become more condensed during aging, due to cross-links forming between sulfur atoms. In this condensed state chromatin is thought to be less accessible to repair enzymes. Therefore, any damage it incurs is less likely to be repaired. Chromatin that is less condensed seems to undergo less damage, or perhaps it is more efficiently repaired. Increased condensation of chromatin is also thought to cause the decreased synthesis of RNA which often occurs during aging. Some evidence suggests that chromatin condensation is also associated with a decrease in the potential of cells to divide with aging. In old lymphocytes the potential to divide can be brought back to younger levels by adding to the culture medium reducing agents that break sulfur cross-links. The reducing agents are thought to eliminate the cross-links that cause chromatin condensation.

Some evidence suggests that an inhibitor substance may be produced in the cytoplasm of aging cells and diffuse into the nucleus, where it inhibits DNA synthesis. For instance, the nuclei of young cells no longer synthesize DNA after they are transplanted into senescent cells, while the nuclei of senescent cells can be induced to resume synthesizing DNA by being transplanted into young cells.

Cytoplasmic Changes

The most consistently reported change that occurs with aging in the cytoplasm is a gradual buildup of *lipofuscin*, the so-called "age pigment" (Figure 3-4). It is felt that this accumulation can affect cell function and thus contribute to aging. For example, cells grown on culture media can be caused to react like younger cells when some of the lipofuscin that has accumulated is removed.

Mitochondrial Changes

Mitochondria may be directly involved in the production of lipofuscin and thus be responsible for the accumulation of this pigment that occurs with aging. The mitochondria of old neurons contain granules in their matrices and show a reduction in the number of folds on the inner membrane as well as some apparent disorganization of their membranes. The altered mitochondria are often found adjacent to dense lipofuscin granules, leading to the suggestion that the pigment is produced by the aging mitochondria. It should be noted, however, that the endoplasmic reticulum, lysosomes, and the Golgi apparatus have also been suggested as sites of lipofuscin formation.

Some lipofuscin granules resemble mitochondria, in that they appear to be surrounded by a double membrane; and some have foldlike structures extending from the inner membrane, much as do mitochondria. These findings suggest that aging may be associated with alterations in the fine structure of mitochondria.

Another rather well established change that occurs with age in mitochondria is a decrease in the number of mitochondria present in postmitotic cells. Since mitochondria are the main sources of metabolic energy in the body, a decrease in their numbers with age can significantly contribute to functional changes associated with aging.

Fig. 3-4 Lipofuscin granules in cardiac muscle.

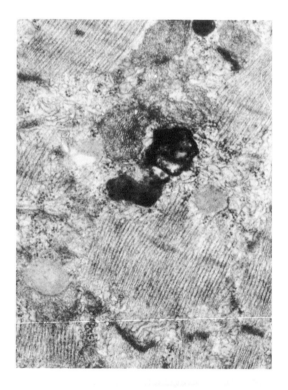

From Junqueiro, L.C., J. Carneiro, and J.A. Long: Basic Histology, *5th Ed. Copyright Appleton and Lange, 1986, p. 50.*

Chapter 3 Cellular Aging

During the sequential chemical reactions which occur on the folds of the inner mitochondrial membrane, free radicals are formed. It is felt that the free radicals may undergo oxidation reactions with the lipids of the membranes surrounding the mitochondria, causing destructive molecular changes in those membranes and thus contributing to the dysfunction of the mitochondria and the aging of the cell. To support this concept, we mentioned in Chapter 2 how adding antioxidants to the diet, which diminishes the oxidation reactions, increases the average life span of mice.

Lysosomal Changes

Lysosomes are essentially a collection of enzymes surrounded by a membrane. The lysosomal enzymes are capable of breaking down a variety of substances, including proteins, nucleic acids, carbohydrates, and fats. Thus, they play an important role in intracellular digestion and the breaking down of foreign substances.

It has been suggested that the action of the lysosomes in digestion and waste removal is less efficient in older cells. As a result, undigested, non-degradable materials can accumulate and damage the lysosomes. In fact, lipofuscin granules are regarded by some researchers as accumulations of undigestible residues of substances not completely broken down by aging lysosomes. Eventually enzymes released from damaged lysosomes may enter the cells and cause the cell to die. A reduction in the efficiency of lysosomes could result from changes in the membrane surrounding each lysosome, or from a reduction in the numbers and activity of the lysosomal enzymes.

Summary

Much of the data concerning cellular aging have been obtained by means of culturing cells in the laboratory. Although one must be cautious about assuming that reactions observed in cultured cells are the same as occur in cells in the body, several lines of evidence indicate that cell-culture data do have some validity and can make valuable contributions to our understanding of the aging processes at the cellular level.

Many known cellular changes with age involve either the synthesis or activities of proteins, including structural proteins or enzymes. Specific cellular changes observed during aging include alterations in the properties of membranes surrounding certain cytoplasmic organelles as well as in the plasma membrane, a progressive increase in the faulty synthesis of proteins, an increase in the formation of certain cross-links between molecules, the accumulation of lipofuscin granules, a decrease in the number of mitochondria, and a reduction in the efficiency of intracellular digestion and waste removal.

The Integumentary System

4

Review of Structure and Function

Epidermis • *Dermis*

Age-Related Changes

Epidermal Changes • *Dermal Changes* • *Hypodermal Changes*

Age-Related Dysfunctions

Lentigo • *Acrochordon* • *Senile Pruritus* • *Senile Keratosis* • *Seborrheic Keratosis* • *Herpes Zoster* • *Decubitus Ulcers* • *Skin Cancer*

Summary

The integumentary system comprises the skin, along with the hair, nails, and various glands located in the skin. This system, particularly the skin, is one of the most conspicuous features of the body and provides obvious reminders that a person is aging. As we age the texture and general appearance of our skin change, and wrinkles and sags appear where our skin was once smooth and tight. These changes, coupled with a gradual graying of our hair, are outward signs which herald aging changes that are occurring in our body. We might attempt to disguise these aging changes in our integumentary system through the use of various creams and hair dyes, but it is doubtful that anything so far on the market will actually delay the changes. Although plastic surgery can provide a more youthful appearance by removing some of the aging changes that have occurred in the skin, it does not actually delay the aging process.

As is the case in all body systems, aging changes in the integumentary system occur at different rates in different individuals. The rate and degree of aging changes that occur in the various components of the integumentary system are influenced by a variety of factors, including heredity, a person's dietary habits, and the levels of various hormones in the body. In addition to these intrinsic factors, extrinsic factors such as the sun and wind can significantly influence aging of the integumentary system—perhaps even to a greater extent than the intrinsic factors. The potential of skin cancer resulting from excessive exposure to the sun has

Chapter 4 The Integumentary System

been widely publicized, and the use of protective sun-shield lotions is becoming common practice. This has long been common knowledge and practice in the senior citizen meccas of the southern and southwest regions of the United States, where the combination of extensive sunshine and older persons has resulted in a large increase in skin cancers.

The aging of an individual's skin can be greatly influence by that person's occupation or recreational preferences. For instance, the skin of those whose occupations require them to spend extended periods in the sun, if not protected, tends to show age changes earlier than that of people whose occupations keep them inside most of the time. In a similar manner, those who engage in activities such as sunbathing or boating are also extensively exposed to the sun and may experience accelerated aging of their skin.

Review of Structure and Function

The components of the integumentary system perform a number of functions, all of which contribute to its single most important function—that of helping to maintain a stable internal environment (*homeostasis*) within the body so that the various cells composing the body are able to function normally. The system forms a protective covering that prevents the loss of water from the underlying tissues and serves as a barrier against the entrance of microorganisms and other foreign substances into the body. Pigment cells in the skin help protect against excessive ultraviolet radiation from the sun. Within the skin are many sweat glands and a rich network of blood vessels, both of which serve as temperature-regulating mechanisms. As body temperature rises the blood vessels in the skin dilate, thereby accommodating a greater volume of blood close to the body surface. In this manner body heat is lost by radiation from the blood to the environment. At the same time, the activity of the sweat glands may increase, causing the body surface to become wet, thereby facilitating the loss of body heat by evaporation. The integumentary system also provides information concerning the external environment to the nervous system through its many specialized receptors that are sensitive to pain, temperature, and touch.

The skin, which is the major component of the integumentary system, separates the body from the external environment by forming an uninterrupted covering over the entire body surface. It consists of two major portions (Figure 4-1). The superficial portion of the skin is the *epidermis*; the

Fig. 4-1 **Structure of the skin and hypodermis.**

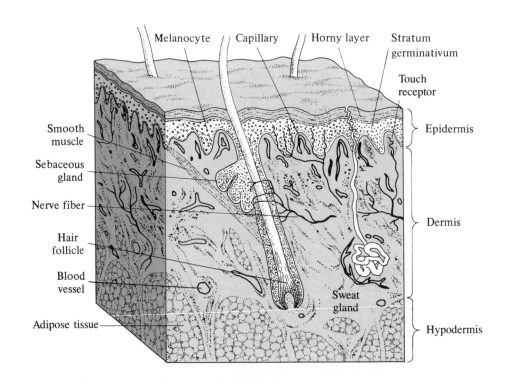

(Adapted from Barrett, J.M., et al., Biology. *Englewood Cliffs, N.J.: Prentice Hall, 1986, p. 321.*

deeper portion is the *dermis*. A layer of loose connective tissue called the *hypodermis* attaches the dermis to the underlying muscles. In many regions fat is deposited in the hypodermis, providing for padding and serving as a fat storage site.

Epidermis

The epidermis consists of several layers of thin, flat cells (squamous cells) that form a tissue referred to as stratified squamous epithelium. It is generally quite thin, but becomes thicker in regions that are subjected to constant pressure or friction, such as the soles of the feet and the palms of the hands. In fact, continued pressure at a particular site causes the epidermis to thicken to the extent that calluses or corns may be formed.

Unlike most tissues, there are no blood vessels or nerve fibers within the epidermis. Because of the lack of blood vessels, nutrients reach the cells of the epidermis, and wastes are carried away from them, only by diffusing from, or to, blood vessels located in the dermis. This indirect method of exchange is adequate for those cells located closest to the dermis. But as these basal cells divide, forcing the daughter cells toward the body surface and thus farther away from the dermal blood vessels, the rates of exchange of nutrients and wastes are not sufficient to maintain the cells, and they die. The cytoplasm of the dead cells is gradually replaced with a harder substance known as keratin. In this manner the outermost layer of the epidermis becomes composed of thin, dead cells containing a horny material.

The color of the skin is determined primarily by the amount and distribution of a dark pigment called *melanin* within the epidermis. The epidermis of dark-skinned people contains more melanin than that of light-skinned people. The blood vessels of the dermis also impart a reddish hue to the skin of light-skinned races. Oriental people contain a yellow pigment in their epidermis in addition to melanin.

Dermis

The dermis is located immediately beneath the epidermis. It is thicker than the epidermis and is composed of dense connective tissue. There are many collagenous fibers and some elastic fibers distributed throughout the dermis. The spaces between these fibers are filled with a matrix that varies in consistency from fluid to semisolid.

In contrast to the epidermis, the dermis is well supplied with blood vessels, lymphatic vessels, and nerves. It also contains *sweat glands* and oil-secreting *sebaceous glands*. Specialized receptors located in the dermis provide information to the nervous system concerning environmental stimuli producing touch, pressure, pain, and temperature changes. These receptors allow us to respond in an appropriate manner to environmental challenges.

Age-Related Changes

Most of the changes that occur in the skin with age do not constitute a threat to one's life or, for that manner, generally do not greatly affect a person's health. However, age-related changes of the skin should not be underrated by those caring for older persons. The changes tend to be so obvious to the person affected as well as to the persons he or she interacts with that they can affect an individual's self-concept. And this, in turn, can affect the person's general attitude and health.

Epidermal Changes
The epidermis tends to become thinner with age, due in part to an increased scaling off of its cells and a declining rate of cellular division that typically accompanies aging. As a result, some of the cells lost from the surface of the epidermis are not replaced. There are reports of increased permeability of the surface cells, allowing substances to pass through this barrier more readily than in younger skin.

There is a decrease in the number of cells in the epidermis capable of producing the pigment melanin. However, the pigment cells (*melanocytes*) present tend to be larger and group together, forming dark pigment plaques called *aging spots* that are typical of older persons.

Dermal Changes
The dermis is a connective tissue layer, and most of the cells within this layer are fibroblasts, which form the fibers of the connective tissue. There is a general reduction in the number of fibroblasts and fibers with aging, and thus the dermis becomes thin and somewhat translucent. At the same time, the collagenous fibers present become larger and coarser. This reduces the amount of space available for storage between the fibers, causing the fat, water, and matrix content of the dermis to diminish with age.

During aging the elastic fibers of the dermis become less resilient due to structural changes resulting from the formation of cross-links. In some locations the elastic fibers may undergo slight calcification, which further decreases their resiliency. These changes in the properties of the elastic fibers cause the skin to be less able to smooth out; thus, wrinkles and sags become common with age.

There is a reduction in the numbers of sweat glands and sebaceous glands due to their gradual atrophy. Therefore, older persons tend to sweat less and have drier, scalier skin. Because older persons do not perspire as much as younger persons, their ability to regulate body temperature is diminished, and they are more likely to suffer from heat exhaustion.

At the same time, there is a generalized reduction in blood flow to the skin, causing the skin surface to be cooler in older persons than in younger persons. The lowered skin temperature slows the growth of the fingernails and toenails. Although the nails grow more slowly, they tend to take on a yellowish color, develop ridges, and become thicker due to the deposition of calcium. This is more noticeable in the toenails, which may also become curved.

With age there is a decrease in the number and activity of hair follicles, causing a generalized loss of body hair which is especially noticeable on the head. However, the hair in the eyebrows, nostrils, and ears of old men may become coarse and grow more rapidly. Because of a concomitant decrease in the number of functioning pigment-producing cells, there is a gradual reduction of pigment in the hair with aging. As the amount of pigment in the hair decreases there is a loss of hair color and the hair becomes gray. In the complete absence of pigments the hair appears white. Heredity plays a role in the loss of hair color, and some people become gray prematurely, while others retain their usual color until quite late in life.

Structural, functional, and numerical changes with age have been reported for some of the dermal sensory receptors. A person's sensitivity to touch diminishes with age in regions of the skin which lack hairs but remains at its usual level in skin with hairs. The data on temperature and pain receptors are mixed and make any conclusions concerning their age-related changes tentative at best. There are indications that the sensitivity of temperature receptors declines with age. Data from pain research are particularly confusing in that some support an increased, others a decreased, and still others an unchanged sensitivity to pain.

Hypodermal Changes

The hypodermis, which is also referred to as the *subcutaneous tissue* because it is located just beneath the skin, is technically not part of the skin. But it undergoes changes in older people that affect the skin, so we will consider those changes. The hypodermis is essentially a layer of loose connective tissue in which much fat is stored. With aging there is a generalized loss of fat from the subcutaneous tissue. This loss is usually most obvious in the face and the limbs. The loss of subcutaneous fat is a major cause of the wrinkles that are common with age and is largely responsible for the emaciated appearance of many older persons. It is the loss of subcutaneous fat which makes a definition of aging that appeared in a recent issue of *Modern Maturity* magazine so on target. The definition stated that "Old age is when, upon getting out of the bath tub, you notice that the full-length mirror is steamed up—and you are glad of it."

The loss of subcutaneous fat also results in a loss of padding. Because of this, as well as the reduction in blood supply to the skin, older persons are more likely to develop pressure sores, especially when bedridden. The sores generally develop in areas where the skin is under constant pressure as it passes over bony prominences. Reduction of subcutaneous fat also diminishes its value as an insulator of the body, allowing greater amounts of body heat to escape and causing the person to feel chilly much of the time. Because of the fat loss and diminished blood supply to the skin, an older person may need to keep a room so warm to be comfortable that younger persons feel uncomfortable.

Age-Related Dysfunctions

Lentigo

After a person is about 50 years old dark brown irregular areas commonly form in the skin, most often on the dorsal surface of the hands and forearms, and on the face. These darkened areas are so common with aging that they are referred to as *senile freckles*, although the technical name for the condition is *lentigo*. The areas, which are flat, result from increased deposition of melanin. With age they gradually increase in size and number and become darker. The actual cause of these pigmented areas is not known. There is not thought to be any relation between their formation and exposure to the sun, and they have no tendency to become malignant.

Acrochordon

Acrochordon is characterized by small pendulous skin growths, commonly referred to as *cutaneous tags*, that are often found on the chest, neck, eyelids, or armpits of older women. They contain dermal connective tissues and blood vessels, and resemble small, benign tumors. They are thought to be associated with hormonal imbalances.

Senile Pruritus

We mentioned earlier that with aging there is a gradual loss of oil-secreting sebaceous glands and sweat glands, as well as a reduction in the water content of the skin. These changes cause the skin to become drier and less pliant and commonly lead to the development of tiny cracks, which cause itching and other discomfort. This condition is called *senile pruritus* (itching). If left untreated, the cracks may worsen and form deeper fissures that exude tissue fluid. A crust may form over the affected areas in severe cases.

Pruritus may be worsened by any external factor which tends to dry the skin, such as low humidity, high temperature, and strong wind. Excessive bathing can also dry the skin and exacerbate the condition.

Senile Keratosis

Senile keratosis, which is also called *actinic keratosis*, is characterized by localized red areas on the skin. The areas are generally flat when they first appear but gradually thicken, become scaly, and change to a yellow-brown color. If peeled off, the scaly surface generally reforms. This condition most commonly affects the middle-aged or elderly, particularly those of fair complexions who have had excessive exposure to the sun. The lesions are more common in men, especially on the face, neck, and forearms, which tend to receive the greatest amount of sunlight.

The lesions of senile keratosis must be carefully watched, as they can be precancerous and remain dormant for many years before giving rise to squamous cell carcinoma. Malignant keratoses tend to become harder as they develop.

Seborrheic Keratosis

Seborrheic keratosis is characterized by the formation of benign epidermal tumors that are generally not precancerous. The growths of seborrheic keratosis begin as oval-shaped raised plaques that have a yellowish hue. They gradually thicken, enlarge, and become brown or black. The term seborrheic refers to a greasy scale that often forms on the surface of the tumors. Although this covering resembles sebum produced by the sebaceous glands of the skin, it is not thought to be actually formed by those glands. The surface layers of the growths, which are most common on the face and trunk, may scale-off if rubbed.

Herpes Zoster

Herpes zoster is a viral disease that is not restricted to elderly persons but is more common in them. The virus that causes this disease, which is also referred to as *shingles*, is believed to be the same virus that causes chickenpox. After entering the body and causing chickenpox when a person is younger, the virus is thought to remain dormant for many years in sensory divisions of spinal nerves—most often those nerves supplying the back and chest. When it becomes reactivated, the virus attacks the sensory nerve fibers and the skin supplied by those nerves.

The disease begins with the person experiencing itching and aching pain along the path of the affected nerves. Eventually, small plaques appear on the skin along the paths of these nerves. They first appear on the back and then extend around the sides to the chest. The plaques are quickly replaced by small fluid-filled vesicles, often within a day. Eventually the vesicles dry down and form a crust, which scales off, leaving pigmented areas where the vesicles had been. Shingles generally runs its course in one to two weeks, but can last considerably longer. Even after the lesions heal the person may experience pain for a number of months.

Decubitus Ulcers

Decubitus ulcers, or *pressure sores*, are cavities of dead tissue that form in the skin. They generally occur in people who are bedridden or otherwise immobilized, such as those confined to a wheelchair or who spend their days sitting rather than moving about. For this reason they are common in paralyzed persons or older persons who have not received proper care. The ulcers most often occur over bony prominences that have little subcutaneous fat between them and the skin, and which are constantly in contact with a surface, such as a bed or a chair. Ulcers of the back, buttocks, and heels are common in bedridden persons. Those who sit for extended periods may develop ulcers on their buttocks, over the ischial tuberosities of the pelvis.

The ulcers can develop rather quickly, so daily skin care is necessary for bedridden or inactive persons. If the ulceration is treated when it is shallow it may respond quickly to treatment. But deeper ulcers, which may completely penetrate the skin, have such extensive areas of tissue death and are so prone to infection that healing may require months of treatment. The ulcers are generally treated successfully with antibiotics, but it may be necessary to surgically remove some regions of tissue surrounding a large ulcer.

Skin Cancer

Cancers of the skin are fairly common. There are a number of different types of skin cancers, some of which originate in the epidermis, and others in the dermis, and still others are associated with the glands of the skin.

Although any new skin growth or any change in the appearance of a preexisting skin growth, such as a wart or a mole, should be carefully watched, most cancers of the skin are not malignant. That is, they are not likely to spread to other areas of the body, and therefore most do not pose a threat to one's life. Effective treatment of any cancer is greatly aided by early detection. Because of their location on the surface of the body, skin cancers stand a better chance than most cancers of being detected early and therefore receiving early treatment.

Basal Cell Carcinoma. This type of skin cancer, which is the most common form, is so named because it develops from cells in the deepest, or basal, layer of the epidermis. Its development is associated with exposure to sunlight; therefore, it is most common in regions of the world known for their extensive sunshine. It is also most prevalent in light-skinned races, who are especially sensitive to the damaging effects of excessive exposure to the sun.

The lesions of basal cell carcinoma, which are only rarely malignant, are small and smooth at first but may enlarge and develop a crust on their surface. If not removed surgically, the growths can invade and destroy the underlying tissue.

Squamous Cell Carcinoma. As the name implies, this type of cancer develops from squamous epithelium. Squamous cell carcinoma is much less common than is basal cell carcinoma, but because it often is malignant and capable of spreading to other parts of the body, it is more dangerous. As with basal cell carcinoma, its development is associated with excessive exposure to sunlight. Because of this, it is more common in older persons, and especially in older men.

The tumor has the general appearance of a wart. It is often in the form of a hard nodule with small reddened areas showing through its surface. In some cases an ulcer may develop in the growth.

Malignant Melanoma. This is a highly malignant and potentially dangerous form of skin cancer. It usually develops in the pigment cells (melanocytes) of a preexisting epidermal mole. Moles have a tendency to be inherited and are generally stable. However, occasionally, perhaps due to chronic irritation, the cells of a mole will begin actively dividing and form a malignant melanoma. For this reason, all moles should be continually examined so that changes in size or texture are detected. Any such change could herald a malignant condition. Early detection and surgical removal of malignant melanomas can extend a person's survival time.

Secondary Skin Cancer. Some cancers that are detected in the skin actually originate in other regions of the body and spread to the skin. The spreading most commonly occurs through the lymph or blood. Such cancers, which are usually in the form of rapidly growing nodules, are referred to as *secondary cancers*. The nodules of secondary skin cancer often appear in groups in the skin overlying the site of the primary cancer. For instance, if the primary cancer is in a breast, the skin nodules tend to occur on the anterior wall of the chest; when the primary cancer is in a kidney, the nodules tend to occur in the skin of the small of the back.

Secondary skin cancers are more common in persons over 50 years old. Because the nodules do not cause symptoms, their presence may not cause alarm and they may be ignored. No new growth on the skin of any person, particularly an elderly person, should be ignored, as discovering a secondary skin cancer may lead to the detection of a heretofore unknown primary cancer.

Summary

Because of its location on the body surface, aging changes of the integumentary system are influenced by environmental factors as well as by changes within the body. The skin tends to become thinner, less pliable, and dryer with age. There is a generalized loss of fat from the hypodermis beneath the skin, which, coupled with the diminished elasticity, causes the skin to become loose, and folds and wrinkles become prominent. The fat loss also causes the body framework to become more obvious, giving an emaciated appearance to older persons.

Although the number of pigment-producing cells diminishes significantly with age, those remaining move closer together to form dark aging spots. Nails become thicker and curved, while growing more slowly. There is a generalized loss of hair, and the remaining hair tends to lose its color and appear gray.

The Skeletal System

5

The skeletal system consists of two types of tissue: bone and cartilage. Each of these tissues has unique structures and functions which we will consider.

We are all well aware of two obvious, but important, functions performed by the bones composing our skeletal system. Bones serve as a framework that supports the soft tissues of the body and provides points of attachment for most of the body muscles. And through the special moveable joints formed where many bones meet, the skeletal system determines the extent and type of movements permitted by the body. But the skeletal system performs several other important functions that are not as obvious, and we may not be as aware of them.

Protection of vital internal organs is a function we take for granted. Many of our most vital organs are located in regions that are protected by the skeletal system. For instance, the skull and vertebral column protect the brain and spinal cord, which constitute the entire central nervous system; and the heart and lungs are protected by the rib cage.

One reason the skeleton provides structural support and protection so well is that bone is very hard and strong. Another function performed by the skeletal system is responsible for this strength and firmness: bone serves as a major storage area for a number of minerals that are vital to many body functions. Calcium, sodium, phosphorus, and potassium are among the more prevalent minerals stored in bone. These minerals must also be maintained at certain concentrations in the blood. As the blood levels of these minerals drop below their optimal levels they can be removed from bone and enter the blood, thus raising their concentrations to the levels necessary for proper functioning of various organs. When the blood levels of these minerals are adequate they are again deposited in bone, where they strengthen the bone and remain until they are needed again to maintain the blood levels.

A final function of the skeletal system that we only appreciate if it malfunctions is the formation of blood cells. Although blood cells are produced by tissues in several different organs during embryonic development, following birth they are formed only within the red bone marrow tissue of certain bones. This is a vital function and it is certainly well protected by the skeletal system.

Changes in the skeletal system with age can significantly alter a person's life-style. Movement can become painful as joints become stiff, and their articulating surfaces roughened or eroded. Posture is often affected as structural changes occur in the vertebral column. And the protection afforded by the skeleton may lessen with age as the bones lose minerals and become brittle and fragile.

Review of Structure and Function

Bone
There are bones of various shapes in the skeletal system, which are generally grouped as short, flat, irregular, and long bones. For purposes of reviewing the terminology associated with bones we will describe only a long bone.

Each long bone has a shaft (*diaphysis*) and two ends, called *epiphyses* (Figure 5-1). The diaphysis contains a central *medullary cavity* that is surrounded by a cylinder of a type of bone referred to as *compact bone*. The medullary cavity is also called the *yellow bone marrow cavity* because fat is stored within it. The walls of the epiphyses, like the shaft, are formed of compact bone. But internally the epiphyses are filled with interconnecting plates of a type of bone that, because of its appearance, is called *spongy bone*. In the epiphyses of certain bones the spongy bone contains *red bone marrow*, where blood cells are produced.

When examined with a microscope the appearance of compact bone is rather surprising. It is not just a formless mass of minerals. Rather, it is seen to be organized into groups of interconnecting canals called

Fig. 5-1   Structure of a long bone

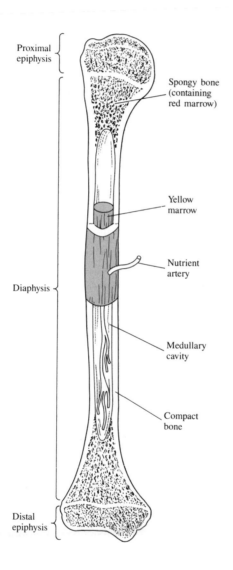

Proximal epiphysis

Spongy bone (containing red marrow)

Yellow marrow

Nutrient artery

Diaphysis

Medullary cavity

Compact bone

Distal epiphysis

haversian systems (Figure 5-2). Each of the haversian systems, which generally run parallel to the long axis of the bone, has a central *haversian canal* that is surrounded by several layers *(lamellae)* of bone. Small cavities called *lacunae* are located between adjacent lamellae. Within each lacuna is a bone-forming cell called an *osteocyte*. Tiny canals called *canaliculi* interconnect the lacunae within each haversian system. The canaliculi allow for the passage of nutrients and wastes between osteocytes in adjacent lacunae. Nutrients are carried to, and wastes carried away from, the osteocytes by blood capillaries located in the haversian canal.

The lacunae are surrounded by a matrix consisting of a framework of collagenous fibers embedded in inorganic salts—principally calcium and phosphate salts. Because collagen fibers are capable of undergoing stretching and twisting, their presence helps bone to withstand those forces. The salts, in turn, allow bone to resist compression. Therefore, while the salts cause bone to be exceptionally strong, the fibers keep it from being brittle.

In the embryo bone formation begins in one of two ways. In some bones a matrix framework containing collagen fibers is first laid down. In other bones a cartilage model of the bone is formed first. Specialized cells appear in the matrix and form bone by replacing the fibers or the cartilage with inorganic salts. Even in adults new bone continues to be formed as old bone is broken down, or resorbed. The continuous formation and resorption of bone serves to replace old matrix, which tends to become brittle, and remodels the bones to better meet changing structural requirements. Thus, as a person gains weight their bones can become thicker and stronger.

A number of factors can influence the development and replacement of bone. One such factor is stress. Since bone is a living tissue, it is capable of undergoing structural changes that cause it to become stronger when subjected to stress. When bone is subjected to heavy loads for a prolonged time, the body responds by depositing increased amounts of collagen fibers and inorganic salts in the bone. On the other hand, in the absence of stress salts may be withdrawn from bone. There are two main kinds of stresses a bone may be subjected to. Gravity constantly stresses the bones, mainly because the skeletal system must support the weight of the body— which is a result of gravity. Stress is also placed on bones by functional forces, such as those that result when contracting muscles exert a pull on bone. This being the case, it is to be expected that as a person becomes older and exercises less and spends more time sitting or perhaps becomes bedridden, bone formation is affected.

Fig. 5-2 The haversian system of compact bone.

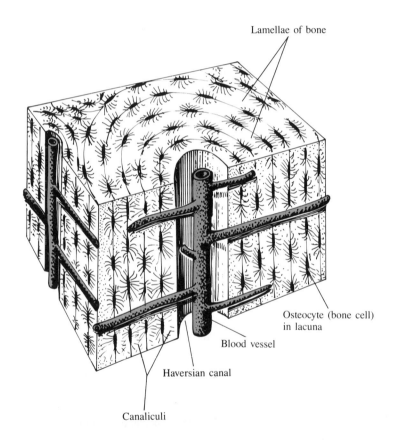

Lamellae of bone

Osteocyte (bone cell)
in lacuna

Blood vessel

Haversian canal

Canaliculi

From Evans, W.F.: Anatomy and Physiology, *3rd Ed. Englewood Cliffs, N.J., Prentice Hall, 1983, p. 50.*

The interactions of two hormones also play an important role in regulating bone development. Elevated levels of *parathormone* from the parathyroid glands causes an increase in the number and the activity of cells that break down bone. When bone is broken down and resorbed calcium is released from the bone. The calcium then enters the blood and raises the blood calcium level. As a balance to this activity, the hormone *calcitonin*, which is released from the thyroid gland, has an effect opposite to that of parathormone. Calcitonin causes the rate of bone resorption to decrease and lowers the blood calcium level. In fact, since calcitonin favors the deposition of minerals, it stimulates the formation of new bone. In a normal person bone is constantly being formed and resorbed as a result of the interactions of these two hormones.

Nutrition also has a great influence on the development of bone. Normal bone development requires a balanced diet that provides the body with a variety of essential substances. One such substance that must be present in the diet is vitamin D. Vitamin D assists calcium across the walls of the digestive tract and into the blood stream. The blood calcium level must be high if bone formation is to occur. Getting older persons to follow a balanced diet often presents a problem, as their appetites tend to be diminished and the condition of their teeth may cause them to have difficulty chewing some foods.

Cartilage

Although most components of the skeletal system are composed of bone, *cartilage* plays an important role in several areas. Like bone, cartilage is composed of matrix in which cells are embedded in lacunae. In cartilage the cells are called *chondrocytes*. And like bone, the matrix contains mostly collagenous fibers. In some types of cartilage elastic fibers are also prevalent. However, instead of being surrounded by calcium and phosphate salts, as is the case in bone, the fibers in cartilage are embedded in *chondrin*, which is a complex formed of protein and carbohydrate molecules joined together. Chondrin forms a firm matrix—although not as firm as the mineral salt matrix of bone—and allows cartilage to serve as a structural support. At the same time, the presence of large numbers of fibers in the chondrin makes a certain amount of flexibility possible in cartilage, which is not allowed to any great extent by the hard matrix of bone. Based upon variations in the fiber content of their matrices, three types of cartilage are identified: hyaline, elastic, and fibrocartilage (Figure 5-3). Hyaline cartilage is the most abundant type.

In contrast to bone, cartilage does not contain blood vessels. The only blood supply to cartilage is provided by blood vessels located in a

Fig. 5-3 Photomicrographs of (a) hyaline cartilage (×300), (b) elastic cartilage (×350), and (c) fibrocartilage (×500).

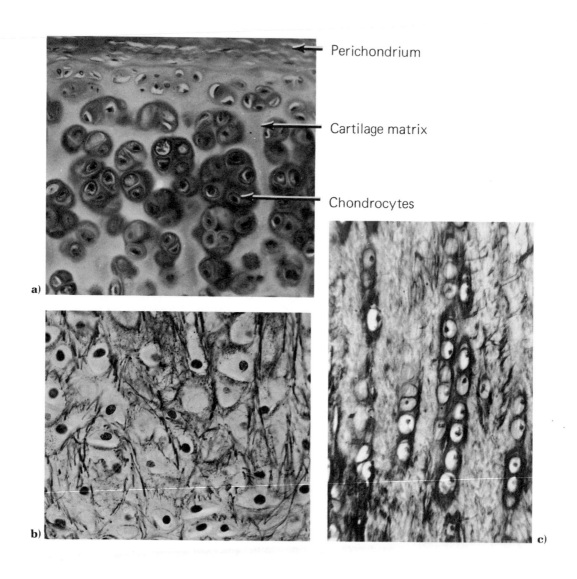

Perichondrium

Cartilage matrix

Chondrocytes

From Junqueira, L.C., J. Carneiro, and J.A. Long: Basic Histology, *5th Ed. Copyright Appleton and Lange, 1986, pp. 131, 136, 138.*

connective tissue layer that surrounds cartilage. Because of this arrangement the survival and growth of the chondrocytes is dependent upon the diffusion of nutrients and wastes through the chondrin of the matrix to and from the blood vessels surrounding the cartilage. This is a less efficient method of exchange than that of bone, where the capillaries within the haversian systems pass close to the osteocytes. As a consequence, when injured, cartilage tends to heal more slowly than bone.

Age-Related Changes

The major age-related change in the skeletal system is the loss of calcium from bone. This loss is more severe in older women than in men. In women, the amount of calcium in the bones steadily decreases after about the age of 30, and it has been reported that by the age of 70 a woman's skeletal system may have lost 30% or more of its calcium. Although calcium is also lost from the bones of older men, their bones contain more calcium than those of women, and men generally do not begin to lose calcium from their bones until after the age of 60.

The actual cause of the calcium loss from bone is not known, and there are no certain methods of preventing the loss. We mentioned earlier that throughout one's lifetime the matrix of bone is continually being resorbed and replaced by new matrix. In elderly persons, however, not only is much calcium lost from bone, but protein synthesis may occur so slowly that new collagen fibers are not formed in the matrix as rapidly as the old fibers are broken down. As the number of collagen fibers decreases, the bone matrix gradually comes to contain a greater proportion of inorganic salts, even though the matrix is also losing calcium. The increased percentage of mineral salts that occurs with aging is thought to be the reason that the bones of elderly persons often become brittle and fracture easily.

When bone is incinerated the collagen fibers it contains are destroyed, and the ash that is left is composed primarily of mineral salts. Incineration of bone provides interesting data concerning the increased percentage of salts as compared with fibers with aging. When bones of infants are incinerated, the ash that remains represents about one-half of the dry weight of the bone. When bones from a middle-aged person are incinerated, the ash represents about four-fifths of the dry weight of the bone, and the ash from old bones equals about seven-eighths of the dry weight of the bone. These figures indicate a significant reduction in the amount of collagen (protein) fibers present in the matrix of bone with aging.

While these changes in the composition of the matrix are occurring, bone resorption proceeds and causes the centrally located medullary cavity of long bones to become enlarged and the compact bone forming the wall of the shaft to become thinner. Resorption may also cause haversian canals to increase in diameter with age. Thus, the decreased ability of bone to withstand stress with increasing age is thought to result from a combination of a loss of mineral salts and collagen fibers, an increase in the percentage of mineral salts in the remaining bone, and an increased porosity of bone due to a failure to replace all bone that has been resorbed.

Bone formation and resorption are complex processes, and just what alters their balance with age is not known. There are a number of possibilities that have been suggested. Perhaps the ability of cells (osteoblasts) to form bone is affected with age. This would explain why resorbed bone is not always replaced in older persons. It is also possible that a hormonal imbalance develops, particularly between parathormone and calcitonin. And perhaps the walls of the blood vessels that supply bone become hardened (sclerosed), thus diminishing the exchange of substances through the walls and affecting the nutrition of bone.

One of the main roles of cartilage in the skeletal system is to contribute to the smooth functioning of the various moveable joints of the body. In most joints the surfaces of the bones forming the joint are covered with an *articular cartilage* (Figure 5-4). Thus, during movement the adjoining articular cartilages rub together, rather than bone against bone. The structure of cartilage makes it much more suitable for this role than bone. In very old people the cartilages of joints often become thinner and show other signs of deterioration, including erosion of the joint surfaces. These changes cause discomfort and restrict movement of the joint. Some of the deterioration of the joint cartilages is thought to be a result of repeated trauma, such as the joints of athletes are subjected to. However, some deterioration must be due to functional changes internal to the body, as persons who have lead rather sedentary lives also commonly experience these joint changes as they grow older.

In some locations, such as between the ribs and the sternum, bones are held together in a joint that is only slightly flexible by rather large areas of cartilage (costal cartilages). These cartilages frequently undergo calcification with age, restricting the flexibility of the rib cage and making breathing more difficult.

Changes also occur with age in the fibrocartilage that forms the intervertebral discs which separate each vertebra of the spinal column.

Fig. 5-4   **Structure of a freely moveable joint.**

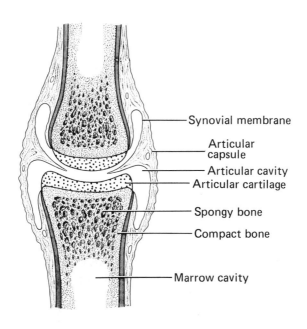

Synovial membrane

Articular capsule

Articular cavity

Articular cartilage

Spongy bone

Compact bone

Marrow cavity

From Junqueira, L.C., J. Carneiro, and J.A. Long: Basic Histology, *5th Ed. Copyright Appleton and Lange, 1986, p. 161.*

Fibrocartilage is more compressible than other types of cartilage and is well suited for providing cushioning while supporting the weight of the body. The center of each disc, which is referred to as the *nucleus pulposus*, is semisolid and thus somewhat softer than the rest of the disc. One common cause of back discomfort at any age is the squeezing of the nucleus pulposus to one side of the disc. This can be caused by trauma, deformity of the vertebral column, or poor posture. The displaced nucleus can cause the disc to protrude, or in severe cases to rupture. If the protrusion or rupture presses on spinal nerves it can cause severe pain along the paths of the nerves and in the regions supplied by the nerves.

After about 40 years of age the cartilage of the discs experiences a gradual loss of cells and water, with the result that the nucleus becomes less mucoid in character. Pigment, which may be lipofuscin, forms in the discs, and calcification of the discs, as well as several other degenerative processes, often begins. It has been reported that all persons over the age of 40 show some deterioration in their intervertebral discs—especially in the lumbar and cervical regions. The increased frequency in back pain in older persons is thought to be associated with these degenerative changes. However, back discomfort is not necessarily progressive with age. There seems to be some strengthening of the outer regions of the intervertebral discs after age 50, thus improving the ability of the disc to resist protrusion or rupture caused by displacement of the nucleus pulposus.

Age-Related Dysfunctions

Arthritis

When considering diseases associated with old age, arthritis is probably one of the first to come to mind. *Arthritis* is a general term that refers to various types of inflammation or degenerative changes that occur in joints. Although arthritic changes can occur at any age, they are much more common in older persons. Accompanying the inflammation of arthritis there may be pathological changes in the membranes surrounding the joint, as well as in the cartilage covering the ends of the bones forming the joint and in the bones themselves. These changes typically cause the joint to swell and make movement painful.

The three most common types of arthritis are osteoarthritis, rheumatoid arthritis, and gouty arthritis.

Chapter 5 The Skeletal System

Osteoarthritis. This is the most common form of arthritis, affecting an estimated 30 to 40 million people in the United States alone. *Osteoarthritis* is a chronic inflammation that causes the articular cartilages covering the ends of the bones in the affected joint to gradually degenerate. For this reason the condition is also referred to as *degenerative joint disease.*

With the degeneration of the articular cartilages, bony spurs develop on the exposed ends of the bones forming the joint. Thus, movement of the joint causes the roughened ends of two bones, rather than two smooth cartilages, to rub together. Consequently, the joint swells and becomes stiff and painful. In chronic osteoarthritis, ligaments supporting the joint may also be damaged, causing the joint to become unstable.

The cause of osteoarthritis is not definitely known. Some of the changes associated with the condition are thought to be partly due to changes that occur during aging in the collagen and elastic fibers of bone and cartilage. It is also possible that reduced circulation to joints may produce degenerative changes in the cartilage of joints. Because osteoarthritis is most common in older people, it is also considered to be due in part to the "wear and tear" that joints are subjected to throughout one's lifetime. Thus, except in a joint that has been injured or has experienced excessive prolonged stress, the condition generally does not show up before middle age. For this reason, the constant stresses placed on joints by excessive body weight or poor posture, and repetitive job-related stresses, are thought to contribute to the development of osteoarthritis. There are also indications that heredity may be a factor.

Osteoarthritis may cause pain and disfigurement in the fingers, but it is more common in the lower limbs and spinal column—both of which bear the body's weight when one is not lying down. Osteoarthritis of the spine may be associated with chronic backache, and in such cases bony spurs may develop on the vertebrae and eventually fuse several adjacent vertebrae together. The fusion of vertebrae stabilizes the spinal column, but limits the movement allowed by the column. It has been estimated that 90% of all people have some joint degeneration by the age of 40, but many are unaware of these early osteoarthritic changes, as they often do not become severe enough to cause symptoms until later in life.

Rheumatoid Arthritis. *Rheumatoid arthritis* is not strictly a disease of old age. It can begin at any age. The first symptoms of the disease often appear before a person is 50 years old. However, rheumatoid arthritis is a common problem with old people, as it tends to become more debilitating with age.

This form of arthritis tends to severely damage the affected joints, which are most often the small joints of the body, such as those in the hands, feet, ankles, elbows, and wrist. The condition is much more common in women than in men.

Most freely moveable joints are surrounded and completely enclosed by a double-layered membrane called the articular capsule. The outer layer of the capsule is formed of a very strong connective tissue. The inner layer is composed of a thinner vascular connective tissue called the *synovial membrane* (Figure 5-4). The synovial membrane produces a thick fluid (synovial fluid) which fills the space within the articular capsule, where it serves as a lubricant for the joint surfaces and provides nourishment for the cartilages of the joint. Rheumatoid arthritis begins with inflammation of the synovial membrane. Because this membrane is highly vascular, the inflammation causes it to become swollen and thickened, producing severe pain when the joint is moved. Prolonged inflammation of the synovial membrane can cause the formation of scar tissue and masses of granulation tissue, which consists of capillaries and fibroblast cells. This abnormal growth is known as a *pannus*.

In severe cases of rheumatoid arthritis the pannus grows over the articular cartilage and destroys it. It may then erode the surface of the bone that lies beneath the cartilage. In time the pannus can expand throughout the joint cavity, causing extensive damage to the joint and its capsule. The growth of the pannus may be so extensive that the ligaments surrounding the joint become inflamed and stretched and eventually may be destroyed. Fibrous tissue gradually invades the pannus; thus the movement of the affected joint is severely restricted. Chronic swelling of the joint causes the tendons that pass over the joint to be pushed out of their normal positions, producing some deformity of the joint. In severe cases, calcification of the pannus may fuse the bones forming the joint, making it immovable.

Although the cause of rheumatoid arthritis is not known, many investigators suspect that a bacterial or viral infection may initiate the disease process. It is also felt that some persons have a genetic tendency to develop the disease. Once the disease process has been initiated rheumatoid arthritis often appears to be an immune disease, in which a foreign substance becomes located in highly vascular tissue—such as the synovial membrane—where it serves as an antigen and causes an inflammatory response by the body's immune system. Or some suggest that, rather than requiring invasion by a foreign substance, rheumatoid arthritis may be an autoimmune disease, where the body's immune system produces antibodies that act against one's own tissues.

Rheumatoid arthritis can become so severe that surgery may be necessary to repair the affected joints, and in some cases the diseased bone of the joint is removed and replaced with a prosthetic device. In other cases the joint is surgically fused, causing it to be permanently immovable but making it stable enough that it can support the body weight and thus, in the case of the knee, be used for walking.

Gouty Arthritis. Gout is an inherited condition in which an excessive level of uric acid builds up in the blood. Uric acid is formed when purines are broken down, and is normally maintained at acceptable levels in the blood by being excreted through the kidneys. Above-normal levels of uric acid in the blood are caused either by an increased production of uric acid or a reduction in the ability of the kidneys to excrete it.

The excessive level of uric acid in the blood causes so much of the acid to enter the body fluids that they become overly saturated and eventually the acid precipitates out of the fluids and forms sodium urate crystals in the soft tissues and joints of the body. When the joints are affected, the condition is called *gouty arthritis*. As the crystals accumulate in the tissues surrounding the joint they cause severe pain and swelling. The attacks usually subside after a few days but often chronically reappear every few weeks or months. The inflammation may become so severe that the cartilage and underlying bone of the joint are eroded.

Gouty arthritis is more common in males, usually first appearing between the ages of 40 and 55 years and often becoming more severe with advancing age. Gout is popularly associated with excessive eating of rich foods and drinking of alcoholic beverages, but it is uncertain whether such a connection really exists. However, since gout is closely related to purine metabolism, a person experiencing discomfort from gout should restrict proteins, which are high in purines, and fats, which tend to impede the excretion of uric acid. On the other hand, carbohydrates seem to enhance the elimination of uric acid and thus can help reduce the symptoms of gout.

Osteoporosis

A common condition in elderly persons, especially in women after menopause, is a gradual reduction in the formation of new bone while the rate of bone resorption remains normal. This produces spotty areas in the bone where much bone matrix has been removed and not replaced. Thus, this condition is referred to as *osteoporosis*, or "porous bone." Osteoporosis is essentially an extreme version of bone replacement that continually occurs normally in adults. For many people this loss of bone may not produce any symptoms, but it can result in diminished height and cause curvature of the spine and backache as vertebrae are eroded and compressed. It often causes a general reduction in the strength of bones, making them more easily fractured.

Any bone may experience the changes of osteoporosis. But it is most noticeable when the vertebrae of the spine are affected, as compression of the vertebrae produces the hunched back and shortening of the trunk that are so common in older women. The femur (thigh bone) bears much of the body's weight, and when affected by osteoporosis fractures of the neck of the femur commonly occur.

The cause of osteoporosis is unknown. As with most diseases of aging, there is probably no one cause. Rather, a number of factors are thought to be involved. One likely factor is a long-term diet deficient in calcium. In fact, because young women tend to be especially weight conscious and avoid fatty foods, including milk and cheese, osteoporosis may begin to develop before the age of 30. Calcium deficiency may occur in older persons even though they attempt to maintain a balanced diet containing an adequate level of calcium, as they are not able to absorb milk and other dairy products as well as younger persons. Calcium absorption by the intestines is hindered by an age-related decrease in the level of vitamin D in the blood. If sufficient calcium is not obtained through the diet, the body attempts to maintain adequate levels in the blood by resorbing bone and putting the calcium that is released into the blood. As we mentioned earlier, if the resorbed bone is not replaced by the formation of new bone, the weakened bone typical of osteoporosis results.

Age-related loss of bone generally begins at about age 40, after which women may gradually lose up to 50% of their skeletal mass over the next 20 to 30 years. During this same age span the rate of bone loss in men is about two-thirds that of women. Because some degree of osteoporosis occurs in 65% of women over age 65 but in only 21% of men, hormonal changes associated with menopause are thought to be a major factor in its development. For this reason, estrogen therapy has been used in postmenopausal women to treat osteoporosis. There is evidence that increasing the level of estrogen in the blood can slow the removal of calcium and other minerals from bone and may actually promote new bone formation. However, estrogen therapy increases a woman's chances of developing cancer of the uterus. A combination of estrogen and progesterone is generally prescribed, as this seems to reduce the likelihood of uterine cancer.

Injection of the hormone calcitonin has recently been approved by the Food and Drug Administration as a treatment for postmenopausal osteoporosis. Calcitonin acts to inhibit bone resorption, thereby reducing bone loss. Taking calcium tablets is also a popular treatment for osteoporosis, but its effectiveness has not been proven and has been frequently questioned. However, several studies have shown that women who have adequate long-term intake of calcium have lower incidences of hip fractures and compression of vertebrae. The studies indicate that postmenopausal women should ingest about 1500 mg of calcium each day. It would require six glasses of milk to reach this level, so calcium tablets provide a more convenient means of assuring adequate calcium intake.

It has also been suggested that inactivity may contribute to the development of osteoporosis. In support of this, it has been shown that the condition is more prevalent in people who are immobilized for prolonged periods, such as those suffering from severe joint disease of fractures. This being the case, exercise should help prevent osteoporosis, and there is evidence that continued weight-bearing activities such as walking yield a long-term increase in bone calcium. A recent study showed that 45 minutes of moderate weight-bearing exercise three times a week greatly slows the loss of calcium in older women and, if continued for a year, can reverse the demineralization that has occurred.

Tumors of Bone
When bone cancer develops in older persons it has generally traveled to the bone through the bloodstream from a cancer located elsewhere in the body—such as the lungs, breast, or prostate gland. Bone cancer can weaken the bone and cause joint symptoms similar to those of arthritis.

Summary

Calcium and other minerals are maintained at adequate levels in the blood in part by being withdrawn from bone. With increased age this withdrawal often occurs at a faster rate than the minerals are deposited, causing a gradual loss of calcium from bone matrix. At the same time, the formation of new collagen fibers in the matrix occurs at a slower rate. As a consequence of these changes, bone tends to become more porous, weakened, and brittle with age.

The cartilages forming the smooth surfaces of joints tend to become thinner and deteriorate somewhat with age. This deterioration, along with erosion of the underlying bone, causes joint disorders to be common in elderly persons. The cartilage that forms the discs between the vertebrae of the spinal column also undergoes degenerative changes with age, resulting in decreased flexibility of the spinal column and increased back pain.

The Muscular System

Review of Structure and Function

    Skeletal Muscle • *Smooth Muscle* • *Cardiac Muscle*

Age-Related Changes

    Skeletal Muscle • *Smooth Muscle* • *Cardiac Muscle*

Age-Related Dysfunctions

    Parkinson's Disease • *Myasthenia Gravis*

Summary

There are over 600 muscles in our body. Some are so small and their actions so obscure that we are generally not aware of them. We take for granted our ability to close our eyes, compress our cheeks, frown, smile, and numerous other rather inconspicuous movements, without giving much thought to the small muscles that make them possible. However, we are well aware of the larger muscles that move our major joints and help us to defy gravity by standing erect and walking or running. In fact, many of us expend considerable time and effort in our younger years attempting to develop these larger muscles in order to improve the appearance of our body. Therefore, when changes in the muscular system with increased age alter our body contours it can be depressing enough to greatly affect our self-image.

Muscle is composed of contractile cells that actively develop tension and shorten. Muscles that are attached to the bones of our skeletal system cross a joint and are connected to a bone on each side of the joint. Thus, when such a muscle contracts and shortens it moves at least one of the bones forming the joint. But some muscles do not attach to the skeletal system. Rather, they are located in the walls of organs, blood vessels, or various other tubes. Contraction of these muscles compresses the organs or tubes they surround, thereby emptying the organ, moving materials within the body, or causing the excretion of some substances through body orifices. The contractions of muscle tissue that make these actions occur also produce significant amounts of heat. Much of this heat is used to maintain body temperature at normal levels.

Review of Structure and Function

There are three types of muscle in the body: skeletal muscle, smooth muscle, and cardiac muscle. Each has a unique structure and performs specialized functions. We want to briefly consider the structure and function of each type of muscle.

Skeletal Muscle

The muscles we are most familiar with are *skeletal muscles*. Most attach to bones and cause all the movements of the various joints of the skeleton. Skeletal muscles are voluntary muscles; that is, their contractions are generally under the conscious control of the individual. Therefore, as a rule, voluntary muscles do not contract unless the person wants them to. However, this is not always the case. In reflex acts, such as removing one's hand from a painful stimulus or maintaining an upright posture, no conscious thoughts are involved. In these cases, the skeletal muscles respond involuntarily. Skeletal muscle contractions are under the control of signals transmitted to the muscle by a portion of the nervous system known as the somatic nervous system.

When viewed microscopically, skeletal muscle cells, which are also called muscle *fibers,* are seen to contain more than one nucleus and have alternating light and dark bands across the cell, giving them a striped, or striated, appearance (Figure 6-1). The bands are the result of thousands of regularly aligned threadlike *myofibrils* oriented lengthwise throughout the cell. The myofibrils are separated into a series of repeating segments known as *sarcomeres* by thin, dark lines that extend across them. Myofibrils are composed of thousands of thinner strands called *myofilaments*. There are two types of myofilaments: *thick filaments*, which are composed mainly of the protein myosin, and *thin filaments*, which consist mainly of three proteins—actin, tropomyosin, and troponin.

When a nerve impulse reaches the surface of a muscle cell, a chemical called *acetylcholine* is released from the nerve into the tiny space (called the *neuromuscular junction*) separating the nerve fiber and the muscle. Acetylcholine depolarizes the cell membrane, and the depolarization is transmitted deep into the cell by structures called transverse tubules. Upon reaching the inside of the muscle cell, the nerve impulse

Fig. 6-1   Anatomy of a skeletal muscle.

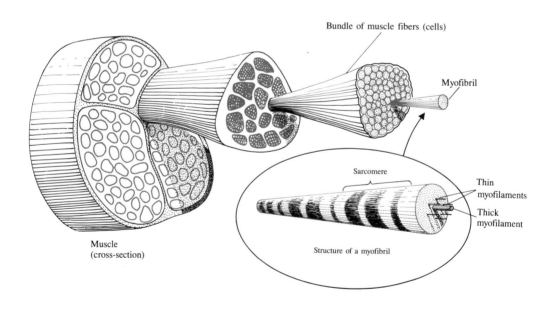

Bundle of muscle fibers (cells)

Myofibril

Sarcomere

Thin myofilaments

Thick myofilament

Structure of a myofibril

Muscle (cross-section)

From Evans, W.F.:   Anatomy and Physiology, *3rd Ed. Englewood Cliffs, N.J., Prentice Hall, 1983, p. 92.*

Chapter 6   The Muscular System

(depolarization) causes the release of calcium ions that were bound to the endoplasmic reticulum of the cell. The free calcium ions cause the troponin and the tropomyosin of the thin filaments to move from their usual positions, in which they had been blocking any interactions between the actin and the myosin of the myofilaments. With troponin and tropomyosin out of the way, actin and myosin react, forming cross bridges between the thick and thin filaments. Using energy obtained from the splitting of a high-energy molecule (ATP), the actin-myosin cross bridges shorten. The shortening of the cross bridges serves somewhat as a ratchet and causes the thin filaments to slide in relation to the thick filaments. The simultaneous sliding of thousands of filaments causes the muscle to shorten, or contract.

Smooth Muscle

The cells constituting some muscle tissue lack the striations that are visible in skeletal muscle cells. These cells, which are called *smooth muscle* cells, have a single nucleus and are shaped differently and are considerably smaller than skeletal muscle cells. Smooth muscle is typically found in the walls of hollow organs and tubes such as the stomach, intestines, and blood vessels, and its contractions regulate the movement of materials through these structures.

In contrast to skeletal muscle, smooth muscle is involuntary muscle. That is, its contractions generally cannot be controlled consciously by an individual. Rather, contractions of smooth muscles are regulated by factors within the muscle itself, by hormones, and by signals transmitted to the muscle by a portion of the nervous system known as the autonomic nervous system.

Smooth muscle cells contain thick and thin filaments, similar to skeletal muscle cells, but the filaments of smooth muscle are not striated or separated into sarcomeres. Nevertheless, cross bridges do form between myosin and actin in smooth muscles, and contraction will not occur in the absence of free calcium ions. Therefore, contraction of smooth muscles is thought to involve a sliding-filament mechanism similar to that of skeletal muscle.

Cardiac Muscle

Cardiac muscle forms the wall of the heart. It is striated, like skeletal muscle, but contracts involuntarily, like smooth muscle. A distinguishing feature that identifies cardiac muscle from skeletal muscle when viewed under the microscope is the presence of darkly staining structures called intercalated discs located at the junctions between adjacent cells (Figure 6-2). Intercalated discs are formed by special cell-to-cell junctions present in cardiac muscle. Contraction of cardiac muscle is thought to involve the same basic reactions as occur during skeletal muscle contraction. However, unlike skeletal muscle, certain cells of cardiac muscle contract spontaneously and rhythmically—without the need for stimulation by the nervous system. Moreover, the depolarization associated with the contraction of a cardiac muscle cell spreads to adjacent cells through the specialized cell junctions at the intercalated discs. It should be noted, however, that the spontaneous activity of cardiac muscle may be modified by nerve impulses carried over the autonomic nervous system, and by chemicals and hormones that travel in the blood (see Chapter 9).

Age-Related Changes

As a person ages he or she becomes aware of a gradual reduction in their strength and endurance, and notices that certain movements may not be as coordinated as they once were. These alterations of muscular functioning can be a depressing aspect of aging.

Some of the changes that occur with age in the muscular system are related to alterations of connective tissues associated with the muscles and the neurons supplying the muscles. Therefore, as we discuss muscular changes within the specific types of muscle tissue, we will point out the changes that may result from factors external to the muscle.

Skeletal Muscle

One of the most obvious age-related changes in skeletal muscle is a general reduction in the total mass of the muscle. The loss of muscle mass is thought to be due to atrophy of muscle fibers, resulting in both a decrease in the number of fibers and in the diameter of the remaining fibers. Muscle fibers are postmitotic, and therefore new fibers cannot be formed to replace those lost. Consequently, many of the lost fibers are replaced by fat tissue. The amount of muscle cells lost and their replacement by fat depends on a number of factors, including the amount of exercise the muscle undergoes and the nutrition of the individual. Heredity also seems to be involved. The muscle fiber loss has been reported to be as high as 30% between the ages of 30 and 80. In some elderly persons fatty replacement may be so extensive that islands of fat become formed between the muscle cells.

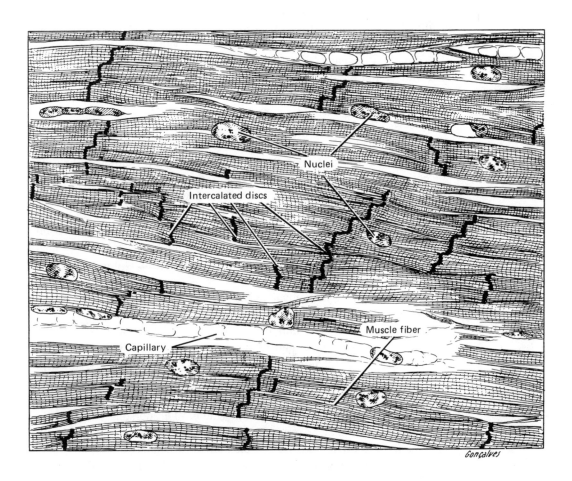

From Junqueira, L.C., J. Carneiro, and J.A. Long: Basic Histology, 5th Ed. Copyright Appleton and Lange, 1986, p. 247.

Correlated with the loss of muscle mass is an age-related reduction in skeletal muscle strength. However, in most persons there is only a small reduction (10% to 20%) in muscle strength up to age 70, after which the reduction becomes greater (up to 50%). The amount of strength loss differs between individuals, depending to a large extent upon the level of activity the person has maintained throughout his or her lifetime. The best defense against muscle atrophy is to use the muscle. Differences in muscle atrophy and strength may occur in different muscles in the same individual, with the more severe reductions occurring in muscles that are less frequently used. Numerous studies have indicated that regular moderate exercise not only slows the rate of muscular atrophy but can also actually increase the strength of the muscles—even in persons in their 70s. Along with the gain in muscle strength the general metabolic activity of exercised muscle cells has been reported to become more efficient. The mitochondria of exercised cells seem to function more effectively, with the result that less lactate accumulates. There are also indications that exercise may favorably affect the ability of nerves to stimulate muscle fibers.

Skeletal muscle fibers can be classed as "fast-twitch" or "slow-twitch" fibers, based upon the speed at which they contract. When we speak of muscle strength we are generally referring to the quick and powerful contractions of fast-twitch fibers. It is significant, then, that fast-twitch fibers seem to atrophy earlier than do slow-twitch fibers, which contract more slowly and thus maintain contractions over a longer period of time. Their slow, somewhat prolonged contractions are used for such things as maintaining posture—which is generally not significantly, if at all, affected until very late in life.

The orderly arrangement of the myofibrils sometimes becomes altered in skeletal muscles in older persons. Instead of their usual longitudinal orientation within the muscle cells, the myofibrils may run obliquely or intertwine into irregular plexuses. They have also been reported to condense into tightly packed balls, leaving areas of cytoplasm free of fibrils. With aging there is a tendency for myofibrils to degenerate and be replaced by lipofuscin or connective tissue. Therefore, there is an increase in collagen in the skeletal muscle of older persons.

Each cell of skeletal muscle normally contains several nuclei, but with aging there is often a decrease in the number of nuclei per cell.

Each motor neuron to a skeletal muscle branches and supplies a number of muscle cells. A single motor neuron and all of the muscle cells it supplies is referred to as a motor unit. There is an age-related loss of motor neurons to skeletal muscle cells, and this reduction in nerve stimulation is considered to be an important cause of muscle atrophy. The reduction in the number of neurons, along with the atrophy of muscle fibers, reduces the size of individual motor units in skeletal muscle. As a consequence, an increased number of motor units must be activated in order to move a particular weight, and thus, moving the weight seems to require increased effort in older persons. At the same time, there is a reduction in the amount of the neurotransmitter substance acetylcholine released by neurons where they approach muscle fibers. This reduction is thought to be due to diminished synthesis of acetylcholine by the nerves with increased age.

Contraction of a skeletal muscle fiber can be divided into three periods: the latent period, between the time a stimulus is applied and the fiber begins to contract; the contraction period, during which maximum tension is produced; and the relaxation period. With aging, all of these periods are lengthened. This results in a tendency for the skeletal muscles of older persons to respond more slowly to stimuli. The lengthening of these periods may be significantly less in muscles that are used regularly.

Smooth Muscle

In the digestive tracts of older persons, smooth muscles in the wall of the tract show an increased tendency to form saclike pouches called diverticula that protrude from the wall. Diverticula may be due to a weakening of the smooth muscle contractions. The pouches tend to become inflamed and produce a condition called diverticulitis, which is especially common in the colons of older persons. The diverticula may also form abscesses or, if severe enough, perforate through the wall of the tract.

In the walls of arteries, smooth muscle cells may gradually accumulate large vacuoles containing material thought to be fats, and collagenous fibers often increase with aging in smooth muscle fibers.

Cardiac Muscle

Cardiac muscle fibers increase in diameter until about age 50, after which they gradually become thinner. It is uncertain how much of an effect, if any, this diminished diameter has on the strength of cardiac muscle contractions. By middle age, there is often an accumulation of fat among the cardiac muscle fibers. As a person becomes quite old there is a tendency for the fatty tissue to be replaced by collagenous and elastic connective tissues, which can interfere with the efficient contraction of the heart.

As is the case with many tissues, with advancing age granules of lipofuscin accumulate in the muscle cells of the heart. The presence of lipofuscin granules in the heart is so consistent that it is referred to as "brown atrophy" of the heart.

Age-Related Dysfunctions

Because smooth and cardiac muscles are important parts of a number of other body systems—such as the digestive and cardiovascular systems—we will discuss several specific age-related dysfunctions involving muscle tissue in other chapters with other body systems. In fact, the two dysfunctions that we discuss here are both closely related to other body systems.

Parkinson's Disease

Parkinson's disease, which primarily affects people over 50 years old, is characterized by uncontrollable contractions of skeletal muscles, producing tremors and rigidity of the muscles. There is often a decrease in normal muscular activities that are usually related to other movements. Thus, persons suffering from Parkinson's disease typically do not swing their arms as much as is normally done while walking and do not change their facial expressions as much with changing emotions.

However, these are only symptoms, and the actual cause of the condition lies in a specific region of the central nervous system. Therefore, we will consider Parkinson's disease in greater detail with the nervous system.

Myasthenia Gravis

Although *myasthenia gravis* can occur at any age, it is more prevalent in older persons. The major symptom of this condition is chronic severe muscular weakness. However, rather than being a dysfunction of the muscle tissue itself, myasthenia gravis is a result of an abnormal response by a person's immune system. For reasons that are unknown, the immune system sometimes acts against the receptors located on the muscle cell membrane that respond to acetylcholine. Recall that acetylcholine, which is produced by neurons, depolarizes the muscle cell membrane and initiates the reactions which culminate in muscle contraction. In myasthenia gravis the immune system renders the receptors less sensitive to acetylcholine. Thus, the muscles do not contract as they normally would in response to stimulation.

Summary

Starting at about age 30 there is a gradual progressive loss of skeletal muscle mass due to atrophy of muscle cells. Many of the atrophied muscle cells are replaced by fat and, eventually, by collagenous fibers. Since fat weighs less than muscle, the normal body weight at age 50 is less than that at age 30. Associated with the decrease in muscle mass, maximal muscular strength may decline by about 50% by the time a person is 80 years old. Muscular atrophy is thought to result in part from an age-related loss of neurons supplying the muscle cells. With atrophy, aging skeletal muscles respond more slowly and with diminished strength.

Cardiac and smooth muscles also show increased accumulations of fat and collagenous fibers with aging, and smooth muscles tend to form more diverticula. Cardiac muscle, in particular, characteristically has increased deposits of lipofuscin.

The Nervous System

7

Review of Structure and Function

Age-Related Changes

Age-Related Dysfunctions

Summary

$\mathbf{T}$here are two body systems that serve primarily as means of internal communication among the cells of the body: the nervous system and the endocrine system. We will consider the nervous system in this chapter, and the endocrine system in Chapter 15.

The nervous system controls the contraction and relaxation of skeleton muscles and smooth muscles. Consequently, it controls body movements, which are regulated by skeletal muscles, as well as the activities of virtually all of the body organs, which contain smooth muscle in their walls. The nervous system also receives, processes, and stores sensory information from outside and inside the body. Information from outside the body is conveyed to the nervous system by means of receptors associated with the special senses of hearing, vision, taste, smell, and touch. The nervous system then correlates this sensory information and initiates messages that cause appropriate responses by the body to the information.

The nervous system is of prime importance in any consideration of the aging process because changes in this system will affect organs in other body systems and can cause general and specific disturbances of many body functions. And, unlike most body cells, nerve cells are generally considered to be *postmitotic*. That is, they do not divide in postnatal life. Therefore, if nerve cells are destroyed or degenerate they cannot be replaced. Aging changes in the nervous system can slow the processing of information by the system and affect a person's memory and ability to learn. These changes, along with changes they cause in other body systems, make aging of the nervous system one of the most feared aspects of growing old.

Review of Structure and Function

In order to understand the aging changes which occur in the nervous system, we must be familiar with the various types of cells constituting the system, and the general organization of the system.

Cells of the Nervous System
Nervous tissue is composed of three types of cells, each with a unique structure and a distinct function:

1. *Neurons (nerve cells)* transmit nerve impulses. Neurons have several processes extending from their cell bodies (Figure 7-1). Those processes in which nerve impulses originate are called *dendrites*. Each neuron generally has several dendrites. The nerve impulses are transmitted by dendrites to the conductive processes, which are called *axons*. There is only one axon per neuron. Axons can be quite long, and they transmit nerve impulses to cells located throughout the body. While a neuron is an individual cell, a *nerve* is composed of the processes of many neurons held together by connective-tissue sheaths.

   There are two main types of neurons. *Motor neurons* carry nerve impulses from the brain or spinal cord to a muscle cell or a gland cell, or from a higher center within the brain or spinal cord to a lower center. In contrast, *sensory neurons* carry nerve impulses from receptors located inside or on the surface of the body to the brain or spinal cord, or from a lower center within the brain or spinal cord to a higher center. In addition, neurons called *association neurons* often are present within the brain and spinal cord. These neurons, which resemble motor neurons, transmit nerve impulses from one neuron to another.

Fig. 7-1 Structure of a typical motor neuron (a) and a sensory neuron (b). The arrows indicate the direction traveled by nerve impulses.

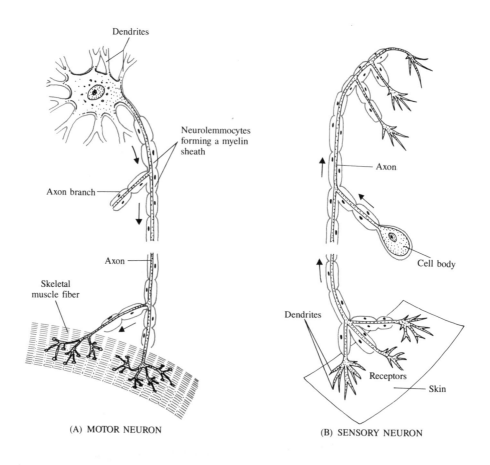

(A) MOTOR NEURON

(B) SENSORY NEURON

From Evans, W.F.: Anatomy and Physiology, *3rd Ed. Englewood Cliffs, N.J., Prentice Hall, 1983, p. 33.*

2. *Neuroglia (glial cells)* are located between the neurons in the brain and spinal cord, and serve to support the neurons as well as being involved in their metabolic activities. There are billions of neurons in the brain and spinal cord, but there is an even greater number of neuroglia.

3. *Neurolemmocytes (Schwann cells)* form a segmented covering called a myelin sheath around the conducting processes of many of the neurons in spinal nerves. Neurons whose processes are covered with neurolemmocytes are referred to as *myelinated neurons. Unmyelinated neurons* lack the neurolemmocyte covering.

When a neuron is not conducting an impulse it is polarized, with the inside of the cell being negative compared with the outside. This polarization is due primarily to an unequal distribution of sodium and potassium ions inside and outside the cell. The unequal distribution of ions results from differences in the abilities of sodium and potassium ions to pass through the cell membrane of the neuron.

When a neuron is stimulated the membrane permeability changes at the site of stimulation, and more sodium ions are allowed to enter the cell. The movement of positively charged sodium ions to the neuron depolarizes the membrane and actually reverses its polarity, with the outside becoming negative compared with the inside at the site of stimulation. This point of negativity of the membrane is called an action potential. The action potential moves along the neuron by depolarizing the region of the cell membrane adjacent to it, and continues in this manner along the entire length of the axon. The moving action potential, which is referred to as a propagated action potential, is a *nerve impulse.*

The point at which the terminal branch of the axon of one neuron appears to contact another neuron is referred to as a *synapse.* Actually, a small gap called the *synaptic cleft* separates the two neurons. In order for a nerve impulse to pass from one neuron to another, chemicals called *neurotransmitters* must be released into the synaptic cleft by the first (*presynaptic*) neuron. The neurotransmitter rapidly diffuses across the synaptic cleft and affects the polarity of the second (*postsynaptic*) neuron. Some neurotransmitters depolarize the membrane of the postsynaptic neuron, thus initiating a nerve impulse in that neuron. Other neurotransmitters hyperpolarize the membrane of the postsynaptic neuron, thereby inhibiting the responsiveness of that neuron. A number of neurotransmitter substances have been identified; however, *acetylcholine* and *norepinephrine* are the most common.

Organization of the Nervous System

The nervous system has a very complex structure, and although there is actually only one nervous system, we can simplify its description by separating it conceptually into various divisions, based on either structural locations or functional characteristics. *Structurally*, the nervous system may be divided into two parts: the central nervous system and the peripheral nervous system.

Central Nervous System. The central nervous system consists of the *brain*, which is encased within the skull, and the *spinal cord*, which is located within the vertebral column. The brain and the spinal cord, which are continuous with one another, are covered by three layers of connective tissue called *meninges*. The meninges provide protection and support for the central nervous system. Separating two layers of the meninges is a fluid-filled space that extends around the entire central nervous system. The fluid is called *cerebrospinal fluid*. Cerebrospinal fluid is also present within the brain in chambers called *ventricles* and in the *central canal* that extends down the length of the spinal cord.

The most conspicuous portions of the brain are the left and right *cerebral hemispheres*, which together are referred to as the *cerebrum* (Figure 7-2). The surface of the cerebrum is formed of rounded ridges called *gyri*, which are separated by furrows referred to as either *fissures* or *sulci*. The outermost region of the cerebrum is composed primarily of nerve cell bodies and unmyelinated axons, and has a grayish color. This surface layer of *gray matter* is called the *cerebral cortex*. The regions of the cerebrum deep to the cortex are composed primarily of myelinated axons and, because of the color imparted by the fat of the myelin, are referred to as the *white matter*.

On the basis of neurophysiological and anatomical studies it has been determined that certain areas of the cerebral cortex are related to specific functions. Among the functional areas identified are a *primary motor area*, whose neurons control the conscious and precise voluntary contractions of skeletal muscles; a *primary sensory area*, in which sensory tracts that carry information concerning temperature, touch, pressure, pain, and proprioception (muscle position sense) terminate; and several *special senses areas*, which receive nerve impulses associated with sight, hearing, smell, and taste. The cerebral cortex also contains a number of *association areas*, whose neurons are involved in processing, integrating, and interpreting sensory information and formulating patterns of motor responses, and which store information—thus providing for a memory.

Deep within each cerebral hemisphere are several masses of gray matter known as the *basal ganglia*. Neurons in the basal ganglia, like those

Fig. 7-2 Lateral view of the surface of the brain, showing the gyri, sulci, and fissures of the cerebral hemispheres, and the cerebellum, brain stem, and spinal cord below the cerebrum.

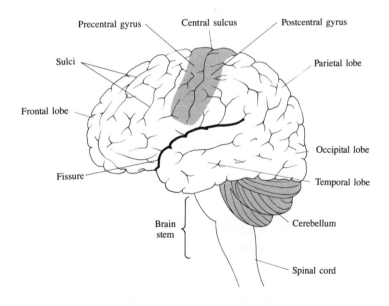

Precentral gyrus Central sulcus Postcentral gyrus

Sulci

Parietal lobe

Frontal lobe

Occipital lobe

Fissure

Temporal lobe

Brain stem

Cerebellum

Spinal cord

Adapted from Barrett, J.M., et al.: Biology. *Englewood Cliffs, N.J.: Prentice Hall, 1986, p. 413.*

Review of Structure and Function

of the primary motor area of the cerebral cortex, are involved in controlling skeletal muscle activity. Disorders affecting basal ganglia neurons result in involuntary contractions of skeletal muscles.

From the base of the brain the central nervous system leaves the skull and continues as the *spinal cord*. The spinal cord serves to conduct sensory nerve impulses to, and motor impulses from, the brain, and processes certain sensory information. Thus, reflex actions called spinal reflexes may occur at the spinal-cord level, without input from centers located in the brain.

The spinal cord, like the brain, is surrounded by the connective tissue meninges and consists of areas of white matter and gray matter—depending upon whether most of the neurons are myelinated or unmyelinated. In contrast to their locations in the brain, in the spinal cord the gray matter is centrally located and is surrounded by white matter.

Peripheral Nervous System. The peripheral nervous system consists of the nerves that travel between the central nervous system and all of the various structures and regions of the body. It includes 12 pairs of *cranial nerves*, which arise from the brain and the brain stem and leave the cranial cavity through openings in the skull, and 31 pairs of *spinal nerves*, which arise from the spinal cord and leave the vertebral canal through openings located between adjacent vertebrae (Figure 7-3).

The peripheral nervous system can be divided *functionally* into afferent (*sensory*) and efferent (*motor*) divisions:

The **afferent division** includes *somatic sensory* neurons, which carry impulses to the central nervous system from receptors located in the skin, in the fascia, and around joints; and *visceral sensory* neurons, which carry impulses from the viscera of the body to the central nervous system.

The **efferent division** of the peripheral nervous system is divided into the somatic nervous system and the autonomic nervous system. The *somatic nervous system* is also called the voluntary nervous system because its motor functions may be consciously controlled. It consists of somatic motor neurons, which carry impulses from the central nervous system to skeletal muscles. The *autonomic nervous system* is an involuntary nervous system. It is composed of visceral motor neurons which transmit impulses to smooth muscle, cardiac muscle, and glands. The autonomic nervous system can be separated both structurally and functionally into two divisions: the *sympathetic division* and the *parasympathetic division* (Figure 7-4). With few exceptions, the actions produced by the two divisions are mutually antagonistic. If one division increases the activity of certain organs the other system generally decreases the activity of those organs, and vice versa.

Fig. 7-3   **Cross section showing the relationship of the spinal cord and the spinal nerves to a vertebra.**

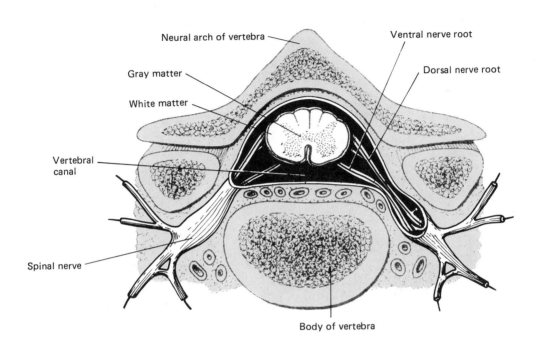

Adapted from Evans, W.F.: Anatomy and Physiology, *3rd Ed. Englewood Cliffs, N.J., Prentice Hall, 1983, p. 172.*

The nerves of the sympathetic division of the autonomic nervous system originate in cells located in the spinal cord segments from the level of the first thoracic nerve to the second lumbar nerve. Therefore, it is also referred to as the *thoracolumbar division*. In general, sympathetic stimulation tends to produce responses that prepare a person for strenuous physical activity, such as may be required in an emergency or other stress-producing situations. Rage and fear are generally accompanied by a widespread activation of the sympathetic division of the autonomic nervous system. For instance, sympathetic stimulation increases heart rate, diminishes digestion, and dilates the bronchi of the lungs, all of which prepare the body for emergency responses.

Review of Structure and Function

Fig. 7-4 The pathways of the automatic nervous system. Presynaptic neurons are shown as solid lines; postsynaptic neurons as dotted lines. The parasympathetic division is represented by the heavy lines, the sympathetic division by the lighter lines.

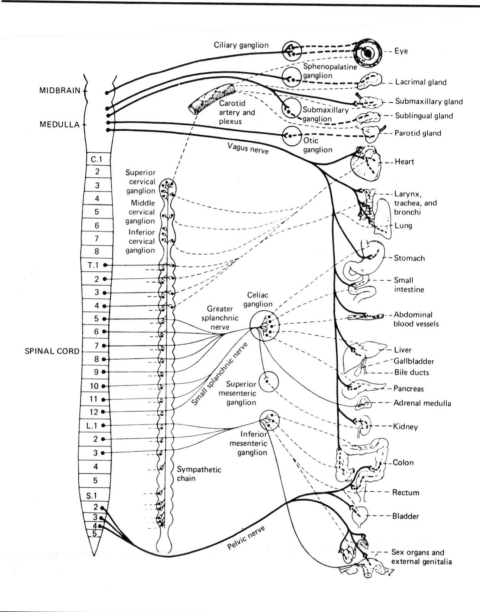

Modified and reproduced with permission from William B. Youmans, M.D.

The nerves that form the parasympathetic division of the autonomic nervous system arise from the brain stem or from the sacral region of the spinal cord. Therefore, it is also referred to as the *craniosacral division*. In general, parasympathetic stimulation tends to produce responses that maintain bodily functions under routine conditions. For example, parasympathetic stimulation decreases heart rate and promotes digestion.

Age-Related Changes

Perhaps the most worrisome age-related change of the nervous system is the loss of nerve cells. In nervous tissue, as in all tissues, many cells die each day in the normal course of aging. However, recall that nerve cells generally do not undergo mitosis, so any neurons lost are not replaced. The fact that nerve cells are not replaced means that there is a gradual reduction in nervous tissue with age. As a result, with aging there are fewer axons in the peripheral nerves and fewer neurons in the central nervous system. How these changes affect the functioning of the nervous system varies among individuals and depends on where the decrease in numbers of neurons occurs.

The loss of neurons in the central nervous system is thought to be largely responsible for the general reduction in brain mass that is commonly associated with aging. However, the loss of neurons is not observed to the same degree in all areas of the brain. For instance, in the cerebellum about 25% of the specialized cells which are responsible for coordinated movements are lost during aging, but there are some areas of the brain in which the number of neurons remains essentially constant throughout life. The loss of significant number of cerebellar cells may affect balance and cause older persons to have difficulty coordinating fine movements.

The data indicate that in humans the brain weight increases up to about age 30, declines slightly in the next several years, and then falls more rapidly with increased aging. A brain may ultimately lose as much as 10% of its maximum weight by the age of 90 years. As the volume of nervous tissue becomes less, the fluid-filled ventricles within the brain enlarge, the gyri forming the surface of the cerebrum become smaller, and the sulci between them widen. When the brain of an older person is examined at autopsy, it is found that both the gray and the white matter are reduced. However, the gray matter seems to diminish faster than the white matter up to 50 years of age; thereafter, the white matter is lost faster than the gray matter.

The most noticeable changes that accompany the reduction of brain mass are those associated with learning new skills. In fact, in older persons there is a greater decline in speed of response and ability to integrate what is observed than there is in verbal ability or memory.

The brain has a large reserve capacity, in that it has more neurons and synapses than are necessary to perform its many functions. The loss of neurons with age would be expected to affect brain functioning noticeably when enough neurons are lost to interfere with this redundancy. Therefore, it would seem that with aging it is only a matter of time until brain functioning becomes diminished. However, some neurons appear to grow new axons and establish new synapses to compensate for damaged or degenerated neurons. In effect, these new nerve cell connections may take over the functions of the lost neurons. Some evidence suggests that the establishment of new synapses with age may result in a net increase in neuron connections in older persons. Since learning requires the formation of new synapses, the fact that this process still occurs in older persons is reassuring. Thus, diminished intellectual ability may not be an inevitable consequence of aging.

However, it is generally accepted that there is a decline in intelligence with aging, and this decline is thought to be associated with the loss of neurons. The decline is so consistent that it is considered normal for an elderly person to experience up to a 25% reduction in verbal ability as compared with a person 30 years old. It should be kept in mind that this is an average loss, and there are widely differing individual changes in nervous-system functioning with age, especially in the intellect. In general, well-educated people tend to retain their intellectual abilities longer than those who are not as educated. For reasons that are not known, there is also a statistical correlation between intelligence and length of life. People with a high intelligence tend to live longer than those less well gifted.

Along with a decline in intellect, memory is also affected by age, perhaps as a result of loss of neurons, but not entirely so. There are two types of memory: long-term memory, which involves things experienced in the distant past, and short-term memory, which involves things experienced within the past few weeks. Long-term memory seems to be less affected with age than short-term memory. In fact, long-term memory sometimes seems to become increased in old persons. They may be able to recall in some detail events that occurred years ago, but are unable to remember much more recent events.

There is some evidence that people with higher intellects retain better memory in old age. And memory seems to be retained better in older persons who continue working or otherwise keep busy after retirement. It seems as if "exercising" the brain helps to maintain its normal functioning.

Other changes noted in the nervous systems of older persons are a decrease in the rate of conduction of impulses by neurons, and an increase in the time required to transmit impulses from one neuron to another—that is, to cross a synapse.

The decrease in conduction rate is thought to be the result of a mild loss of myelin from the sheaths surrounding neurons. The increased time required for a nerve impulse to cross a synapse is thought to be due to decreases that have been noted in several classes of enzymes that are related to the neurotransmitters released into the synapses. Some studies indicate there may also be a significant reduction in the number of receptors on the postsynaptic neurons that are sensitive to the neurotransmitters. One such study reported a loss of 40% of a specific type of receptor between 60 and 90 years of age. The effective transmission of an impulse across a synaptic cleft depends as much upon having enough receptors for the transmitter substance on the postsynaptic neurons as it does on having sufficient transmitter substance released by the presynaptic neurons. Therefore, the increased time required to cross a synapse by nerve impulses may well be a result of the combination of both of these factors.

Based on tissue staining techniques, it has been reported that certain regions of the brain show a reduction with age in the number of dendrites and small dendritic spines which extend off of the dendrites. This would cause a decrease in the number of synapses, which would hinder transmission of impulses between neurons. However, as we mentioned earlier, there is evidence that the dendrites of some neurons are able to undergo increased development and establish new synapses, even in older persons. In an attempt to interpret these two opposed findings, it has been suggested that a reduction in dendrites may be typical only of dying neurons.

An intracellular change associated with aging that is noted within some neurons, as well as in other types of cells, is the accumulation of lipofuscin in membrane-bounded granules. We mentioned earlier that lipofuscin, which is composed of lipids cross-linked with proteins, is so common in old cells that it is referred to as the aging pigment. In some neurons the lipofuscin occupies so much of the cytoplasmic volume that it is assumed to displace significant quantities of cellular organelles, perhaps leading to cell dysfunction and death. However, the suggestion that lipofuscin is harmful to a cell has never been directly demonstrated and is not accepted by all researchers.

The Golgi complex often deteriorates in aging neurons, and there is a decrease in the amount of darkly staining material referred to as *chromatophilic substance* (Nissl bodies) that is located in the cytoplasm of neurons. The chromatophilic substance, which has the appearance of rough endoplasmic reticulum, contains RNA. Therefore, its disappearance could signal a decline in metabolism within the neurons. Vacuoles containing small granules develop in the cytoplasm of some neurons.

Another age-related change, which occurs primarily in neurons located in the cerebral cortex and in a portion of the brain called the hippocampus (associated with memory), is the development of neurofibrillary tangles and neuritic plaques. A *neurofibrillary tangle* is an abnormal mass of fibrils or microtubules that develops in the cytoplasm of some neurons. These tangles, which have been found only in humans, become more prevalent after age 60 and are present in just about everyone after age 80. It has been suggested that the tangles may interfere with the flow of cytoplasm within the cell and thus affect metabolism in aging neurons. *Neuritic plaques* are situated between neurons rather than within neurons, as are the tangles. The plaques have a central core of protein surrounded by numerous abnormal axons, degenerating mitochondria, and multi-layered residual bodies.

The significance of the neuritic plaques and neurofibrillary tangles is not known, but although they are present in only small numbers in the functional elderly, there are large numbers present in people who are senile. Consequently, there seems to be a direct relationship between the number of plaques and tangles present and the degree of mental disability. Plaques and tangles are present in significant numbers in patients suffering from Alzheimer's disease. Because elderly persons may have some plaques and tangles without exhibiting any mental problems, there seem to be threshold values for the numbers of plaques and tangles that must be exceeded before intellectual and personality deterioration occurs. It should be noted that neurofibrillary tangles are not entirely unique to the aging brain. They are also present in the neurons of people suffering from Parkinson's disease and mongolism (Down's syndrome).

There are about ten times as many glial cells as neurons in the nervous system. There does not seem to be a single general trend in glial cells with aging. Some reports indicate that, in contrast to neurons, the number of certain types of glial cells increases with age in some regions of the brain. However, other types of glial cells have been reported to decrease in number with age. Degenerative changes that occur in glial cells with aging may affect the metabolism of the neurons by interfering with the supply of nutrients that reach the neurons from capillaries.

Neurons of the sympathetic nervous system secrete the neurotransmitter norepinephrine, which initiates the stress-related responses characteristic of this system. With aging, there is a progressive increase in the amount of norepinephrine in the blood, when measured with the person at rest and lying down. When a person stands up, the amount of norepinephrine in his or her blood normally increases, thereby accelerating the heart rate and maintaining sufficient blood flow to the brain in the upright position. When an older person changes from a recumbent to an upright position, the level of norepinephrine in the blood increases even than it does in a younger person. There is also a greater than normal increase in norepinephrine when an older person eats large amounts of sugar, is exposed to severe cold, or exercises.

The elevated level of norepinephrine in the blood may be a result of a general increase in the activity of the sympathetic nervous system in older persons, causing so much norepinephrine to be produced that all of it cannot attach to receptors on the neurons. The excess norepinephrine may pass through the walls of nearby capillaries and enter the circulatory system.

It is also possible that receptor cells may become less sensitive to norepinephrine with age. It has been suggested that the diminished contraction force characteristic of the left ventricle of the heart with age may be in part due to a decreased responsiveness of the heart to stimulation by norepinephrine. Such a decreased sensitivity would cause sympathetic neurons to produce even more norepinephrine in a further attempt to cause normal levels of responsiveness. Thus, the increased norepinephrine levels that occur with aging may not be caused by changes in the sympathetic nervous system; rather, they may be a part of compensatory mechanisms that are necessary to maintain adequate blood flow in older persons when subjected to some form of stress.

The data on age-related changes in the parasympathetic nervous system are contradictory, with some suggesting stability of function and others indicating changes in various reactions initiated by this division of the autonomic nervous system.

Age-Related Dysfunctions

Decreased Reflex Responses
A common dysfunction of the nervous system with aging is a general decrease in reflex responses. Although most deep-seated reflexes appear

to remain relatively intact up to age 60, there is a tendency for the more superficial reflexes to show a gradual decline before this age. And various studies have reported the absence of jerk reflexes of the ankle, knee, biceps muscles, and triceps muscles in a significant percentage of subjects over 70 years old. By age 90, all jerk reflexes are generally absent.

Declining Autonomic Responses

Other common aging dysfunctions involving the nervous systems result from a decreased ability of the autonomic nervous system to bring about responses to changing environmental temperatures. The heat-producing and heat-loss mechanisms of the body do not perform as effectively in older persons. Consequently, maintaining a normal body temperature when the environmental temperature is below 68° F (20° C) is more difficult for an older person. And under conditions of elevated environmental temperatures there is an increased mortality rate from heat prostration in the elderly. Aging changes in the autonomic nervous system are partially responsible for older persons requiring longer to return to a normal pulse rate following exercise. And loss of control of anal and urethral sphincters, which are controlled by the autonomic nervous system, is more common in older persons.

Parkinson's Disease

Parkinson's disease is a fairly common central nervous system disorder of older persons. It is chronic and slowly progressive, generally developing after age 50. For reasons that are not known the condition is more common in men than women.

One symptom typical of Parkinson's disease is useless contractions of skeletal muscles, causing muscle rigidity and tremors. The person also experiences difficulty initiating movement and then moves slowly with a distinctive shuffling gait while leaning slightly forward. Speech is slow, and there may be some drooling from the mouth and watering of the eyes. There is often a loss of facial expression.

Parkinson's disease is caused by changes affecting the basal ganglia of the cerebral hemispheres. It is thought to occur when cells of the basal ganglia fail to properly metabolize the neurotransmitter *dopamine*. In Parkinson's disease, the level of dopamine in the basal ganglia is lower than normal. Dopamine is unable to cross the blood-brain barrier which regulates the exchange of substances between the cells of the brain and the cerebral blood vessels; therefore, the administration of dopamine is not an effective treatment for the disease. What has been most effective is the administration of *L-dopa*, which is a precursor of dopamine. L-dopa is able to cross the blood-brain barrier and enter the brain cells, where it is converted into dopamine and helps overcome the deficiency of dopamine.

The administration of L-dopa reduces muscle rigidity and tremors, and improves posture and speech. The masklike facial appearance is generally not improved, however. This is unfortunate because it, along with the speech disorders, can cause people to think a person with Parkinson's disease is mentally affected, when in most cases their intelligence levels remain normal.

A new procedure involving the surgical transplantation of tissue from an adrenal gland of a fetus into the brain of a person afflicted with Parkinson's disease in an attempt to restore the production of dopamine has produced promising results. However, this procedure is still in the experimental stage and more information is needed concerning long-term effects before it can become a routine treatment for Parkinson's disease.

Organic Brain Syndrome

Organic brain syndrome is a general term for a group of brain disorders that increase with age and cause memory changes, intellectual defects, behavioral disturbances, and other signs of dementia (i.e. mental deterioration). It has been estimated that up to 10% of the total population over 65 years of age are affected by one or more of the changes included in this syndrome, and there is an even greater prevalence in persons over 80 years old.

Some forms of organic brain syndrome are caused by nutritional deficiencies and are reversible with proper treatment. Others involve brain deterioration and thus are irreversible. Atherosclerosis of the blood vessels of the brain is a primary cause of some cases of the irreversible forms of the syndrome. In these cases brain degeneration occurs as a result of localized ischemia (deficiency of blood). However, sometimes the ischemia lasts only a short time, resulting in mental or functional impairment that is only temporary and does not cause brain degeneration. The most common irreversible conditions associated with organic brain syndrome are Alzheimer's disease and senile dementia.

Alzheimer's Disease. *Alzheimer's disease*, which affects about 40% of geriatric patients who have dementia, exhibits the same psychological and neurological symptoms as occur in senile dementia. The two conditions are distinguished primarily by age of onset, with Alzheimer's disease generally appearing before the age of 65—thus it is sometimes referred to as *presenile dementia*.

Three stages of Alzheimer's disease have been defined. Some researchers have further subdivided it into seven more specific stages, but the general classification will best serve our purposes. Among the earliest symptoms are impairment of recent memory, spatial disorientation, and a lessening of spontaneous emotional responses. As the disease progresses and enters the second stage, higher learning functions deteriorate, and the abilities to read, write and calculate are lost. The person becomes confused, loses track of time, and eventually is unable to recognize his or her spouse or members of the family. In the final stage the person experiences seizures and becomes unable to speak appropriately.

Among the most noticeable changes that occur in the brains of Alzheimer's patients is the presence of neuritic plaques and neurofibrillary tangles. There is also a deficiency of acetylcholine-releasing neurons, which is thought to be a result of degeneration of neurons.

There is a tendency for Alzheimer's disease to be inherited, and recently researchers have isolated two genetic markers on chromosome 21 that may aid in identifying the gene responsible for the condition. Interestingly, a gene that is responsible for the formation of the neuritic plaques has also been identified on chromosome 21. If the plaques prove to be the cause of Alzheimer's disease, rather than merely a symptom, it may be possible to treat the disease by developing a drug that will stop plaque production.

Senile Dementia. The symptoms of *senile dementia* are quite similar to those of Alzheimer's disease. A primary difference between the two conditions is that senile dementia generally does not become noticeable until after the age of 65.

People suffering from senile dementia exhibit memory loss and repeat the same stories or statements over and over. They become careless in personal hygiene and appearance, lose muscle coordination, and may fall repeatedly. In advanced stages of dementia the patient may be unable to eat without assistance and may lose control of urination and bowel movements.

Cerebrovascular Accident

Cerebrovascular accident, or *stroke*, is a common aging dysfunction that causes neural symptoms, although it originates as a disease of the cardiovascular system. A stroke occurs when a blood vessel to the brain is obstructed or ruptures and the flow of blood to the region of the brain supplied by the vessel is reduced. The reduced flow of blood does not provide an adequate amount of oxygen to the cells of the affected area, causing them to deteriorate and often producing permanent brain damage. The blockage of a blood vessel may be due to either a buildup of fatty deposits inside the vessel or a blood clot that becomes lodged and blocks the vessel. Rupture of a vessel is generally due to elevated blood pressure or a weakened vessel wall.

The neurological effects of a stroke vary, depending on the site and extent of brain damage. If the lesions are confined to a small area of the brain, symptoms of the stroke may go unnoticed, whereas larger strokes may cause paralysis or even death. Because most of the nerve tracts connecting the brain and the spinal cord cross, the symptoms produced by a stroke appear on the opposite side of the body from the side of the brain in which the lesion occurred. The incidence of strokes is higher in the black population then in the white population, in both males and females.

Multi-infarction Dementia

Atherosclerosis of blood vessels leading to the brain may cause periods of decreased blood flow alternating with periods of adequate blood flow, resulting in repeated ministrokes. The ministrokes may cause damage to such small regions of the brain that the person is not aware of the strokes. However cells in the affected regions of the brain do die, producing deteriorated areas called infarcts. If the ministrokes continue the person may begin to show symptoms similar to Alzheimer's disease, including memory loss. This condition is referred to as *multi-infarction dementia*. Just being somewhat absentminded does not necessarily mean a person is suffering from multi-infarction dementia, but it can be an early symptom of brain damage.

Summary

Nerve cells die during aging, and are not replaced. Consequently, there is a general reduction in nervous tissue mass with age. This loss of neurons is thought to contribute to a slight decline in intelligence, lessened ability to learn new skills, and memory loss.

Nerve impulses are conducted at decreased rates in older persons and require more time to cross synapses. The delay at the synapses is thought to be due to a decrease in the amounts of neurotransmitters released and a reduction in the number of receptors sensitive to the neurotransmitters. The data are mixed as to whether there is an actual decrease in the number of synapses with age.

Within aging neurons lipofuscin granules accumulate, Golgi complexes deteriorate, the amount of chromatophilic substance decreases, and neurofibrillary tangles develop. Neuritic plaques form between aging neurons.

The Special Senses

8

The Eye

Review of Structure and Function

Age-Related Changes

Age-Related Dysfunctions

Presbyopia • *Blindness* • *Glaucoma* • *Cataracts* •
Senile Macular Degeneration • *Detached Retina*

The Ear

Review of Structure and Function

Age-Related Changes

Age-Related Dysfunctions

Presbycusis • *Tinnitus* • *Deafness* • *Dizziness*

continued

Taste

Review of Structure and Function
Age-Related Changes

Smell

Review of Structure and Function
Age-Related Changes

Summary

Information concerning our external environment is received through specialized sensory receptors for vision, hearing, equilibrium and balance, taste, and smell. The receptors for vision are located in the eyes; those for hearing, equilibrium, and balance are located in the ears; the receptors for taste are in the mouth and throat; and the receptors for smell are located in the nose. These receptors monitor the environment by transforming light waves, sound waves, fluid movement, or chemical stimuli into nerve impulses that are transmitted to the brain over sensory pathways. The cerebral cortex processes the sensory input and the stimuli are perceived as objects, sounds, body position and movement, tastes, or smells.

The functional capabilities of these special senses may be altered with aging, and thus older people are often unable to detect as much sensory information from their environments as can younger people. We begin our consideration of aging in the special senses with the eye.

The Eye

Perhaps the most cherished of the special senses, and certainly the one upon which we rely most heavily, is vision. To better understand the aging changes that occur in our ability to see we need to know how the eyes are constructed and function.

Review of Structure and Function

The eyes are located within the bony orbits of the skull. Each eye is in the form of a sphere with a wall consisting of three layers, or tunics (Figure 8-1). The outer tunic is composed primarily of fibrous connective tissue. The eye is lined internally with a nervous-tissue tunic; and separating the connective-tissue and the nervous-tissue tunics is a region that is amply supplied with blood vessels.

Except for its anteriormost region, the fibrous tunic is white and opaque and is called the *sclera*. The connective tissue of the sclera provides a strong wall for the eye and helps maintain its shape. The most anterior region of the fibrous tunic is clear and is called the *cornea*. The cornea is curved more than the sclera; consequently, the front of the eye bulges somewhat. In order to enter the eye, light must pass through the cornea.

The vascular tunic, which is internal to the fibrous tunic, is composed of three structures: the choroid, the ciliary body, and the iris. The *choroid*, which lines most of the sclera, is heavily pigmented and contains many blood vessels. Where it approaches the cornea, the choroid forms a ring called the *ciliary body*. Within the ciliary body are smooth muscles called *ciliary muscles*. Anteriorly the vascular tunic forms a thin muscular diaphragm called the *iris*. The pigmentation of the iris is responsible for eye color. A round opening called the *pupil* is located in the center of the iris and allows light to enter the eye.

The *retina*, which is the innermost tunic of the eye, consists of an outer pigmented layer and several inner nervous-tissue layers. The nervous-tissue layers contain photoreceptor cells called *rods* and *cones*, which are the actual receptors for light. Nerve fibers from the rods and cones undergo several synapses in the retina, after which they converge

Fig. 8-1   Structure of the eye.

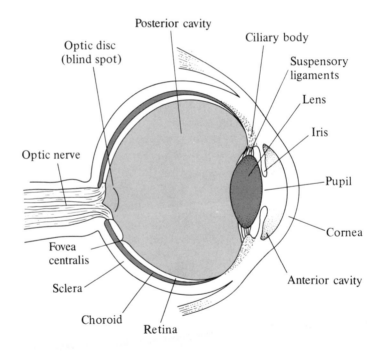

Adapted from Barrett, J.M., et al.: Biology. *Englewood Cliffs, N.J.: Prentice Hall, 1986, p. 460.*

Chapter 8   The Special Senses

and exit through the rear of the eye as the *optic nerve*. The optic nerve transmits nerve impulses from the rods and cones to nerve tracts which ultimately terminate in the visual cortex on the posterior surface of the brain, where they are interpreted visually. The point of exit of the optic nerve from the eye lacks photoreceptors and is called the *optic disc* (blind spot). Blood vessels that supply the retina also enter or leave the eye through the optic disc. Valuable information concerning a person's health can be obtained by examining these vessels with an instrument called an ophthalmoscope. A slightly yellow region known as the *macula* lies laterally to the optic disc. The macula contains a depression called the *fovea centralis*. The fovea, which contains cones but no rods, is the portion of the retina where the ability to distinguish details on objects (i.e. visual acuity) is the greatest. If your eyes are functioning properly, looking directly at an object will focus the image of the object on the fovea.

The *lens*, which is located behind the pupil, is a biconvex structure that is somewhat elastic. By changing shape, the lens aids in focusing the light that enters the eye onto the retina. It is held in place by a fibrous suspensory ligament that attaches it to the ciliary body of the choroid. The lens separates the interior of the eye into an anterior cavity in front of the lens and a posterior cavity behind the lens. The anterior cavity contains a clear fluid called the *aqueous humor* that is produced by cells of the ciliary body. The posterior cavity contains a gelatinous mass called the *vitreous humor*, which is composed of a network of collagenous fibers and long protein molecules.

Several structures located outside of the eye contribute in various ways to its function. Therefore, we want to briefly consider the eyelids, the conjunctiva, the lacrimal apparatus, and the extrinsic eye muscles.

The *eyelids* are skin-covered structures that can close over the anterior surface of the eye, thus protecting it from external objects. They also block most light from entering the eye when closed and reduce the evaporation of fluid from the surface of the eye. The eye is kept moist by the blinking of the eyelids that occurs repeatedly and automatically, spreading tears across the surface of the eye. Covering the insides of the eyelids and the anterior surface of the eye itself is a clear, thin, protective layer of epithelium called the *conjunctiva*.

Located in the upper lateral region of each orbit is a *lacrimal gland*, which secretes tears onto the surface of the conjunctiva. Most of the tears evaporate, but any excess fluid flows to the medial corner of the eye where it passes through two small openings which lead, eventually, into the nasal cavity.

Eye movements result from the contractions of six straplike skeletal muscles that originate from the orbit and insert on the sclera of the eye. These muscles are under voluntary control by means of nerve fibers that travel in three cranial nerves.

Light rays that enter the eye are bent (refracted) when they pass through the cornea, again when they enter the aqueous humor, and still more as they enter and leave the lens. In an eye that is functioning normally, the lens, by changing shape, adjusts the bending of the light rays as necessary to focus the images on the fovea centralis of the retina. Focusing problems can be caused by an irregularly shaped cornea (astigmatism), an elongated eyeball (nearsightedness), a shortened eyeball (farsightedness), or by a lens that is unable to properly change shape.

Age-Related Changes

Some people maintain near-normal sight well into old age. As I write this my mother is 81 years old and does not need glasses. However, there are a number of changes that often occur with age that cause most older persons to have some visual problems. General changes in the eye that are considered typical of aging include a slight shrinkage of the eye, an increase in the amount of connective tissue present, degeneration of some cells, and reduced blood supply. These changes do not occur rapidly, and their rate of development tends to vary considerably in individuals. For this reason, changes in the eyes do not necessarily indicate similar rates for aging in other parts of the body; the eyes may be functionally older or younger than a person's chronological age.

Among the less serious age-related changes of the eye is a loss of fat and elastic tissue from around the eyes and a thinning of the skin in the eyelids. These cause the formation of wrinkles at the corners of the eyes. The skin of the eyelids also tends to sag, producing hanging folds on the upper lids, and may cause "bags" below the eyes.

With aging the conjunctiva tends to become roughened, thinner, and more fragile. As a result, older persons report the feeling of sand in their eyes and experience more small hemorrhages beneath the conjunctiva. The sclera becomes somewhat yellow with age and may develop small spots that become transparent, allowing the pigments of the choroid to show through. The cornea becomes more translucent with age, which tends to increase its refractive power. At the same time, the curvature of the cornea changes, causing its surface to be less spherical. Thus, astigmatism is common in older persons. A white or yellowish ring called the "senile ring" is frequently seen around the outer circumference of the cornea. The cornea also becomes less sensitive to pain. Aging changes in the choroid cause its surface against the retina to become uneven and more fragile. It may undergo spotty thickening. With aging, the ciliary body produces less aqueous humor, thus affecting the nourishment and cleansing of the lens and cornea. After the age of 45, the ciliary muscles steadily lose mass due to atrophy of muscle cells.

The data concerning the effect of aging on the numbers of photoreceptor cells in the retina are contradictory. Some studies report a general decrease, whereas others report no decline. However, there is less efficient removal by the retina of the debris remaining from metabolic reactions caused by the exposure of the photoreceptors to light and of lipofuscin, which accumulates in the retina. Excessive amounts of these waste products may affect the functioning of the photoreceptors and cause their degeneration.

Due to the breakdown of its collagenous fibers, the vitreous humor becomes more fluid, usually beginning by the age of 50. As a consequence, the vitreous may shrink, and parts of it may detach from the retina. The parts that remain attached may exert tension on the retina, causing nerve impulses that are interpreted as light flashes. The vitreous may also become more opaque with aging, reducing the amount of light reaching the retina. Thus, older persons generally require more light in order to see well.

The iris has a tendency to become hardened with aging, and its color fades due to cellular atrophy. Atrophy of the dilator muscles in the iris reduces the size of the pupil. Thus, the pupil is no longer able to dilate fully, and the amount of light that reaches the photoreceptors of the retina by age 70 may be only one-third of the amount that reaches them during youth. The inability of the pupil to dilate fully can also contribute to poor drainage of the aqueous humor, resulting in increased pressure within the anterior chamber of the eye and a greater likelihood of glaucoma.

The lens becomes yellowed and less transparent with age. As a result it becomes more difficult for the person to discern certain color intensities, especially those in the blue, green, violet end of the spectrum, as they are filtered out by the increase in yellow pigments.

The lens is one of the few body structures that experiences increased cellular growth with age, and this causes most of the aging changes characteristic of the lens. As new fibers are laid down on the outside surface of the lens the older fibers are squeezed toward the center, and the lens flattens. Since the old fibers remain while new ones are added, the lens thickens and becomes more dense. This process continues on into old age, and by the age of 70 the lens may be about three times thicker than it originally was. At the same time the capsule surrounding the lens thickens and becomes less permeable, and the lens tends to harden and lose some of its elasticity. Thus, the lens is less able to change shape and its ability to bend light rays is diminished. The end result is at best farsightedness, and at worst cataracts. We will discuss these conditions in more detail later in this chapter.

As new cells develop on the surface of the lens and the old fibers are compressed, the central cells become crystalline and form very small opaque regions. These opacities do not affect visual acuity, but they do produce a hazy effect that reflects light, and small, bright light sources may produce so many reflections that they interfere with vision.

The blood vessels of the retina and the choroid often undergo atherosclerosis with aging. The hardening of the walls of the vessels is usually mild and causes no significant problems. But if it progresses sufficiently, vision can be impaired. Sclerosis of the choroid vessels can be detected by examining the eye with an ophthalmoscope.

The visual pigments of the photoreceptor cells are destroyed by light. When a person moves from a bright environment into a dark environment the visual pigments must be restored before the receptor cells function properly and the person is able to see effectively. This rebuilding process is known as dark adaptation. With aging the chemical processes involved in dark adaptation are slowed somewhat, and adaptation takes longer and is not as complete as in youth. As a result of several of the aforementioned age-related changes, a person's ability to distinguish details on the objects viewed begins to decline progressively by about age 50. It is not uncommon to have an 80% loss of visual acuity by 85 years of age.

Age-Related Dysfunctions

Presbyopia

Presbyopia is probably the most common age-related dysfunction of the eye, affecting many people after about age 40. The condition, which is also known as farsightedness of older persons, is the result of a gradual loss of lens elasticity, a flattening of its shape, and an increase in its density. As a result, the lens loses some of its ability to change shape and bend the light rays when viewing near objects. The ability of the lens to accommodate for near vision is absent or greatly reduced in most persons by the time they are 55 years old. As the ability of the eye to accommodate for viewing near objects diminishes, a person must hold reading materials farther and farther from the eye in order for them to be focused onto the retina. As this condition progresses, a point will be reached where reading material will have to be held so far from the eye that the letters are too small to be read. Because of presbyopia, most people need reading glasses or bifocals, which also correct for distant vision, by the time they are in their forties. The reading glasses mechanically compensate for the loss of lens accommodation and focus near objects properly on the fovea.

Blindness

Most people do not become blind as a result of aging, but the incidence of blindness does increase with age. In one study the onset of blindness occurred 54% of the time in people over 65 years of age. There are a number of causes of blindness in older persons. It is beyond the purpose of this book to consider them in any detail, but we will discuss glaucoma, which is a rather frequent cause of blindness.

Glaucoma

Glaucoma is perhaps the most serious eye disease that is associated with aging, being most common in persons over 40 years of age. If left untreated it can cause blindness. The disease is the result of elevated pressure within the eye. The pressure is caused by deficient drainage of aqueous humor from the anterior cavity of the eye. As a result of the diminished drainage, the fluid is formed faster than it can be eliminated, and the pressure within the eye increases. The elevated pressure can squeeze shut blood vessels within the eye, causing degeneration of the retina and resulting in blindness.

Glaucoma may develop for unknown reasons or as the result of eye disease or injury. In some cases it is thought to be due to inherited factors which predispose the person to the condition. Glaucoma may develop suddenly and last only a short time; or it may develop so slowly that the eye is damaged by the time the person is aware of the condition.

A person developing glaucoma experiences blurred vision, with circles of light surrounding light sources. There is often pain and watering of the eye. These symptoms may be accompanied by severe headache and nausea. An early specific indication of glaucoma is a gradual loss of peripheral vision. As a result, objects that are off to the side of the visual field go unnoticed. In time, so much of the visual field is lost that only objects in a person's direct line of sight are visible. This is referred to as "tunnel vision." If left untreated the condition will become progressively worse and lead to total blindness.

Glaucoma cannot be cured, but it is possible to reduce the pressure within the eye before it becomes high enough to cause damage to the retina by treatment with drugs or eye drops or by surgically providing a drainage pathway for the aqueous humor. Thus, persons over the age of 40 should have periodic eye examinations that include tests for glaucoma.

Cataracts

Cataracts are rather common. About 90% of people over age 70 are said to have some degree of cataract formation, not all of which affects vision. A cataract is a cloudy or opaque lens, often altered to the degree that vision is impaired because of interference with the passage of rays of light through the lens.

Earlier we mentioned that the lens is composed of fibers, and new fibers continue to be formed—even in old age—while the old fibers are not removed. The continuous formation of lens fibers causes the older fibers to be compressed; thus the transparency of the lens is gradually diminished, and it takes on a yellowish hue. As cataract formation continues, vision may become blurred and dimmed.

The most effective treatment of cataracts is surgical removal of the lens. After the lens is removed, vision may be restored to almost normal by the use of lens implants, contact lenses, or special eyeglasses.

Senile Macular Degeneration

Senile macular degeneration is the degeneration of the macular area of the retina, which is the area that permits an individual to distinguish detail. This condition is not entirely age dependent, but is more common in older persons. Unlike glaucoma, macular degeneration does not affect the peripheral vision. Rather, there is a loss only of central vision, making it difficult to distinguish the fine detail of the objects viewed.

Unfortunately, macular degeneration does not respond to medical or surgical treatment. The use of magnifying devices—either hand-held or incorporated into eyeglass lenses—have proved beneficial in overcoming the loss of visual acuity.

The cause of senile degeneration of the macular region is not known. Diabetes mellitus and hypertension affect this region of the eye, so the development of macular degeneration may be related to those conditions in some persons.

Detached Retina

The retina is composed of two layers: an outer pigmented layer and an inner nervous-tissue layer. The nervous-tissue layer is attached to the pigmented layer posteriorly only around the optic nerve and anteriorly in the vicinity of the ciliary body. The rest of the retina is loose from any attachment, being held in place largely by pressure from the tamponlike effect of the vitreous humor.

During aging the vitreous humor becomes more fluid and shrinks slightly, pulling away from the retina. This diminishes its support of the retina, and it is not uncommon for older persons to experience a *detached retina*, with the nervous-tissue layer separating from the pigmented layer. This separation interferes with vision in the detached portion.

Because of diffusion across the gap separating the two layers the retina resists degeneration for several days and can become functional again if the detachment is repaired. The two layers can be reattached surgically or by means of a laser.

The Ear

The ear contains receptors that transform sound waves into nerve impulses which are interpreted as sounds by the brain, as well as receptors providing information concerning balance and equilibrium.

Review of Structure and Function

For descriptive purposes, the ear can be divided into external, middle, and inner regions (Figure 8-2).

The *external ear* is composed of a funnel-shaped *auricle* that collects sound waves and helps localize the source of sound, and a

Fig. 8-2   Structure of the ear.

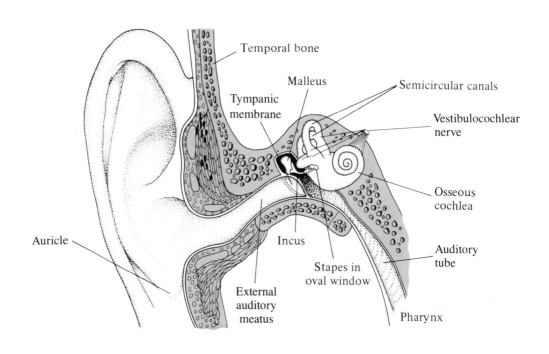

Temporal bone

Malleus

Semicircular canals

Tympanic
membrane

Vestibulocochlear
nerve

Osseous
cochlea

Auricle

Incus

Auditory
tube

Stapes in
oval window

External
auditory
meatus

Pharynx

Adapted from Barrett, J.M., et al.: Biology. Englewood Cliffs, N.J.: Prentice Hall,
1986, p. 454.

Chapter 8   The Special Senses

passageway called the *external auditory meatus*, that directs the sound waves from the auricle to the eardrum. The auricle has an elastic cartilage framework covered with skin. The meatus is lined with skin and has fine hairs surrounding its entrance. Oil-secreting and wax-secreting glands empty into it.

The *middle ear* is a small air-filled chamber located in the temporal bone of the skull. It is separated from the external auditory meatus by a taut membrane called the eardrum or *tympanic membrane*, and from the inner ear by a wall of bone. There are two small membrane-covered openings in this wall, the *oval window* and the *round window*. Another small opening connects the middle-ear chamber with the *auditory tube*, which leads to the nasopharynx. The middle-ear chamber and the auditory tube are lined with mucous membranes that are continuous with the mucous membrane of the throat. For this reason, infections of the throat can spread via the mucous membrane to the middle-ear chamber.

Three small bones called *ossicles* form a flexible bridge across the middle-ear chamber, between the tympanic membrane and the oval window. They serve as a lever system that picks up vibrations of the tympanic membrane and transmits them to the oval window, which leads into the inner ear.

The *inner ear* is also located in the temporal bone, but is medial to the middle ear. It consists of a series of canals (the osseous labyrinth) which are hollowed out of the bone. Within these bony canals, and following their courses, are membranous canals (the membranous labyrinth). The membranous canals are filled with a fluid called *endolymph* and are suspended in a fluid called *perilymph*.

The bony canals of the inner ear are divided into three areas called the cochlea, the semicircular canals, and the vestibule. The membranous canal within the tightly coiled *cochlea* contains the *spiral organ* (organ of Corti), which is associated with *hearing*. The three *semicircular canals* are arranged at right angles to each other. Within each canal is a membranous *semicircular duct* which contains receptor cells that detect certain movements of the head. The *vestibule* contains receptor cells located within spherical compartments of the membranous labyrinth called the *utricle* and *saccule* which also detect the position and movement of the head. Thus, the semicircular ducts, the utricle, and the saccule provide information related to *equilibrium* and the sense of *balance*.

If a sound is to be heard the vibratory movements of sound waves traveling in air must be transferred to the fluids within the inner ear. This is accomplished when vibrations of the eardrum cause the middle ear bones to vibrate and push against the oval window. Movement of the oval window initiates waves in the perilymph surrounding the membranous inner ear structures, and in the endolymph within them. The fluid waves, in turn, activate specific regions of the spiral organ that coincide with the rate of vibration of the sound waves. Thus, sound waves of a specific frequency always cause the same region of the spiral organ to vibrate more intensely than other regions, making it possible for the brain to determine the pitch of the sound. Activation of the spiral organ causes nerve impulses to travel over the vestibulocochlear nerve from the activated region to a specific region of the cerebral cortex, where they are interpreted as sound.

Age-Related Changes

Most age-related changes that occur in the outer ear do not affect hearing. The auricle may become longer and wider and lose some flexibility. The external auditory meatus becomes wider, and the skin lining it becomes dry and fragile. Consequently, it cracks more easily, causing bleeding and crusting. The hairs protecting the entrance to the meatus become stiffer. One change that can affect hearing is the accumulation of excessive ear-wax. Because the activity of sweat glands within the meatus is diminished with age, the wax becomes drier and is less likely to be removed in the course of normal activities. It is estimated that about one-third of the cases of hearing loss in older persons, especially losses in the low frequency tones, is caused by a buildup of earwax.

Like the outer ear, age-related changes in the middle-ear structures have little effect on hearing. Although some fibers in the tympanic membrane may become sclerosed, the membrane generally becomes thinner and less rigid; and the joints between the ossicles may ossify and thus become less freely moveable. Both changes tend to interfere with the transfer of sound vibrations to the inner ear, but generally not to the extent that it is noticed clinically.

The gradual loss of hearing that often begins by the age of 40 is due mostly to changes that occur in inner-ear structures. It is not uncommon to have some degeneration of spiral-organ cells and the cells of the sensory ganglia associated with the organ by the age of 50. This degeneration is due, at least in part, to a thickening of the walls of capillaries supplying the cochlea, resulting in a decreased nutrient supply to the spiral organ.

The vestibulocochlear nerve, which innervates the structures of the inner ear, is composed of two divisions: the cochlear division, which is associated with hearing; and the vestibular division, which is associated with balance and equilibrium. A decrease in the number of nerve fibers has been reported in both divisions in persons over 45 years old, thus affecting balance and equilibrium as well as hearing. Balance is further affected by a reduction in the number of sensory cells in the utricle, saccule, and semicircular ducts. These reductions may begin at 50 years of age and are especially noticeable after the age of 70. Neurons in the cerebellum that receive sensory information concerning balance and equilibrium from inner-ear structures are also lost, contributing to diminished balance information.

Age-Related Dysfunctions

Presbycusis

Presbycusis is the term used to indicate the loss of hearing that typically occurs with aging. Hearing loss is often noticeable by the age of 50, and the sensitivity to the higher sound frequencies is the first to be impaired. A young child can hear high-pitched sounds with frequencies of about 20,000 cycles per second, but the upper range for a person 65 years of age is about 8000 cycles per second. With advancing age there is also diminished sensitivity to the lower sound frequencies. However, in most elderly people the hearing loss does not become severe.

There are several forms of presbycusis, each due to age-related changes in different inner-ear structures. The most common form is thought to be due to degeneration of the sensory hair cells of the spiral organ. In other forms the nerve fibers supplying the spiral organ, or the cells that line the cochlea, degenerate. One form of presbycusis is thought to be caused by structural changes in the membrane on which the spiral organ is located, interfering with the vibrations of the membrane.

The speech patterns of most people do not utilize the high frequencies that are first affected by presbycusis, so the ability to understand spoken material may at first be normal. But as the condition progresses the ability to hear the common speech frequencies is also diminished, and when the pattern of speech is interrupted, the rate of speaking is changed, or background noise interferes, the ability to understand conversation is affected.

Tinnitus

Tinnitus is the condition of having constant background noise in the ears, the so-called ringing of the ears. The noise is generated somewhere within the auditory system—but how or where is not known. About 10% of people over 65 years of age complain of tinnitus, which seems to be more common in women than in men.

Deafness

Deafness is not common in older persons, but it becomes more prevalent with aging. There are two types of deafness: conductive deafness and nerve deafness.

Conductive deafness occurs when the transmission of sound waves through the external or middle ear is hindered or blocked. The interference might be caused by a physical blockage of the external auditory meatus by earwax or a foreign object, inflammation of the tympanic membrane, calcification of the joints between the ossicles, or thickening of the oval window. All of these diminish the vibrations reaching the inner-ear structures. Because there is no damage to the receptor cells of the spiral organ or the nerve pathways to the brain, hearing aids of the type that transmit sound waves to the inner ear through the bone of the skull rather than via the middle-ear structures can be helpful in conductive deafness.

In *nerve deafness* the loss of hearing results from disorders that affect the receptor cells of the spiral organ, the neurons of the vestibulocochlear nerve, or nerve pathways within the central nervous system. Ordinary hearing aids will not help correct nerve deafness, but improvement is possible by means of a *cochlear implant*. This procedure uses a small microphone to serve as an ear. The microphone transmits sounds that it picks up to a stimulator unit worn on a belt. The stimulator processes the signals it receives from the microphone and converts them into weak electric signals, which are sent to an induction coil attached to the outside of the skull. The electric current travels from the induction coil along a fine implanted electrode to the inner ear, where it produces activity in the vestibulocochlear nerve. This activity is interpreted in the brain as sound sensations. A cochlear implant makes it possible for a person suffering from nerve deafness to hear, but the sounds perceived by the brain are very different from those of normal hearing.

Dizziness

Older people tend to have a greater tendency to be troubled with *dizziness*. This generally involves an illusion of movement, such as a sensation that the external environment is revolving. There can be a number of causes for dizziness. Often it results from inflammation of the parts of the inner ear associated with balance and equilibrium (semicircular ducts, utricle, and saccule) or the nerve fibers of the vestibulocochlear nerve, which carries impulses from these structures.

Episodes of dizziness may cause older persons to appear disoriented and to feel less secure. To compensate, while standing or walking they may adjust their stances in order to provide more stability by spreading their legs and holding their arms away from their bodies.

Taste

It is important for elderly persons to maintain adequate nutritional levels. Nutritional deficiencies can seriously affect one's quality of life, even to the extent of causing mental symptoms similar to those of senile dementia. Nutritional levels are best maintained by eating a balanced diet containing the proper proportions of the various types of foods (see Chapter 12). However, it is often difficult for elderly persons to follow such a diet, as they may be living alone and lose their motivation to eat, and their appetites may be diminished. Elderly persons report that one reason they often do not eat a complete meal is that the food no longer tastes good. Thus, the sense of taste can have a significant effect on one's nutritional status and overall health.

Review of Structure and Function

The receptors for taste are sensory cells located within spherical structures called *taste buds*. Each taste bud contains about 50 sensory cells. Most taste buds are located on the surface of the tongue, but some are found on the roof of the mouth and in the throat. The cells of a taste bud are continually dying and, unlike most other neural cells, are replaced by new sensory cells. Each receptor cell is thought to live for only about one week. Sensory nerve fibers from the receptor cells carry impulses to the brain primarily over two cranial nerves. In order to evoke a taste sensation, a substance must dissolve in the fluids that bathe the tongue and interact with the receptor cells of the taste buds in such a way that they generate a nerve impulse in the sensory nerve fibers.

Four primary taste sensations have traditionally been identified—sweet, salty, bitter, and sour—with each taste being detected best in specific regions of the tongue surface. However, there does not seem to be a corresponding specificity of taste receptor cell types. Each taste receptor cell is thought to interact with a variety of different substances that belong to more than one of the specific taste categories, although it may be maximally stimulated by one particular category. It has been suggested that taste cells possess several different types of receptor sites that react with different types of molecules, each reaction generating nerve impulses in the sensory nerve fibers leading from the receptor cell to the brain. It is apparent that taste is a more complex phenomenon than we generally consider it to be.

It should be kept in mind that much of what is commonly considered to be "taste" actually also involves the stimulation of olfactory receptors. This is the reason food does not have much taste when you have a congested nose and are unable to smell. Any interference with taste reception may be in part due to olfactory problems.

Age-Related Changes

With aging there is a general decrease in taste perception that is more noticeable in the ability to taste certain substances than others. It has been suggested that this decline is due to a decrease in the number of taste buds that begins shortly after maturity and continues into old age. However, other studies report little, if any, decline in the number of taste buds until after 75 years of age. Rather, it is suggested that the diminished taste perception with aging may be due to changes in the processing of taste sensations in the central nervous system.

Other factors that may contribute to the reduction in taste sensation in older persons are a decrease in the volume of saliva secreted and the formation of fissures and furrows on the tongue. Reduction in saliva could interfere with dissolving foods so they can react with the receptor cells, and the fissures and furrows may make taste buds less accessible to the dissolved molecules.

Smell

The sense of smell serves a number of functions, including protective functions by providing warnings of smoke, gas, and noxious substances. But a sense of smell is of particular importance in older persons because of its close relationship with the sense of taste. In order for a person to enjoy food and eat a balanced diet, it must taste good. And in order for food to taste good, it must smell good.

Review of Structure and Function

Smell, like taste, is a chemical sense. The receptors for smell are specialized neurons located in the nasal mucosa of the upper portion of the nasal cavity. These neurons have two processes. One process has fine projections extending into the mucous lining of the nasal cavity. The other neural process travels within the olfactory nerve to the olfactory bulbs on the underside of the brain.

To be detected, an odorous substance must dissolve in the mucous layer covering the receptors and interact with them. It is thought that the dissolved substances depolarize the receptors, resulting in the generation of nerve impulses that are conveyed over the olfactory nerves to the brain, where they are interpreted as a particular smell.

Age-Related Changes

It is thought that, like taste receptors, olfactory sensory cells are replaced by new cells as they die. If so, there should be no decrease in their number with age. However, some studies have reported such a decrease. Perhaps not all of the sensory cells that degenerate are replaced. A loss of neurons in the olfactory bulbs during aging has also been reported. For whatever reason, the sense of smell begins to decline in most people by middle age and continues to decline gradually into old age.

Summary

The most significant effects of aging on the eye are due to increased thickness, opacity, and yellowness of the lens and a reduction in pupil size. Small opaque regions that reflect bright light may develop in the lens. The refractive power and the curvature of the cornea change with age, and a white "senile ring" often forms around the cornea.

The data concerning the effects of aging on photoreceptors are not clear, but debris and lipofuscin granules do accumulate in the retina. The vitreous humor shrinks slightly, removing some of its support of the retina. There is some increase in the time required to rebuild visual pigments when entering a dark environment from a bright environment.

Although excessive earwax accumulates in older persons and can affect hearing, age changes of inner-ear structures cause most hearing problems. Degeneration of the sensory cells of the spiral organ is thought to commonly occur with age, and the loss of nerve fibers in the vestibulocochlear nerve affects both hearing and balance.

There is a general decline with age in taste perception and the sense of smell. It is unclear whether these reductions are due to a decrease in the number of receptor cells, or to other factors.

The Circulatory System

9

Review of Structure and Function

Blood • *Heart* • *Blood Vessels* • *Lymphatic System*

Age-Related Changes

Blood • *Heart* • *Blood Vessels*

Age-Related Dysfunctions

Ischemic Heart Disease • *Myocardial Infarction* • *Angina Pectoris* • *Cardiac Arrhythmias* • *Congestive Heart Failure* • *Atherosclerosis and Arteriosclerosis* • *Hypertension*

Summary

In order for the cells of the body to survive, grow, and function properly they must receive a constant supply of oxygen and various nutrients and have an efficient means of disposing of the waste products formed by their metabolic activities. The structures constituting the circulatory system provide for these cellular needs.

The circulatory system becomes increasingly important as a person ages, since diseases of the system are a significant problem for many older people. In fact, diseases of the heart and the blood vessels are the major cause of death in the United States and most other developed countries. The two top causes of death, heart disease and stroke, are both associated with dysfunctions of the circulatory system. It is estimated that more than 9% of the total population will die from diseases of the heart or blood vessels. And a large proportion of the people who survive such diseases are disabled to varying degrees. These people often require long-term care, which contributes to the high cost of caring for an aging population.

The circulatory system can be subdivided into the cardiovascular and lymphatic systems. The *cardiovascular system* includes the *heart* and the *blood vessels*. Rhythmic contractions of the heart provide the force necessary to propel blood through the blood vessels. The *lymphatic system* consists of *lymphatic vessels* that collect tissue fluid from the tiny spaces separating the cells of the body and carry it to the vessels of the cardiovascular system, and *lymphoid organs*, that filter the lymph and play a role in the immune responses of the body. The lymphoid organs include the tonsils, the thymus, the spleen, lymph nodes, and lymphoid nodules.

We will review the normal structure and function of the heart, the blood vessels, and the lymphatic system in this chapter, but will consider the role of the lymphatic system in immune reactions in more detail in Chapter 10.

The cardiovascular system is a closed system of heart chambers and blood vessels that form a circular path throughout the body. Blood is confined within the heart and the vessels and repeatedly travels through the heart, into arteries and arterioles, then through capillaries into venules and veins, and back to the heart. Under normal conditions, blood does not leave the vessels, although some of the fluid portion (plasma) of blood does pass through the walls of the capillaries and becomes tissue fluid. However, this fluid is also returned to the cardiovascular system, either reentering the capillaries or entering the vessels of the lymphatic system.

Review of Structure and Function

Blood

Blood is the fluid component of the circulatory system and serves as the means of transporting substances to and from the body cells. It consists of a number of structures called *formed elements* suspended in a liquid called *plasma*. The plasma is mostly water, but contains hormones, proteins, carbohydrates, amino acids, lipids, gases, and various ions and metabolic end products.

The formed elements in blood include red blood cells, several types of white blood cells, and platelets. The red blood cells are by far the most numerous type of cell in the blood. They contain an oxygen-binding pigment called hemoglobin and function primarily to transport oxygen from the lungs to the tissues. There are at least five types of white blood cells in the blood. Each performs somewhat different functions, but they essentially serve to protect the body against invasion by foreign substances and remove debris that results from dead or injured cells. Platelets are involved in blood clotting, which serves a vital role in preventing hemorrhages. The blood cells are formed from precursor cells in the red bone marrow located within certain bones.

Heart

The *heart* functions primarily as a pump. In order to do so, it must have chambers that receive blood and chambers that deliver blood, and valves that direct the flow of blood through the chambers. It must also be capable of contracting strongly in order to force the blood out of the heart and through the vessels. The propulsive force of the heart is made possible by its wall, which is composed of cardiac muscle and is referred to as the *myocardium*.

The heart contains four chambers: right and left *atria*, which serve as receiving chambers, and right and left *ventricles*, which serve as delivery chambers. The atria are separated from one another by a muscular wall called the *interatrial septum*, and the ventricles are separated by an *interventricular septum* (Figure 9-1).

The right atrium receives venous blood from the veins of the body through large vessels called the *superior* and *inferior venae cavae* and delivers blood to the right ventricle through the flaplike *right atrioventricular valve*. The right ventricle delivers the blood it receives from the right atrium to the blood vessels of the lungs through the *pulmonary trunk*, which divides into right and left pulmonary arteries, each of which supplies a lung. The blood passes through the cuplike *pulmonary semilunar valve* as it leaves the right ventricle and enters the pulmonary trunk. The left atrium receives blood that has been newly saturated with oxygen in the lungs through four *pulmonary veins* and delivers this blood through the *left atrioventricular valve* to the left ventricle. The left ventricle, in turn, propels the blood through the *aortic semilunar valve* into the *aorta*, which delivers it to the various vessels that supply the entire body. In the first part of the aorta, just behind the cusps of the aortic semilunar valve, are openings that lead into the *coronary arteries*, which supply oxygenated blood to the heart muscle. Having the coronary-artery openings in this location ensures that the heart is the first organ to receive newly oxygenated blood.

Contraction of the heart chambers is referred to as *systole*, and the increased blood pressure this causes is *systolic pressure*. *Diastole* refers to the period when the heart chambers are relaxed, and the reduced blood pressure during this period is *diastolic pressure*. Although nerves supplying the heart can increase or decrease its rate of contraction, the impulses they carry do not actually cause the heart to contract. Rather, the heart contains two small masses of specialized muscle cells that initiate the impulses which cause it to contract. Other specialized cells conduct these impulses throughout the myocardium so that the heart contracts in a coordinated manner. One of the specialized masses, called the *sinuatrial node (SA node)*, is located in the wall of the right atrium. The SA node

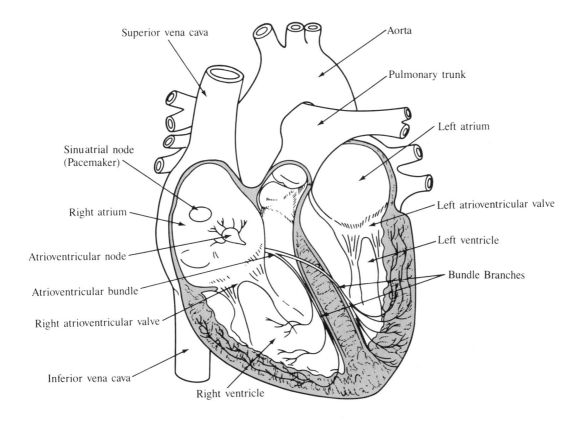

Adapted from Mulvihill, L.M.: Human Diseases: A Systemic Approach. *Bowie, Md., Brady, 1980, p. 39.*

Review of Structure and Function

depolarizes spontaneously about 70 times each minute, generating a nerve impulse with each depolarization that causes the heart to contract. Consequently, the rate and rhythm of heart contractions is determined by the rate of depolarization of the SA node. For this reason, it is also referred to as the *pacemaker* of the heart.

The nerve impulses generated by the SA node spread from cell to cell throughout the myocardium of the atria, causing both atria to contract. However, the impulses cannot pass from the atria to the ventricles because a fibrous connective tissue partition that separates the ventricles from the atria does not depolarize, and thus blocks the nerve impulses generated by the SA node.

This blockage is bypassed by means of a second group of specialized cells called the *atrioventricular node* (*AV node*), which is located within the interatrial septum, just above the connective tissue partition. The stimulatory impulses from the SA node, which cause the atria to contract, also depolarize the AV node. Impulses generated by the depolarization of the AV node travel down the interventricular septum over specialized conducting cells called the *atrioventricular bundle*. Upon reaching the apex of the heart, the fibers of the bundle enter the walls of both ventricles and terminate in small branches on the muscle cells of the ventricles. Conduction over the bundle fibers is rapid; therefore the ventricles contract very soon after the atria contract.

The AV node cells, like the SA node cells, can also depolarize spontaneously. However, their rate of spontaneous depolarization is about 50 times per minute, as compared with 70 times per minute in the SA node. Therefore, under normal conditions the AV node does not generate impulses because it is depolarized by impulses from the SA node before it would depolarize spontaneously. Under pathological conditions that delay the transmission of impulses from the SA node to the AV node, the AV node may spontaneously depolarize. This can result in unsynchronized contractions of the atria and the ventricles.

Blood Vessels

Upon leaving the heart, blood enters the blood vessels, which transport it to all parts of the body. The exchange of nutrients, gases, hormones, metabolic end products, and other substances between the blood and the tissue fluid occurs across the walls of certain of these vessels. Ultimately, the vessels return the blood to the heart.

The walls of blood vessels vary in thickness, due to modifications in certain vessels of the three layers of tissues that typically constitute their walls (Figure 9-2). The middle of these layers is composed of smooth

Fig. 9-2 Photomicrograph of two small arteries (right) and veins (left).
Notice that the arteries have thicker walls than the veins (× 150). **I**
indicates an internal layer of elastic fibers; **M** is a smooth muscle
layer; **A** is a connective tissue layer.

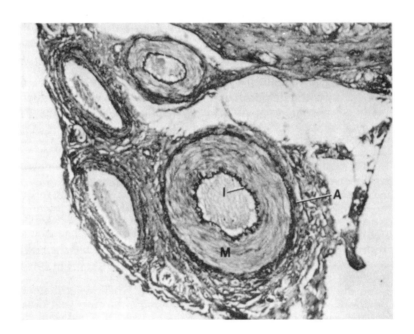

From Junqueira, L.C., J. Carneiro, and J.A. Long: Basic Histology, *5th Ed. Copyright
Appleton and Lange, 1986, p. 264.*

Review of Structure and Function

muscle. The muscle is lined internally with a layer of epithelium called the endothelium, and covered externally with a thin layer of connective tissue. *Arteries* have the thickest walls, and the blood pressure within them is higher than in any of the other vessels. The walls of the largest arteries, such as the aorta and its major branches, contain the three typical layers, with an especially thick muscular layer containing many elastic fibers. During ventricular contraction, these elastic fibers are stretched as blood is ejected from the heart under pressure. During ventricular relaxation, the elastic recoil of these fibers helps maintain some pressure within the vessels.

Arteries lead into *arterioles*, which are smaller in diameter and although they have a fairly thick muscular layer have relatively few elastic fibers in their walls. Arterioles play a major role in regulating the flow of blood into the capillaries because they are capable of *vasoconstriction*, which further reduces their inside diameters and restricts the flow of blood into the capillaries, and *vasodilation*, which increases their inside diameters and allows blood to freely enter the capillaries. *Capillaries* have tiny diameters and very thin walls, consisting of only a single layer of endothelial cells covered by a very thin layer of connective tissue. As a consequence, most substances pass rather freely through their walls, and capillaries are the sites at which the exchange of materials between the blood and the tissue fluid takes place.

Capillaries drain into *venules*, whose walls are thicker than those of capillaries but also lack the smooth muscle layer. Blood from the venules enters *veins*, which have progressively increasing inside diameters and, like arteries, have walls composed of the three basic layers. However, these layers are thinner than they are in arteries, and therefore the walls of veins are considerably thinner than those of arteries. Coinciding with the thin walls, the blood pressure within veins is lower than it is in arteries. The pressure is so small within some of the larger veins that the flow of blood back to the heart could not be maintained if it were not for the presence of valves in these large veins, particularly the veins of the lower limbs. The valves allow blood in the large veins to flow only toward the heart.

Lymphatic System

The lymphatic system, consisting of an extensive network of vessels, lymph nodes, and lymphoid organs, is the means by which tissue fluid is collected from between the cells, filtered, and transported to the cardiovascular system. In the course of the exchange of materials that occurs across the walls of the blood capillaries, about three more liters of fluid (plasma) move out of the blood and into the tissue spaces between the body cells each day than reenter the blood capillaries. This excess fluid is referred to as *tissue fluid*, and is the source of *lymph*. If tissue fluid were allowed to accumulate between cells, the tissues would swell, producing pressure and pain. However, instead of accumulating, tissue fluid passes through the extremely thin walls of blindly ending lymphatic capillaries located in the tissue spaces and enters the lymphatic system. The lymphatic capillaries join together to form progressively larger lymphatic vessels, which generally travel alongside arteries and veins. The lymphatic vessels pass through one or more lymph nodes and then empty into either the *thoracic duct* or the *right lymphatic duct*. Both ducts empty into veins of the cardiovascular system (Figure 9-3). Thus, the lymphatic system returns excess tissue fluid back to the blood stream.

Lymph picks up many foreign particles and microorganisms from between the cells and transports them to the lymph nodes. As lymph flows slowly through the nodes many of the foreign substances it contains are destroyed by specialized cells (phagocytes) located in the nodes. In addition, lymph nodes contain other cells (lymphocytes and plasma cells) that produce antibodies capable of destroying certain foreign substances known as antigens. In this way, lymphoid organs are involved in immune reactions. We will discuss this involvement in Chapter 10.

Age-Related Changes

Blood

There appear to be no major changes in the blood cells or platelets with aging, although there are some subtle changes that affect their fragility. The life spans of the cells remain essentially the same as in younger persons. There also are no major age-related changes in the osmotic pressure or chemical composition of the plasma. Blood volume generally remains fairly stable until about 80 years of age, after which it may diminish slightly. In older persons who are healthy, red blood cell count, hematocrit value, and hemoglobin concentration remain within the normal range up to about 65 years of age. The total concentration of plasma proteins tends to decrease with age, but the concentration of the protein fibrinogen rises by approximately 25% by age 70. The increase in fibrinogen tends to maintain the osmotic pressure of the blood and may raise its viscosity somewhat.

Fig. 9-3 The lymphatic system, showing major lymphatic vessels, lymph nodes, and the thoracic and right lymphatic ducts.

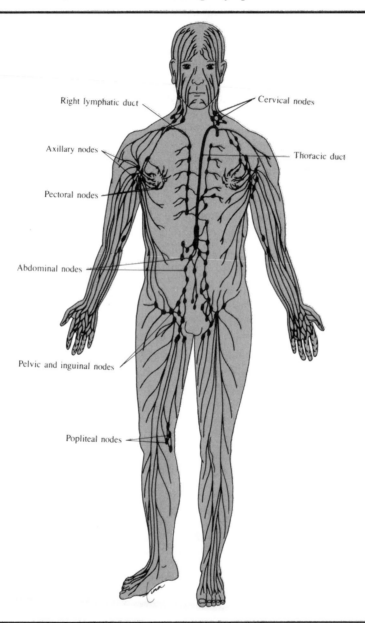

Right lymphatic duct

Cervical nodes

Axillary nodes

Thoracic duct

Pectoral nodes

Abdominal nodes

Pelvic and inguinal nodes

Popliteal nodes

From Rice, J.: Medical Terminology with Human Anatomy. *Norwalk. Ct., Appleton and Lange, 1986, p. 133; adapted from Evans, W.F.:* Anatomy and Physiology, *3rd ed. Englewood Cliffs, N.J., Prentice Hall, 1983, p. 291.*

The amount of active red bone marrow diminishes with age and is replaced with yellow marrow, which does not form blood cells. As a consequence, the total capacity for blood cell formation is reduced in the elderly. The rate of blood cell formation generally remains adequate for normal blood cell replacement, but may be insufficient to produce new cells fast enough to maintain their levels following severe hemorrhage or other conditions causing extensive destruction of blood cells.

Heart

In the absence of heart disease, the size of the heart in elderly people remains essentially the same as it was in middle age, or it may become slightly smaller. The decrease in heart size is mostly due to a reduction in the muscle mass of the left ventricle because of reduced demands placed on it by lower levels of physical activity with aging. However, because diseases of the heart and blood vessels are so common in older persons, the heart is, in fact, often enlarged with age. The enlargement may be the result of a general increase in the volume of the heart chambers or an over-development of the heart muscle.

There is a general reduction in the number and size of cardiac muscle cells with aging. This reduction is correlated with a progressive loss of cardiac muscle strength and a reduction in the volume of blood the heart is capable of pumping with each contraction. These reductions occur because, like all muscle cells, cardiac muscle cells are postmitotic and are not replaced as they die or degenerate. Some of the loss of strength by cardiac muscle may be due to a progressive reduction of capillaries supplying the myocardium. This reduces the oxygen supply to the heart muscle and affects its ability to contract.

Age-related structural changes in the heart include an increase in the amount of fat deposits on the surface of the heart, and accumulation of lipofuscin pigment in the muscle cells. The lining of the heart (*endocardium*) tends to become thicker due to deposition of connective tissue and fat, and hard white patches (*sclerosis*) may form. The heart valves, which are leaflike folds of the endocardium, tend to thicken and become more rigid due to the formation of fibrous plaques on their leaflets. Fibrous plaque formation on the heart valves has been reported in people as young as 30 years old, but it is most prevalent after age 60. Calcification of the valves, especially the left atrioventricular valve, also is not uncommon after 60 years of age. Diseases of the heart valves are noted in over 30% of the postmortem examinations of persons older than 75. Although any valvular disease is potentially serious, the age-related changes in the valves are usually minor enough that they do not become clinically significant and therefore are generally not a major problem for most older persons.

Structural changes also occur with aging in the conducting system of the heart. This system is composed of the SA and AV nodes, and the interventricular bundle, over which impulses are carried to the myocardium from the AV node. The most common changes are an increase of elastic and reticular fibers among the conducting cells, and infiltration of fat into the nodes and the interventricular bundle. It is uncertain whether these changes adversely affect conduction rate; however, the electrocardiogram (EKG) patterns of older individuals show characteristic differences from those of younger people which may be due in part to fibroses in the conduction system of the heart.

In addition to these physical changes in the heart, there are several functional changes that occur with aging. Both systolic and diastolic blood pressures tend to increase with age. Systolic pressure reaches its maximum around 75 years of age and remains at that level. Diastolic pressure generally reaches its maximum level by 65 years of age and then may gradually decrease. In young men, a systolic pressure of 120 mm Hg and a diastolic pressure of 80 mm Hg (written as 120/80) are considered normal. In older men a systolic pressure of 160 mm Hg and a diastolic pressure of 90 mm Hg (160/90) is still considered to be within a normal range.

Among the more serious changes in heart functioning is a progressive decrease in the maximal amount of oxygen that can be delivered to, and used by, working muscles. This capacity, which limits muscular activity, is referred to as the *maximum oxygen consumption* and is considered to be one of the best measures of cardiovascular functioning—although it also involves the respiratory and muscular systems. A person with a high maximum oxygen consumption not only has a strong heart but also has large-capacity lungs and a good blood supply to his or her muscles. Maximum oxygen consumption begins to decrease at about age 30 and has been reported to reach as much as a 40% reduction by 65 years of age. Contributing to the decreased maximum oxygen consumption is a reduction with aging in the heart rate at rest and in the maximum heart rate during strenuous exercise. Resting heart rate declines steadily from about 140 beats per minute in a newborn to about 70 beats per minute in a young adult, and generally decreases still more after 60 years of age.

The volume of blood pumped per minute by either ventricle is referred to as *cardiac output*. Cardiac output is equal to the heart rate multiplied by the stroke volume, which is the volume of blood pumped by one side of the heart per beat. The average stroke volume in a young person is about

75 ml. Since the resting heart rate is generally about 70 beats per minute, cardiac output in a young person under resting conditions is about 5 liters per minute (75 ml x 70 = 5.25 liters). Under these conditions, all the blood in the body is pumped through the heart each minute. With aging, the stroke volume decreases, largely due to a progressively reduced capacity of the left ventricle. As a result of decreased heart rate and stroke volume, cardiac output has been estimated to decrease about 1% per year after 20 years of age. The reduction in cardiac output results in less blood flowing through the arteries and, thus, reduced oxygen available to the cells—which reduces the maximum oxygen consumption.

Under conditions of strenuous exercise, cardiac output can be greatly increased—up to 30 liters per minute in a young, highly trained athlete. The maximum increase possible beyond the resting cardiac output is referred to as *cardiac reserve*. With aging there is a progressive decrease in cardiac reserve.

Although the progressive reduction in cardiac output and maximum oxygen consumption with age seem to present a rather bleak outlook for maintaining activity levels in older persons, they do not necessarily mean that physical activity needs to be reduced to match the capabilities of an aging cardiovascular system. Numerous studies have shown that the rate of loss of maximum oxygen consumption can be reduced significantly if a high level of physical activity is maintained. Especially encouraging are the findings that individuals as old as 70 years can increase their maximum oxygen consumption by following an endurance exercise training program, and the intensity of training necessary to achieve this improvement is lower than is necessary in younger persons. One study reported a 30% increase in maximum oxygen consumption in previously sedentary 60-year-olds who followed an exercise program of walking, jogging, and cycling for one year.

These findings accentuate the importance of following a continuous exercise program, preferably beginning by middle age. Older persons who have followed such a program can increase their maximum cardiac output volumes by increasing the contractility of the left ventricle. At the same time, it has been shown that there is also an improvement in their peripheral circulation, producing an increased flow of blood, and, consequently, oxygen, to the skeletal muscles.

However, even if a program of regular exercise is not followed, the aging changes that occur in a person's heart generally do not hinder it from functioning adequately to maintain the reduced level of activity characteristic of most older persons. Only a disease condition, such as one that causes reduced blood flow through the coronary arteries to the heart muscle, reduces the capacity of the heart to maintain normal activities.

Blood Vessels

One of the most common changes with age in blood vessels, especially in the larger arteries, is a reduction in the elasticity of their walls. This reduction not only affects the capacity of the arteries to rebound after being stretched by the systolic pressure but also reduces their ability to resist stretch. One study reported a 50% reduction in the elasticity of the arteries in a 70-year-old as compared with those of a 20-year-old.

One cause of the diminished elasticity is a progressive reduction in the elastin content of the walls of arteries and a concomitant increase in collagenous connective tissues. A layer of collagen often appears in the aorta as early as age 40. Furthermore, the elastin of older persons tends to bind calcium, and calcification of elastin also reduces the elasticity of arterial walls. Increased collagen in the walls of arterioles may also reduce their internal diameter to the extent that peripheral resistance is increased and blood flow is hindered.

The internal diameter of arteries may also be narrowed in older persons by a gradual accumulation of lipids in their walls. However, studies indicate that following a regular exercise program will decrease the plasma levels of cholesterol, lipids, and low-density lipoproteins. The levels of all of these compounds tend to be increased with age, which is thought to be largely responsible for lipid accumulation in the blood vessel walls. Moreover, the level of high-density lipoproteins, which transport lipids to the liver for excretion from the body, is increased in those who exercise regularly. Therefore, it appears as if regular exercise can reduce lipid accumulation in arteries.

The walls of veins may become thicker with age because of an increase of connective tissue and calcium deposits. The valves of veins may also show an increase in connective tissue and some deposition of fat on their leaflets. Because of the low blood pressures in veins, these structural changes are not thought to significantly affect cardiovascular functioning.

Probably the most common functional effect of the age-related structural changes that occur in the walls of blood vessels is their contribution to an increased systolic blood pressure, even in the absence of any circulatory-system disease. Blood pressure is determined by the amount of blood pumped out of the heart (cardiac output) and the peripheral resistance that the blood encounters in the vessels (i.e. blood pressure = cardiac output x peripheral resistance). A number of things can affect peripheral resistance, including the elasticity and the internal diameter of the arteries.

Elasticity determines the vessel's capacity to stretch and rebound in response to alterations in blood pressure as the heart beats and relaxes. The internal diameter affects the flow of blood through the vessels. Because cardiac output decreases with age, blood pressure would also decrease if the peripheral resistance did not increase. The decrease in elasticity and internal diameter of the arteries gradually increases peripheral resistance and are, in part, responsible for a gradual increase in blood pressure with age.

Age-Related Dysfunctions

There are numerous dysfunctions that occur in the circulatory system, and most of them begin well before a person reaches old age. However, the dysfunctions we will discuss here tend to be more common in older people, so there is an age-related aspect to them.

Ischemic Heart Disease

Tissue that does not receive a supply of blood which is adequate to maintain its cells is said to be *ischemic*. The end result of ischemia is malfunction or degeneration of the tissue affected. *Ischemic heart disease*, which is also known as *coronary artery disease*, is the result of insufficient blood flow through the coronary arteries to the heart muscle. The deficiency of blood supply interferes with contractions of the cells in the deprived regions of the heart or, if severe enough, causes them to degenerate. The reduced blood flow is due to a narrowing or constriction of the coronary arteries. Even in the absence of pathology, the maximum blood flow through the coronary arteries decreases by about 65% by age 60.

Because of the progressive decrease in coronary-artery blood flow, the incidence of ischemic heart disease increases with age and is the major cause of heart problems and death in older persons. It is present in about 12% of women and 20% of men over 65 years of age. The most frequent cause of diminished coronary blood flow is plaques that develop in the lining of the vessels. We will discuss plaque formation in more detail when we consider atherosclerosis. As the plaques enlarge, they protrude into the vessels and partially block blood flow. The plaques may eventually enlarge enough to completely block the vessel.

An additional problem that may occur with plaque formation in the coronary arteries is that the plaque may enlarge to the extent that it protrudes through the lining of the blood vessel and comes in direct contact with the flowing blood. Because the surface of the plaque is roughened, blood platelets adhere to it, causing fibers to be formed, and blood cells become entrapped in the fibers. These reactions form a local blood clot called a *thrombus*, which narrows the lumen of the vessel. A further danger is that the clot may break away from its attachment on the plaque and flow to a smaller, more peripheral branch of the coronary artery, where it may completely block the vessel. Regions of the heart supplied by the blocked vessel may be immediately deprived of blood. A blood clot that travels within a vessel to a region other than where it was formed is called an *embolus*.

Symptoms produced by a sudden blockage of a coronary artery are referred to as a heart attack. Some cases of sudden blockage are thought to be the result of a local spasm of the artery. It has been suggested that the spasm could be caused by irritation of the muscles in the wall of the artery by plaque formation.

The amount of damage to the heart from ischemia, caused either by partial constriction of a coronary artery from plaque formation, or by sudden blockage from an embolus, is determined largely by the extent of development of new blood vessels which bypass the blocked region. Such vessels provide collateral circulation that allows blood to reach tissues which would otherwise be deprived of blood. In an artery that is being slowly blocked, collateral branches may develop, connecting the smaller branches of the artery and thus negating the blockage to some degree.

When a sudden blockage occurs, the sizes of any collateral branches that had previously developed increase to their maximum diameters within a few seconds. Although these collateral vessels allow some blood to reach the threatened regions of the heart, they are usually so small and the blood flow through them so restricted that they are able to maintain the affected regions for only a limited time. Generally, within a few hours the vessels enlarge and collateral blood flow begins to increase. The volume of flow reaching the affected regions may double by the third day and reach almost normal levels within a few weeks. It is because of the development of collateral vessels that a person may recover from an episode of coronary-artery blockage.

The usual treatment for a blocked coronary artery has been bypass surgery in which a portion of an artery from another region of the body is grafted to the coronary artery and used to direct blood around the blocked portion. However, several experimental techniques for removing blood clots from within blood vessels have shown promise. One such technique involves the injection of chemicals (e.g. streptokinase and urokinase) which rapidly dissolve the clot, thus restoring blood flow through the vessel. At the same time a small catheter with a tiny balloon on its tip is often maneuvered through the vessel to the location of the clot. After the clot is softened by the chemicals the balloon is inflated, compressing the clot and further opening the vessel. This procedure is called balloon angioplasty. Another experimental method uses laser beams transmitted through fine glass fibers within a catheter to remove the clot.

Ischemic heart disease is the cause of the next two dysfunctions we will consider: myocardial infarction and angina pectoris.

Myocardial Infarction

Immediately after an acute coronary-artery blockage, blood flow ceases in the coronary vessels beyond the blockage. Except for any small amounts of flow from collateral vessels, the region of the heart supplied by the blocked vessel is completely cut off from its blood supply. This region, which has either no blood flow or so little flow that it is damaged, is said to be *infarcted*—and the condition is referred to as a *myocardial infarction*, or more commonly, a *heart attack*. The damaged or dead cardiac muscle cells do not conduct impulses in the same manner as normal cells; therefore, the presence of infarcted areas can be detected by an electrocardiogram. Thus, an EKG can provide information concerning the extent of heart damage caused by the infarction.

Acute myocardial infarction can cause death for a number of reasons, depending upon the location and extent of the damage. In some cases, so many muscle cells are severely damaged or destroyed that cardiac output becomes too small to sustain the person's life. In other cases, the infarcted regions of the heart may deteriorate to the extent that the heart wall is weakened and ruptures. If the infarction affects the muscles of the ventricles, a decrease in cardiac output may result that reduces arterial pressure and blood flow, and blood may accumulate in the veins—either in the pulmonary veins from the lungs or in the systemic veins draining the rest of the body. For this reason, a person who seems to be recovering well following a myocardial infarction may suddenly develop acute congestion of the lungs several days after the infarction and die within a few hours.

Angina Pectoris

Angina pectoris refers to short episodes of cardiac pain that result from progressive constriction of the coronary arteries. The pain, which is described as dull, pressing, and constricting, appears whenever the heart is called upon to contract more strenuously than can be supported by the restricted coronary blood flow. Consequently, most people who have chronic angina pectoris feel the pain when they exercise or when they experience emotions that accelerate the heart rate. The pain is usually located deep in the center of the chest but is also often reported as feeling as if it were on the surface of the body, especially in the left arm and shoulder, the neck, and the side of the face.

The incidence of angina attacks are often reduced in older persons as compared with younger persons. This is thought to be due in part to the reduced physical activity typical of older persons, and the more extensive development of collateral circulation around the restricted vessel that is more likely to have developed in elderly persons. Treatment of angina generally involves the use of drugs that either dilate the arteries or block the receptors that stimulate the sympathetic nervous system. Recall that the sympathetic nervous system tends to accelerate the heart rate.

Cardiac Arrhythmias

The heart normally contracts in a regular manner that produces a predictable sequence of heartbeats. Irregular beats that occur outside the normal sequence are referred to as *cardiac arrhythmias*. Arrhythmias may occur at any age, but are more common in older persons, and not all cases of irregular heartbeats are considered to be pathological.

Arrhythmias may result from extra systoles, when an atrium or ventricle contracts more often than it should, or from delayed heartbeats, when the chambers contract less frequently than normal. In a resting adult the heart normally beats about 70 times each minute. A heart rate below about 60 beats per minute is referred to as *bradycardia*. Bradycardia is generally not considered to be pathological. *Tachycardia*, where the resting heart rate is over 100 beats per minute, is more serious. A heart rate that is very fast does not allow adequate time for the ventricles to fill properly. Consequently, they contract when only partially full, and the movement of blood through the heart is impaired.

Under certain pathological conditions the atria or the ventricles may contract very rapidly and, at times, incoordinately. When the contractions occur at up to 300 beats per minute and are somewhat coordinated, the condition is referred to as *flutter*. When the contractions are extremely rapid, occurring more than 300 times per minute, and are incoordinated, it is called *fibrillation*. Like tachycardia, flutter and fibrillation do not allow time for proper filling of the heart chambers, and blood is not moved efficiently through the heart.

Congestive Heart Failure

Congestive heart failure is a condition in which the heart is unable to pump enough blood to meet the needs of the body. Therefore, it is also referred to as *cardiac insufficiency*. The condition itself is not actually a disease; rather, it is a result of other cardiovascular diseases that have damaged the heart to the extent that it can no longer function efficiently. For instance, congestive heart failure may result from muscular damage caused by a heart attack's impairing the ability of the heart to contract; valvular diseases may interfere with movement of blood through the heart and place a chronic increased work load on it; or congestive heart failure may be due to prolonged high blood pressure. The result of all of these conditions is that the heart is unable to perform normally and cannot maintain an adequate supply of blood to the body. Heart failure is indicated by a decrease in cardiac output or by accumulation of blood in the veins, with increased venous pressure.

Kidney function is profoundly affected in congestive heart failure. Because of the small cardiac output, production of urine is reduced and fluid is retained, causing an increase in the volume of tissue fluid and blood. In response to the increased volume of blood the capillaries and veins become dilated, and the heart must work harder to move blood through the congested vessels; thus, it increases in size (hypertrophies). After several months to several years of this distension and excessive work, the cardiac muscle fibers gradually lose their strength and the heart can no longer effectively empty one or both of its ventricles.

The symptoms associated with congestive heart failure depend upon which chamber, or chambers, are affected. For example, if the left ventricle is failing, the right ventricle may continue to pump the usual volume of blood into the pulmonary vessels. But blood returning from the lungs is not pumped efficiently into the systemic vessels by the failing left ventricle (i.e. cardiac output is reduced), and the organs do not receive adequate blood flow. Because the failing left ventricle does not empty completely, blood backs up and accumulates in the pulmonary vessels, causing the pressure within the lung capillaries to become elevated. The pulmonary capillary pressure can reach the level where fluid is forced out of the capillaries and into the lungs, causing pulmonary congestion (edema), which is potentially fatal. Persons with pulmonary congestion experience shortness of breath and have difficulty breathing, especially while lying down. It is often more comfortable for them to sleep with their upper body elevated by several pillows.

Since the cardiovascular system is a closed circuit, the pulmonary congestion caused by failure of the left side of the heart will eventually back up into the right side of the heart and cause it to become distended and overworked. In time, the right side of the heart may also fail.

Compensatory mechanisms occur during the development of congestive heart failure that may allow the cardiac output to be maintained within normal levels for a while. For instance, as the heart begins to fail, the sympathetic stimulation to the heart muscle increases, which strengthens the contraction of the chambers and helps maintain cardiac output. At the same time, the reduction in urine production by the kidneys as the heart fails increases the blood volume, causing a greater than usual venous return to the heart. The heart chambers are stretched by the increased venous return and respond by contracting more forcefully. Congestive heart failure does not have a favorable prognosis, but it can be helped with drugs that increase the contractile strength of the cardiac muscle and eliminate excess fluid from the body. Surgical repair of defective valves or other structural problems can also reduce the severity of heart failure.

Atherosclerosis and Arteriosclerosis

The presence of degenerative changes called plaques on the inner surface of the walls of arteries is rather common in older persons and is known as *atherosclerosis*. The plaques are composed of several types of tissue, including connective tissue, lipids, and abnormal smooth muscle cells. The plaques of atherosclerosis can gradually narrow or completely block blood vessels, restricting the flow of blood to the regions supplied by the vessels. And because they are rough, plaques may cause blood clots to form within the vessels. Thus, as we indicated earlier, atherosclerosis of a coronary artery may contribute to ischemic heart disease.

In advanced cases, atherosclerotic plaques can become hardened by the deposition of calcium, and fibrous tissue may proliferate in the arterial walls. This leads to a condition known as *arteriosclerosis*, or "hardening of the arteries." The changes in the arterial walls with arteriosclerosis greatly reduce their elasticity. Consequently, the vessels are less able to expand and recoil in response to the blood-pressure changes that occur as the heart contracts and relaxes. As a result, in severe cases of arteriosclerosis the pressure within the vessels becomes excessively high during systole and falls unusually low during diastole. Because of their reduced elasticity, the walls of arteriosclerotic arteries are subjected to excessive stress and may become weak. Weakened areas of the vessel wall may dilate, forming a balloonlike *aneurysm*, which may rupture when the blood pressure increases.

Hypertension

Hypertension, or high blood pressure, is not restricted to older persons, but its incidence tends to increase with age. It has been estimated that about 30% of the population in industrialized societies suffer from hypertension by the age of 65. Elevated blood pressure is potentially serious because it can contribute to heart attack, heart failure, kidney damage, or rupture of blood vessels. There is no one level above which the pressure is considered to be pathologically high, but in general, systolic arterial blood pressures above 170 mm Hg and diastolic pressures above 90 mm Hg (170/90) are considered to be hypertensive.

The most common causes of hypertension in older persons are atherosclerosis and arteriosclerosis. Because these conditions decrease the diameter and elasticity of the arteries, the heart must contract harder if it is to maintain normal blood flow to the various organs, which, in fact, it is generally unable to do. The additional work load imposed upon the heart by atherosclerosis and arteriosclerosis results in high blood pressure and can eventually lead to heart failure.

High blood pressure may damage the kidneys and affect their functioning. And if the arteries supplying the kidneys develop plaques and lose elasticity, blood flow may be diminished and cause areas of ischemia in the kidneys. The decreased urine output that may result from damage or inadequate blood flow to the kidneys causes the blood volume to increase and the heart to work harder, thus increasing blood pressure.

Atherosclerosis and arteriosclerosis are not the only causes of high blood pressure. Excessive dietary intake of sodium or an excessive retention of sodium by the body are also thought to contribute to some cases of hypertension. Elevated blood pressure can often be lowered and maintained at more normal levels with various medications.

It is generally accepted that high blood pressure is not an automatic consequence of aging and need not be as prevalent as it is in well-developed countries. This conclusion is reached from studies indicating that, by comparison, persons living in less-developed countries tend to have a significantly lower incidence of hypertension and heart disease. It has been suggested that in the populations of the more highly developed regions a number of factors common to the life-styles of people contribute more to the development of hypertension and heart disease than does aging. Among these factors are obesity, lack of exercise, excessive intake of salt, and smoking.

Summary

There are no major changes in blood volume, composition, or components with age. Although a decrease in active red bone marrow reduces the capacity for production of blood cells in older persons, they are generally able to maintain adequate levels of blood cells under normal conditions.

As a result of cardiovascular disease, the heart of an older person is often enlarged, while becoming progressively weaker and less able to maintain cardiac output at the level it was when he or she was younger. The endocardium becomes thicker, and fat is deposited on the surface of the heart. The heart valves thicken and may undergo some calcification. Blood pressure tends to increase with age, and stroke volume, heart rate, and cardiac reserve volume become smaller. In the absence of a regular program of exercise, there is a progressive decrease in maximum oxygen consumption with age, which may limit muscular activity.

Aging diminishes the elasticity of blood vessels, and there is a tendency for calcium to be deposited in their walls. The inside diameter of arterioles may be narrowed as collagen thickens their wall, thus increasing peripheral resistance to blood flow and tending to elevate blood pressure. Accumulations of fat may partially occlude arteries.

The Immune System

10

Review of Structure and Function

Bone Marrow • Thymus • Spleen • Lymph Nodes • Tonsils • Lymphocytes and Plasma Cells

Age-Related Changes

Bone Marrow • Thymus • Spleen • Lymph Nodes • Tonsils

Age-Related Dysfunctions

General Decrease in Immune Responses

Summary

$\mathbf{A}$s people grow older they become more susceptible to disease. Since the immune system is a main line of defense against invasion of the body by bacteria, viruses, fungi, or other foreign substances, deficiencies of the system may increase the incidence of disease. Consequently, searching for changes that occur in the immune system with aging has become a major direction of research.

The data from many studies indicate that several facets of the immune responses seem to decrease with age. These findings have led to suggestions that there may be an association between the function of the immune system, the aging process in general, and age-related diseases. In fact, in what will most certainly prove to be a bit of an overstatement, it has been suggested by some authors that hormones secreted by the thymus gland, which is an important organ of the immune system, may be the long sought "fountain of youth."

Review of Structure and Function

The immune system is not a distinct entity like the other systems of the body. Rather, it involves the actions of specific cells in various tissues, certain types of cells that leave the vessels and affect specific target tissues, and various large molecules that circulate in the blood or lymph. Most of the components of what we refer to as the immune system are studied as parts of other body systems, especially the circulatory and lymphatic systems. Specifically, the immune system consists of the bone marrow, the thymus gland, the spleen, lymph nodes, and the tonsils.

Bone Marrow

Bone marrow is located in central cavities with various bones. There are two types of bone marrow: yellow marrow, which consists primarily of fat deposits, and red marrow, which is colored by the presence of hemoglobin. Red bone marrow is the site of blood-cell formation and serves an important role in the immune responses.

Red bone marrow consists primarily of immature blood cells intermixed with some fat cells and connective-tissue fibers and surrounded by thin-walled blood sinuses. After maturing in the bone marrow, the various blood cells pass through the walls of the sinuses and enter the blood, in which they circulate throughout the body. Both red and white blood cells are produced from precursor cells located within the red bone marrow, but certain of the white blood cells differentiate further in the thymus gland, spleen, or lymph nodes. We will consider these cells later in this chapter.

Thymus

The *thymus* is a mass of lymphoid tissue located beneath the sternum. During early childhood it may extend from the level of the heart up to the base of the neck. The gland is covered with a connective-tissue capsule, from which partitions divide it into small lobules. The lobules consist mostly of a type of white blood cell called *lymphocytes*, but some *macrophages* are also present. Macrophages are active phagocytes, moving by ameboid movements into connective tissues and lymphoid organs, where they engulf and destroy foreign matter.

Spleen

The *spleen* is the largest of the lymphoid organs. It lies to the left of the stomach and extends upward to the diaphragm. It is covered with a strong fibrous capsule and subdivided by connective-tissue partitions into several compartments.

Two types of lymphoid tissues are located within the compartments. Most of the tissue is red pulp, which is composed of blood sinuses surrounded by red blood cells, blood platelets, lymphocytes, and macrophages. Scattered through the red pulp are small masses of white pulp, which consists primarily of lymphocytes. As blood passes through the spleen it filters through the lymphoid tissues. The spleen also serves to remove old, abnormal, or damaged blood cells and platelets from the blood.

Lymph Nodes

Lymph nodes are small masses of lymphoid tissue that are located along the course of the lymphatic vessels. Groups of lymph nodes occur in certain regions. Each node is surrounded by a connective-tissue capsule, which extends inward and subdivides it into several compartments. The compartments contain numerous lymph sinuses surrounded by masses of lymphocytes and macrophages. Lymph enters the node through lymph vessels, slowly filters through the sinuses, and continues to travel toward the blood vascular system through other lymph vessels.

Tonsils

The *tonsils* are small masses of lymphoid tissue embedded in the lining of the pharynx and nasopharynx. A protective ring is formed around the pharynx by the palatine tonsils, the pharyngeal tonsils, and the lingual tonsils.

Tonsils differ structurally from lymph nodes in that they do not contain sinuses; thus, lymph is not filtered through them. Rather, the tonsils are surrounded on their outer surface by networks of lymph capillaries.

Lymphocytes and Plasma Cells

The white blood cells responsible for the defense afforded by the immune system are called *lymphocytes*. When substances enter the body lymphocytes recognize them as being foreign to the body and react against them, attempting to either neutralize or destroy them.

Lymphocytes are produced from precursor cells located in the red bone marrow. After entering the blood, many of the lymphocytes pass into lymph vessels and accumulate in the spleen and lymph nodes. While passing through the spleen and nodes lymph is exposed to the lymphocytes, which are active in immune responses, and to two cell types that are derived from lymphocytes, *plasma cells* and *macrophages*. Thus, the cells of the spleen and lymph nodes act upon any foreign substances present in the lymph—in effect, filtering the lymph.

Lymphocytes also accumulate in small groups immediately beneath the linings of the respiratory and digestive tracts, providing a defense against bacteria, viruses, and other foreign substances that may enter the body through inhalation or ingestion. Examples of such accumulations are the tonsils, the appendix, and small masses of lymphoid tissue on the intestine called Peyer's patches.

Although lymphocytes are similar in appearance, functionally there are at least two types. One type, called *B cells*, develop into plasma cells, which initiate the antibody–antigen responses, thereby serving to resist invasion by bacteria, toxins, and other foreign substances. This protective reaction by B cells is referred to as *humoral immunity*. The second type of lymphocyte, called *T cells*, are responsible for *cell-mediated immune responses*, in which the foreign substances are destroyed by direct contact with the T cells. Examples of cell-mediated immune responses include the chronic inflammatory responses caused by delayed hypersensitivity, rejection of foreign tissues—such as organ transplants—and specific immune responses to invasion by viruses, fungi, and parasites.

During embryonic development certain cells in the red bone marrow become stem cells which divide and differentiate to produce all the various types of blood cells. Some stem cells produce daughter cells which differentiate into lymphocytes. Some of the lymphocyte precursor cells travel to the thymus gland; others travel directly to the spleen, lymph nodes, and tonsils.

Those lymphocyte precursor cells which travel from the red bone marrow to the thymus gland undergo further development into T cells in the thymus before entering the general circulation. Those precursor cells which leave the red bone marrow and develop further in lymphoid tissues other than the thymus gland give rise to B cells (Figure 10-1). Both B cells and T cells continually circulate in the blood, tissue fluid, and lymph, and at any one time large numbers are present in the lymph nodes, spleen, and other lymphoid tissues.

The presence of foreign antigens stimulates B çells in the lymphoid tissues to transform into plasma cells that synthesize the appropriate antibody for the specific antigen which triggered the transformation. The antibodies are released into the blood and lymph and interact with the antigen, inactivating or destroying it (Figure 10-2). Not all of the stimulated B cells develop into plasma cells and form antibodies. Some develop into "memory cells," which allow the immune system to produce antibodies more quickly in response to subsequent exposure to the same antigen.

Fig. 10-1 Formation of T cells and B cells from precursor cells located in the red bone marrow.

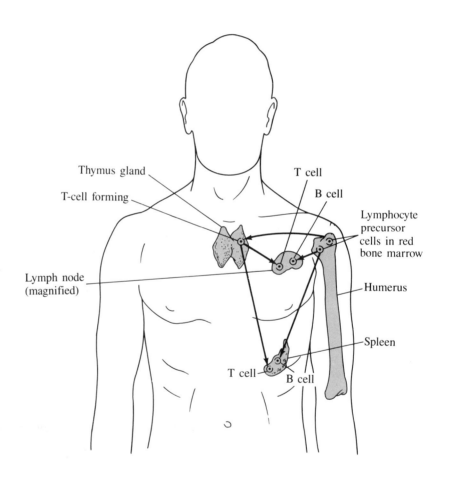

Fig. 10-2 A humoral immune response. B cells stimulated by a foreign antigen develop into plasma cells, which produce antibodies against the specific antigen. Some stimulated B cells remain in the lymph nodes and serve as memory cells.

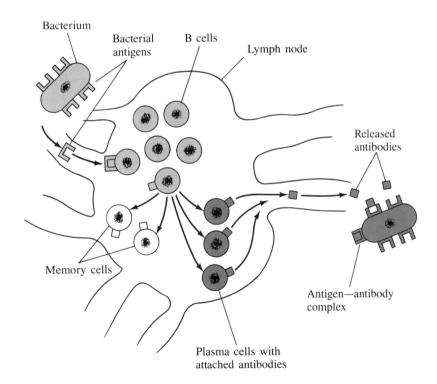

Fig. 10-3   A cell-mediated immune response. T cells stimulated by a foreign antigen form effector T cells, which attack and destroy the cells bearing the foreign antigens. Some stimulated T cells remain in the lymph nodes and serve as memory cells.

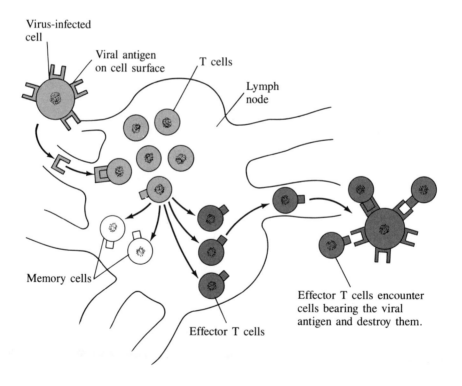

Actually, B cell stimulation and antibody production are more involved than we have described them. In most cases, other cells, such as macrophages and a class of T cells called "helper T cells," are also thought to be involved in transforming B cells into plasma cells, which actually produce the antibodies.

In contrast, antigens on the surface of body cells infected by a virus stimulate T cells to transform into an active form called *effector T cells*. The effector T cells enter the blood and lymph and directly attack and destroy the virus-infected cells (Figure 10-3). In a similar manner, T cells may also provide specific immune resistance to fungi, parasites, and intracellular bacteria, and play a major role in the rejection of tissue transplants. Some of the activated T cells remain in the lymphoid tissue and serve as "memory cells" that facilitate cell-mediated immune response to future infections by the same virus or other foreign agent.

Age-Related Changes

It is well established that most lymphoid tissues undergo structural changes with advancing age, reaching their maximal development at about puberty, and slowly regressing after that time. It has proven more difficult to correlate the structural changes with age-related alterations in immune responses.

Bone Marrow
As we mentioned in Chapter 9, there is some reduction in the amount of active red bone marrow with age. However, enough stem cells remain to produce a supply of blood cells that is adequate to replace those lost due to completion of their normal life cycles. Consequently, functioning of the immune system has not been shown to be adversely affected by an age-related decline in lymphocytes.

Thymus
The thymus reaches its maximum size in early childhood, begins to decrease in mass during the late teen years, and continues to decrease progressively with age. By the age of 50, the cellular mass of the thymus may be only 10% of its original mass, but it generally does not degenerate completely.

Degeneration occurs in cells in the outer regions (cortex) as well as deep within (medulla) the gland. The cortex, which constitutes about 50%

of the gland in a newborn, may degenerate until it represents only 6% of the adult gland. The cells of the medulla may also constitute only 6% of the adult thymus, down from 20% in the gland of a newborn. Most of the adult gland is composed of connective tissue.

As the composition of the thymus gland changes with age, it produces lesser amounts of a group of hormones called *thymosins*. The thymosins are thought to be responsible for the differentiation of T cells. Consequently, the ability of the thymus to transform precursor lymphocytes into T lymphocytes declines with age, and increased numbers of immature T cells appear in the blood. T cell functioning also seems to be adversely affected by the diminished levels of the thymosins.

Although the total number of B lymphocytes in the blood does not change significantly with age, there is an age-related decline in antibody–antigen reactions—which depend primarily on the responsiveness of B cells. One study reported a decrease of over 85% in production of antibodies to a specific antigen between the ages of 20 and 70. The decline in B cell activity may be due, in part, to a decrease in the number or activity of "helper T cells," which assist in plasma cell formation.

Spleen

The average weight of the spleen has been reported to increase up to about age 30 and decreases only after 50 years of age. Much of the decrease is in the lymphoid tissues (red and white pulp) of the organ, while the connective tissue covering the organ and separating it into compartments increases in older persons. Several studies report that the decrease in lymphoid tissue in the spleen reaches a plateau between ages 51 and 65. After 65 years of age, the spleen weight falls steadily.

Studies involving animals which had their spleens removed report a significant increase in their life expectancies. These results would indicate that the spleen may be an important factor in age-related immune dysfunctions, which can shorten one's life.

Lymph Nodes

The lymphoid tissue in lymph nodes reaches its maximum development during childhood and gradually diminishes after puberty. However, the size of the nodes does not change greatly with age because connective tissue in the nodes increases and replaces the lost lymphoid tissue. In some older nodes large fluid-filled cavities develop.

The nodes of older persons generally contain more macrophages than do the nodes of younger persons. The macrophages often have large masses of deep brown pigment and clear vacuoles within them. Because of the differences in the number and appearance of the macrophages, along with more subtle differences in lymphocytes and plasma cells, it is possible to identify a node as being from an elderly person by microscopic examination.

Tonsils

Although tonsils are present in elderly persons, they do tend to decrease in size with age. The decline occurs at different rates in the various tonsils. For instance, the palatine tonsils have been reported to reach their maximum size at about 12 years of age, after which they begin to gradually decline. The pharyngeal tonsils are usually almost completely atrophied in an adult.

Because most of the decreased size of the tonsils is due to a reduction in the amount of lymphoid tissue they contain, the number of lymphocytes present in the tonsils decreases appreciably with age. It is not certain whether the lymphocytes are in such short supply that the immune functions of the tonsils are affected.

Age-Related Dysfunctions

General Decrease in Immune Responses

The interactions of the immune system are very complex and not enough information is available to permit a detailed consideration of the specific dysfunctions of the various components of the system with aging. Suffice it to say that there is a general decrease in immune sensitivity in older persons, including a reduction in cell-mediated and humoral immune responses. However, at the same time, there is a tendency for autoimmune reactions to increase. That is, in older persons the ability of their antibodies to recognize their own body tissues is diminished.

Recall that one theory concerning the cause of rheumatoid arthritis, which is common in older persons, is that the condition is the result of an autoimmune response. Such a reaction involves the production of antibodies that attack the body's own tissues. It has been suggested that, in persons suffering from rheumatoid arthritis, antibodies are produced in response to degradation of tissues in their joints. The antibodies attack the joint tissues, destroying them and producing an inflammatory reaction. Thus, it appears as if immune dysfunctions which affect the ability to recognize deteriorated body tissues as not being foreign to the body may contribute to arthritis, and perhaps to certain other diseases in older persons. There have been several suggestions as to what would cause such an immune dysfunction. Among the more popular suggestions is that mutations of stem cells cause the production of altered lymphocytes that are incapable of properly identifying one's own body cells.

It is not known what causes the decreased responses by the immune system with aging, but they could be due to any of several alterations, including a decrease in the number of precursor cells which give rise to the various types of lymphocytes. Or, the supply of precursor cells may be adequate, but their ability to divide and differentiate into normal T lymphocytes or B lymphocytes may be diminished. In fact, there is some evidence that the decline in immune function that accompanies aging is due primarily to changes in the T-cell component, and that B-cell changes are minimal. Another possibility has been introduced by experiments which indicate that old animals contain suppressor cells or factors that inhibit immune responses. Whether these factors are present in humans has not been determined.

Summary

Accompanying the decrease of lymphoid tissue in all lymphoid organs with aging is a general decline in immune responses, including both cell-mediated and humoral immunity. This general decline is thought to be due to a reduction in the number of T cells and reduced activity of B cells, whose numbers remain fairly stable with age.

The components of the immune system also become less able to recognize the body's own cells in older persons, making them more susceptible to autoimmune responses.

The Respiratory System

11

Review of Structure and Function

Age-Related Changes

Age-Related Dysfunctions

Summary

All cells in the body require a constant supply of oxygen to enable them to carry on their various metabolic activities. They must also have a means of removing the carbon dioxide produced as an end product of these activities. The organs of the respiratory system, along with those of the circulatory system, serve these needs.

The organs of the respiratory system are affected more by environmental factors than are the organs of most other body systems. Respiratory organs are almost constantly exposed to various pollutants in the air, and respiratory infections are so common that they may contribute to the aging process of the respiratory system. Therefore, it is difficult to identify which changes in the system are normal aging changes and which are due to repeated, chronic exposure to environmental factors.

The lungs contain the sites at which air, containing oxygen, and blood, containing carbon dioxide, come in close enough proximity so that an exchange of gases may occur between the two media. Blood is supplied to these exchange sites through the pulmonary arteries from the right ventricle, while air flows through a complex series of conducting passageways to reach the sites. We want to become familiar with these passageways.

Review of Structure and Function

The respiratory system consists of the nasal cavity, the pharynx, the trachea, bronchi, alveoli, and the lungs.

Nasal Cavity

Air enters the respiratory system either through the *nasal cavity* or the mouth and passes into the pharynx, which is a common chamber at the rear of the mouth used by the respiratory and digestive systems (Figure 11-1). Paranasal sinuses, which are air spaces located in several of the bones of the skull, drain into the nasal cavity. The nasal cavity and the paranasal sinuses are lined with a continuous *mucous membrane*. The mucous membrane is well supplied with blood and is kept moist by a thick fluid called *mucus* that is secreted by glands in the membrane. Consequently, the membrane warms and moistens the air as it is inhaled. The layer of mucous covering the mucous membrane also protects the respiratory system by trapping any small particles that are not stopped by the hairs guarding the entrance into the nose. Small hairlike cilia are also present on the surface of the membrane and these move in rhythmic waves to carry the mucus and the particles trapped by it to the pharynx, where they can be removed by coughing or swallowing.

Infections or allergic responses may cause the blood vessels of the mucous membranes of the nasal cavity to dilate. This, in turn, causes the membranes to swell and increases mucous secretion. These responses produce a congestion that interferes with breathing and may cause a "runny nose."

An infection of the nasal mucous membrane can spread into the mucous membranes of the paranasal sinuses, causing them to swell and blocking their connections with the nasal cavity. Because they can no longer drain into the nasal cavity, inflamed sinuses fill with mucus and become painful. The infection can also spread from the nose to the mucous membrane of the pharynx, producing a "sore throat." From the pharynx, infections can spread through the mucous membranes into the passageways leading to the lungs or the middle-ear cavity.

Pharynx

Air from the nasal cavity enters the *pharynx*, which also has openings leading to the mouth, the middle ear, the esophagus, and the trachea. Thus, the pharynx is used by both the digestive and respiratory systems.

Fig. 11-1 Organs of the respiratory system.

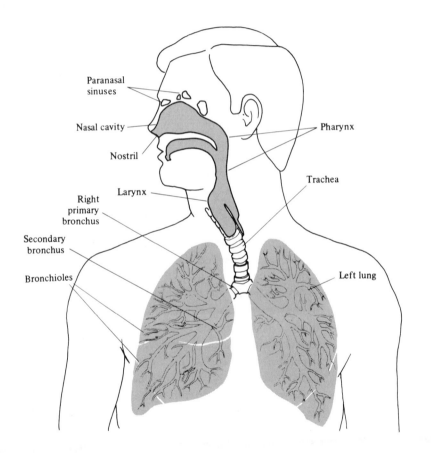

Paranasal sinuses

Nasal cavity

Nostril

Larynx

Right primary bronchus

Secondary bronchus

Bronchioles

Pharynx

Trachea

Left lung

Adapted from Barrett, J., et al.: Biology. *Englewood Cliffs, N.J., Prentice Hall, 1986, p. 238.*

Chapter 11   The Respiratory System

Consequently, swallowing and breathing must be coordinated to prevent food from entering the respiratory system from the pharynx.

Trachea

From the pharynx, air passes through the *larynx* (voice box) and enters the tubelike *trachea*. Both the larynx and the trachea have smooth muscles and cartilage frameworks in their walls. The cartilage forms several plates in the larynx and a series of C-shaped rings in the trachea. These frameworks serve to prevent the larynx and the trachea from collapsing; thus, they keep the airways constantly open.

The trachea descends into the chest along the anterior surface of the esophagus. It, like most of the respiratory organs, is lined with a ciliated mucous membrane. As we mentioned earlier, the cilia beat upward, carrying foreign particles trapped in the mucus away from the lungs to the pharynx, where they can be eliminated from the body.

Bronchi

As it passes behind the aortic arch, the trachea divides into two smaller branches called the left and right *primary bronchi*. The primary bronchi divide into still smaller tubes called *secondary bronchi*, each of which leads to a lobe of a lung. The secondary bronchi, in turn, branch into many smaller *tertiary bronchi*, which further branch repeatedly into tubules called *bronchioles* (Figure 11-2). The bronchioles subdivide into smaller and smaller tubules, ultimately ending in thin-walled air sacs called *alveoli*. The many respiratory tubes formed from the series of branchings the bronchi undergo is known as the bronchial tree.

The walls of the primary bronchi, like those of the trachea, contain smooth muscle and cartilage rings. In the smaller branches the cartilage rings gradually become reduced, and the walls of the bronchioles contain no cartilage and are surrounded only by smooth muscle. In certain allergic responses, such as asthma, the muscles of the bronchioles undergo spasms. Because there are no cartilage rings present in their walls, the air passageways are squeezed shut by the muscle spasms, making breathing very difficult during an asthma attack.

Alveoli

The bronchioles terminate in tiny balloonlike air sacs called *alveoli*. The alveoli are surrounded by many blood vessels, and it is here that gaseous exchange occurs between the air and the blood. The air in the alveoli is separated from the blood in the pulmonary capillaries by a very thin

Fig. 11-2   Microscopic structure of the division of the bronchi into alveoli, their blood supply, and lymphatic drainage.

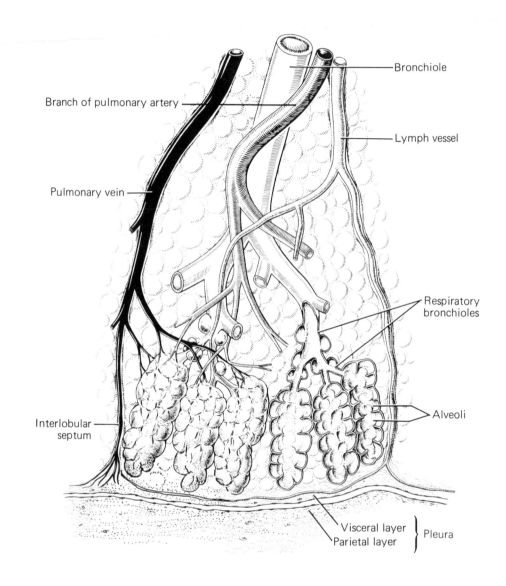

Based in part on Cormack, D.H.: Ham's Histology, *9th Ed. Philadelphia, Lippincott, 1988.*

respiratory membrane consisting primarily of the alveolar epithelium and the endothelium of the capillaries.

The surfaces of the alveoli, like those of the other structures in the bronchial tree, are moist. The molecules of a liquid are strongly attracted to one another, producing a cohesiveness referred to as surface tension. The surface tension of the fluid that coats the alveoli tends to reduce the size of the alveoli and thereby resists their expansion, as occurs during inspiration. If the fluid were pure water, the surface tension within the alveoli would be so great that expansion of the lungs during inspiration would require extreme muscular effort. However, cells within the alveoli produce a substance called *pulmonary surfactant* which reduces the surface tension of the fluid and greatly lessens the muscular effort necessary to expand the lungs.

Lungs

Each *lung* has a pointed apex that is located at the top of the thoracic cavity, behind the clavicle, and a broad base that rests on the upper surface of the diaphragm. The diaphragm separates the thoracic cavity from the abdominal cavity and provides much of the force necessary to accomplish breathing. The walls of the lungs lack muscles but contain elastic fibers which provide a certain amount of resiliency to the lungs.

The lungs are divided into lobes; the right lung has three lobes while the left has only two. In addition, each lung is subdivided by connective partitions into smaller units called *bronchopulmonary segments*. The segments are important because disease tends to be confined to a segment by the partitions, and it is possible to surgically remove a diseased segment while leaving the rest of the lobe intact.

Each lung is enclosed in a double-walled sac called the *pleura*. The very narrow space between the two layers is called the *pleural cavity* and is filled with *pleural fluid*. The pleural fluid acts as a lubricant to reduce friction between the two layers of the pleura during respiratory movements and also serves to create a surface tension which couples the two layers together. Because the inner layer of the pleura is tightly attached to the lungs and the outer layer to the wall of the thorax, and the two layers of the pleura are held together by pleural fluid, outward movements of the thoracic wall cause the lungs to expand.

In order for diffusion of oxygen and carbon dioxide to occur across the respiratory membrane of the alveoli, fresh air must be repeatedly brought into the lungs and the air already within the lungs must be removed. This ventilation of the lungs is accomplished by inspiration and expiration.

During *inspiration* the volume of the thoracic cavity is increased by contracting the diaphragm and elevating the ribs. The increase in thoracic-cavity volume decreases the pressure within the lungs (*intrapulmonary pressure*) to the point where atmospheric pressure causes air to enter the pharynx and pass to the lungs.

During *expiration* the volume of the thoracic cavity is decreased by relaxing the diaphragm and the muscles which elevated the ribs during inspiration. Therefore, expiration is passive, involving only the relaxation of muscles, whereas inspiration is active, requiring the contraction of muscles. Relaxation of the inspiratory muscles allows the elastic recoil of the chest wall to reduce the volume of the thoracic cavity. This, plus the elastic recoil of the lungs, increases the pressure within the lungs and forces air out of them. Contraction of certain skeletal muscles is involved in forced expiration, such as occurs during exercise. Therefore, forced expiration is active rather than passive.

A number of measurable volumes are significant in lung functioning and tend to be altered with aging. Because it is not possible to exhale all the air from the lungs, about 1200 ml always remains within them. This air, which never leaves the lungs, is called the *residual volume* (Figure 11-3). *Tidal volume* refers to the 500 ml of air that moves into and out of the lungs with each breath during normal, quiet breathing. During a forced inspiration, about 2100 ml in females and 3000 ml in males of additional air can be inspired beyond the 500 ml inspired as tidal air. This represents the *inspiratory reserve*. The sum of the tidal volume and the inspiratory-reserve volume is called the *inspiratory capacity*. Additional air can be forced out of the lungs following a normal passive expiration of the tidal volume. This *expiratory reserve* is about 800 ml in females and 1200 ml in males. The residual volume and the expiratory-reserve volume represent air which does not leave the lungs under usual conditions. Therefore, their sum is referred to as the *functional residual capacity*.

The maximal amount of air that can be moved into and out of the lungs with a deep inspiration followed by a forced expiration is called the *vital capacity*. The vital capacity is the sum of the inspiratory-reserve volume, the tidal volume, and the expiratory-reserve volume. In healthy young adults the vital capacity ranges from about 4400 ml in females to 5900 ml in males. Vital capacity plus the residual volume represents the total capacity of the lungs.

Clinically, one of the most significant measurements of lung functioning is the amount of air which can be moved into and out of the lungs by forced breathing during a given period of time. This volume is referred to as the *maximum breathing capacity*. Maximum breathing capacity

Fig. 11-3   Lung volumes and capacities.

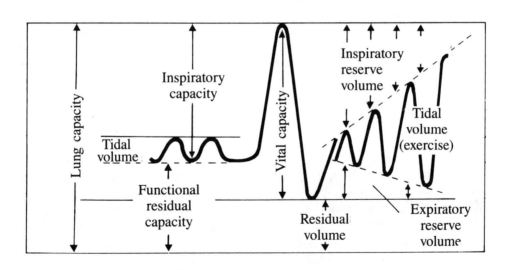

From Clarke, D.H.: Exercise Physiology. *Englewood Cliffs, N.J., Prentice Hall, 1975, p. 158.*

depends greatly on the degree of *compliance* in the lungs. Compliance is a measure of the resistance of the lungs to expansion during inspiration. Because the elastic fibers in the walls of the lungs tend to resist stretching, lung compliance provides an indication of the strength of elastic recoil of the lung wall. Any condition that lessens the resistance of the lungs to expansion increases their compliance. Thus, a reduction in elasticity will increase the compliance of the lungs.

When removed from the chest, the lungs are almost twice as distensible as they are when in the thorax. This is because, like the lungs, the thoracic cage also resists expansion and must be stretched in order for the lungs to be expanded. That is, the compliance of the thoracic cage also affects lung expansion. Structural abnormalities, such as kyphosis (hunchback) or severe scoliosis (lateral curvature) of the vertebral column may reduce the expansibility of the thoracic cage, thus hindering expansion of the lungs and reducing their compliance.

Another measurement of the efficiency of the respiratory system that is clinically useful is the *minute respiratory volume*. This measurement is equal to the respiratory rate (in breaths per minute) multiplied by the volume of air that enters the respiratory passageways with each breath (i.e. the tidal volume). Since the normal tidal volume is about 500 ml, and the normal respiratory rate is about 12 breaths per minute, the normal minute respiratory volume is about 6 liters per minute. The minute respiratory volume will be caused to vary from this normal level by any condition which alters either the respiratory rate or the tidal air volume. As we will see, both of these parameters are commonly altered with aging.

Age-Related Changes

One common sign of aging is when a person cannot maintain as high a level of physical activity as he or she was once able to. Although changes in the muscular and circulatory systems contribute to this functional decline, a major cause is the decreased ability of the respiratory organs to acquire and deliver oxygen to the arterial blood. The impairment in oxygen delivery is the result of a number of age-related changes in various respiratory structures, which we now want to consider.

Trachea and Bronchi
The cartilage in the walls of the trachea and bronchi undergo a progressive calcification, causing them to become increasingly rigid with aging.

At the same time, the smooth-muscle fibers in the walls of the tiny bronchioles tend to be replaced with fibrous connective tissue, which is unable to contract or to stretch. Consequently, the bronchioles become less distensible. These changes, together with a reduced elasticity of the lungs and the wall of the thorax, cause a gradual decrease in maximum breathing capacity and in vital capacity, beginning at about 20 years of age. For instance, the maximum breathing capacity decreases steadily from 165 liters per minute at 25 years to about 75 liters per minute at 85 years of age. Showing the same trend, the vital capacity has been reported to begin to decrease at about 40 years of age, and by age 70 it may be only about 60% of its original volume. Accompanying the decreased vital capacity is an increase in the volume of residual air in the lungs.

With increasing age the epithelial cells of the mucous membrane lining the trachea and bronchi show degenerative changes, and there is a decrease in the activity of the cilia of these cells. There is also a decrease in the phagocytic activity of the macrophages in the lining. The result is a less efficient cleaning of the respiratory tract lining and less effective protection against foreign particles inhaled with the air.

Alveoli
Although the number of alveoli remains essentially constant in elderly persons, there is a gradual deterioration of the walls separating adjacent alveoli. The loss of alveolar walls increases the size of the alveoli and reduces the functional respiratory surface across which gaseous exchange occurs. The reduction has been estimated to be almost 3 sq ft per year from youth to old age. At this rate, a person would have about 150 sq ft less functional respiratory surface at age 70 than he or she had at age 20.

Cross-linkages develop between collagen fibers in the walls of the alveoli, and the ratio of collagen fibers to elastic fibers is gradually altered. These changes diminish the ability of the alveoli to expand during inspiration. As a result, with aging, alveolar ventilation is diminished.

Changes also occur with age in the chemical composition of the substances that fill the space separating the alveoli and the capillaries. The changes tend to impede gas exchange between the alveoli and the lung capillaries. Consequently, with aging a lower percentage of the oxygen available in alveolar air is able to pass to the lung capillaries, causing a decrease in the level of oxygen saturation in arterial blood. Declining oxygen levels in the blood is the main age-related functional change in the respiratory system.

Lungs

With aging, the lungs lose some of their elastic recoil and thus offer less resistance to expansion. The loss of lung elasticity seems to result more from alterations of composition and structure of elastic and collagen fibers than from a reduction of elastic fibers. In fact, it has been reported that the amount of elastic fibers in the lungs increases with age, even while elastic recoil gradually diminishes.

We mentioned earlier that reduced oxygen levels in arterial blood leaving the lungs is the major functional change that occurs in the respiratory system of older persons. Contributing to the reduced oxygen saturation is an unequal distribution of air within the lungs. Even in young people there are areas in the lungs where the volume of inspired air that reaches the region is insufficient to completely oxygenate the blood supply of that region. Consequently, blood leaves the region only partially saturated with oxygen. These regions do not usually cause problems in younger persons because, in their lungs, sufficient blood is completely saturated with oxygen to dilute the partially saturated blood. One such area where air and blood supply are not balanced is the lower portions of the lungs, which, because of gravity, receive a disproportionately large volume of blood. Because of the age-related reduction in elastic recoil of the lungs, older persons often do not sufficiently ventilate the alveoli of these lower lung regions. Consequently, a large volume of oxygen-poor blood leaves the lungs from these regions and dilutes the highly oxygenated blood from other regions, contributing to an overall reduction in oxygen saturation of arterial blood.

Age-related changes in lung functioning also appear to be associated with a person's height. One study reported that with aging, taller men experienced a greater reduction of forced expiratory-reserve volume than did shorter men. It was proposed that gravity causes more distortion in the larger lungs of the taller men and thus has a greater effect on elastic recoil and the rate of air flow.

Tidal volume and the rate of respirations remain fairly constant; therefore, no significant change generally occurs in minute respiratory volume with age. However, because the ability of alveoli to expand is progressively diminished, the air within the alveoli is not exchanged as efficiently as in a younger lung, and less of the tidal air comes in contact with the functional alveolar surface, where gas exchange occurs. Thus, even with respiratory minute volume remaining constant, less oxygen-rich air reaches the alveoli of older persons. Compounding this problem, older persons do not increase their respiratory rates in response to lowered levels of oxygen in the blood to the extent that they did when younger. It is not clear whether this is a result of diminished stimulation of the respiratory muscles by the sympathetic nervous system, or a lessened ability of the respiratory muscles to respond to sympathetic nerve stimulation. Curiously, alteration of respiratory rates in response to variations of carbon dioxide concentrations in the blood does not seem to change significantly with age.

Structural Changes

Some of the age-related changes in respiratory functioning are the result of general structural changes the body undergoes.

It is not uncommon for older people to develop a rounding of the thoracic region of the vertebral column, and in some cases an actual kyphosis, due to the loss of calcium from the vertebrae and a progressive weakening of muscles of the neck and back. The hunching over reduces the volume of the thoracic cavity and makes it more difficult for the lungs to expand. At the same time, the cartilage connecting the ribs to the spinal column and sternum tends to calcify, causing these joints to become stiffer with age. There is also an age-related decrease in the fibers of the muscles of the thorax that are involved in respiration, and in the diaphragm. Combined, these changes in the skeleton and respiratory muscles cause increasing rigidity of the wall of the thoracic cavity, making respiration more difficult and less efficient. Since the chest wall of older persons cannot expand to the extent that it can in younger persons, the volume of air that can be moved during respiration is reduced.

Because of the diminished elasticity of the lungs, the increased stiffness of the rib cage, and changes in the normal spinal curvatures, more muscular work is required to move air into and out of the lungs. Consequently, older persons tend to rely more on the diaphragm for inspiration in order to circumvent the extra effort required to expand the stiffened rib cage. However, because the diaphragm separates the abdominal cavity from the thoracic cavity, contraction of the diaphragm is affected by pressure within the abdominal cavity. Thus, in an old person, breathing can be noticeably affected by changes in intraabdominal pressure. For this reason, older persons may find breathing more difficult when lying on their backs. This position increases intraabdominal pressure, which, along with the stiffness of the rib cage, makes it difficult for them to increase the volume of their thoracic cavity and ventilate their lungs adequately. Elderly persons generally find it easier to breath if their upper body is elevated by several pillows.

While discussing several body systems—particularly the skeletal, muscular, and circulatory systems—we mentioned that age-related changes can be delayed, or perhaps even reversed, by a continued program of exercise. However, in considering the effects of exercise on respiratory functioning, it must be kept in mind that there are no muscles in the walls of the lungs. Only the diaphragm and the respiratory muscles of the chest wall have the potential of being strengthened by exercise. It is unclear whether exercise has any significant effect on lung elasticity, which, as we have seen, is an important factor in respiratory functioning.

The data indicate that, while exercise may increase the maximum volume of air that can be moved through the lungs (i.e. maximum breathing capacity), it does not seem to improve the minute respiratory volume or the lung volume. Therefore, tidal volume and vital capacity are not improved by exercise.

Age-Related Dysfunctions

Some of the dysfunctions of the respiratory system that are more common in older people may not be so much the result of aging as the result of many years exposure of the system to environmental factors, such as air pollution and smoking. Excessive and prolonged exposure to air pollutants may destroy the epithelium lining the trachea, bronchi, and alveoli, and in severe cases may damage the capillaries supplying the alveoli.

The most frequently occurring pulmonary disorders can be classified as either restrictive or obstructive diseases. *Restrictive* diseases are those that hinder the expansion of the lungs. Such restriction can result from diminished elasticity of the lungs or decreased flexibility of the thoracic cavity. We discussed such restrictive conditions earlier in the chapter and indicated how they may reduce the vital capacity of the lungs and impede their ventilation.

The dysfunctions we want to consider now are *obstructive* diseases, which involve the respiratory airways and generally cause an increased resistance to airflow.

Emphysema
Emphysema is a condition in which excessive air accumulates in the lungs as they lose their ability to ventilate properly. It develops very gradually in response to other respiratory problems, such as chronic bronchitis, smoking, or other pulmonary irritants. Therefore, emphysema is much more prevalent in older persons.

Chronic irritation of the bronchial tree by smoke or by repeated respiratory infections may cause the cilia of the mucous membrane lining the airways to become paralyzed and deteriorate. Other cells in the lining are stimulated by the irritation and produce excessive amounts of mucus within the airways to the lungs. The person suffering from pulmonary irritation develops a persistent cough in an attempt to rid the body of the excessive mucous secretions.

As the condition continues, the excessive mucus hinders airflow through the lungs, and air becomes trapped in the alveoli. Eventually the trapped air causes the alveoli to remain inflated, even following exhalation. Thus, the flow of air into and out of the alveoli during respiration is reduced and the supply of fresh air containing oxygen to the alveoli is diminished.

The alveoli eventually become overinflated, which damages and often destroys their walls. The damaged walls of the alveoli are replaced in part by fibrous tissue, across which gaseous exchange cannot occur as readily as it did across the respiratory membrane. Therefore, in persons suffering from emphysema, the surface area across which the exchange of oxygen and carbon dioxide can occur may be greatly reduced, and the level of oxygen in their blood may not be high enough to sustain even mild physical effort. At the same time, the elasticity of the lungs is gradually diminished, making expiration of the air within them difficult. People suffering from emphysema often have a very low maximum breathing capacity and a high residual air volume.

There are, therefore, two basic problems facing the victim of emphysema. The distended alveoli cause the lungs to be "fixed" in inspiration, and the walls of the alveoli have deteriorated to the extent that they no longer provide an adequate surface area for normal gas exchange. The disease cannot be reversed, and gradually worsens. In the later stages, positive-pressure oxygen therapy is often used to force oxygen into the alveoli.

Emphysema places an extra load on the heart as it attempts to pump more blood to the lungs in an effort to compensate for the deficiency of oxygen in the blood leaving the lungs. Consequently, many persons who suffer from emphysema actually die as the result of heart failure.

Bronchitis

Bronchitis is an acute or chronic inflammation of the bronchial tree. It is generally caused by bacterial infection or by irritants, such as smoke, in the inhaled air. In bronchitis, as in emphysema, the lining of the air passageways responds to the irritation by producing excess mucus. The mucus may become so abundant that it hinders the phagocytic activity of macrophages in the tract and the self-cleaning action of cilia lining the airways. In severe cases the mucous membrane of the airways may become swollen and partially block the bronchi. As the mucus secretions accumulate within the bronchi, they are removed by coughing, which can become persistent and irritating.

Chronic bronchitis is generally a result of long-term exposure to environmental irritants and therefore is more common in older persons. When chronic bronchitis leads to the development of emphysema, the condition is referred to as *chronic obstructive pulmonary disease.*

Pneumonia

Pneumonia is an inflammation of the lung in which the alveoli become filled with a fibrinous exudate containing some blood cells. This causes the affected portion of the lung to become less spongy and restricts air from reaching the alveoli, making it very difficult for gaseous exchange to occur. Although pneumonia is not a disease of only older persons, death resulting from it is most frequent in those over 65 years of age.

Most cases of pneumonia are caused either by one of several viruses or by the *pneumococcus bacterium.* However, the inhalation of foods or other foreign bodies that obstruct a bronchus can also cause a similar inflammation, which is referred to as *aspiration pneumonia.* If complete, the obstruction can cause a lung to collapse, and fluids may accumulate within it, contributing to the development of infection. Aspiration pneumonia is more common in older persons, especially in those who are bedridden and are not fully conscious.

Tuberculosis

The bacterium that causes *tuberculosis* usually enters the body with inspired air; therefore, tuberculosis of the lungs is the most common form of the disease.

Phagocytes within the lungs destroy some of the bacteria, and many of those that remain alive are isolated within small nodules called tubercles by the formation of fibrous walls around them. Bacteria that are not killed by phagocytes or completely walled off may destroy lung tissue and cause the infection to spread throughout the lung. As the infection spreads, fibrous tissue replaces the destroyed lung tissue, reducing the elasticity of the lung and interfering with the diffusion of gases across the walls of the alveoli. The end result is a reduced vital capacity and difficulty in breathing.

Although the incidence of tuberculosis has declined in the general population, it is still an important health problem in older persons. The reason for this is because today's elderly persons have lived through a time period when the chances of their being exposed to the bacterium that causes tuberculosis were rather high. Therefore, it would not be unusual for them to have inhaled the bacterium into their lungs. Once within the lungs, the bacteria may have been isolated within tubercles without causing outward signs of the disease. Then, after remaining dormant for many years within the tubercles, the bacteria may escape from them and reinfect the lung. This *reinfection tuberculosis* is generally what occurs in older persons.

Because tuberculosis is less common among the general population today, the number of persons exposed to the bacterium is decreasing and fewer young people are developing tubercles in their lungs. Therefore, it is possible that fewer of tomorrow's elderly persons will develop reinfection tuberculosis.

Pulmonary Embolism

An embolus is a blood clot that flows freely within the blood vessels. The danger associated with an embolus is that if it reaches a vessel whose diameter is too small to allow it to pass through, it may partially or completely block the vessel. This reduces the blood flow to the tissues supplied by the vessel and may cause the tissues to die.

A *pulmonary embolism* refers to a clot that blocks a branch of a pulmonary artery. No matter where the embolus originates in the body, the danger of pulmonary embolism is always great because the embolus will travel freely in large veins to the right side of the heart, and the first small vessels it will enter are branches of the pulmonary artery. Thus, the tendency is for emboli to become lodged in these small branches and restrict blood flow to some region of the lungs.

Emboli can occur at any age, but they are more common on older persons who are bedridden. Patients lying immobile in bed have a greater tendency to develop blood clots, especially in the veins of the legs, because the rate of blood flow through their vessels is reduced.

Summary

With aging, the elasticity of the lungs is diminished, the trachea, bronchi, and the wall of the thorax become more rigid, and changes in the normal spinal curvatures may reduce the volume of the thoracic cavity. Consequently, breathing requires more effort in older persons, and the maximum breathing capacity and vital capacity are reduced.

The alveolar walls tend to deteriorate gradually, reducing the respiratory surface available for gaseous exchange. Although the rate of respirations and the amount of air moved with each breath generally do not change much with aging, the air within the alveoli is not exchanged as efficiently as in younger persons, and less of the inhaled oxygen-rich air reaches the alveoli.

These changes all contribute to a reduction in the amount of oxygen reaching the lung capillaries in older persons, thereby reducing older persons' capacity for physical activity.

The Digestive System

Although the digestive system, like the other body systems, usually functions quite adequately in older persons, gastrointestinal disorders such as indigestion, heartburn, loss of appetite, and constipation increase with age—and these symptoms are a constant worry to many older persons. In addition, the threat of cancer of the digestive system increases with age. Some digestive symptoms are considered to be the result of "normal" aging, whereas others may be caused by pathological changes that need not occur in the elderly.

Every cell in the body must receive a constant supply of energy in order to remain alive and perform its particular functions. Food taken into the body through the digestive system serves as this energy source. Most food, however, must be broken down into simpler molecules before it can become available to the cells. Thus, the digestive system must alter the ingested food so that it is in a form which can cross the wall of the digestive system and enter the blood, which distributes the altered food to the body cells.

Three major categories of foods are acted upon by the digestive system: (1) *Carbohydrates*, which include sugars and starches, are composed of ring-shaped molecules of carbon, hydrogen, and oxygen. They serve as a major energy source for body activities. When ingested as simple sugars, carbohydrates are readily assimilated by the body.

However, many carbohydrates in foods are in the form of more complex molecules, such as starch and glycogen, and must be broken down to simple sugars before they can enter the bloodstream. (2) *Fats (lipids)* consist of three chains of carbon atoms with numerous attached hydrogen atoms and a few oxygen atoms located at one end of each chain. Each carbon chain is a *fatty acid*. The three fatty acids are joined together into a single molecule by an alcohol called glycerol. Therefore, fats are also called *triglycerides*. Fats are incorporated in the structure of many things, such as the cell membrane, and serve as an energy reserve for the body. In order to be assimilated, fats must be digested so that the three fatty acids are released from the glycerol. (3) *Proteins* are the third category of foods. They are large, complex molecules formed by the joining of smaller molecules called *amino acids*. There are 20 different amino acids in the body, each identified as such by the presence of an amino group (NH_2) and a carboxyl group (COOH). Eight of the amino acids must be present in the diet for optimal growth to occur. These are called *essential* amino acids. The remaining twelve amino acids are considered to be *nonessential* amino acids, in that the body can manufacture them from the essential amino acids. Proteins serve as the main structural units of the body and form enzymes which are vital for many chemical reactions. Proteins must be digested to free amino acids or short chains of amino acids before they can cross the wall of the digestive tube and enter the bloodstream.

The digestive system is essentially a tube called the *gastrointestinal tract* that extends from the mouth to the anus. Food within the tract is chemically broken down (*digested*) by secretions which enter the tube from various glands. Many of the digestive glands consist of single cells and are located within the lining of the digestive tube. In contrast, the liver and pancreas are large glands whose digestive secretions are transported to the tube within ducts. Various regions of the gastrointestinal tract perform specific mechanical and chemical functions in the digestion of food. These regions are identified as the mouth, the pharynx, the esophagus, the stomach, the small intestine, and the large intestine (Figure 12-1).

In a properly functioning digestive system, food within the gastrointestinal tract is moved along the tract while it is mechanically changed into a form that aids chemical digestion. The tract then absorbs the digested food, allowing it to enter the circulatory and lymphatic systems. Finally, any indigestible substances and waste products are eliminated from the body by defecation.

Fig. 12-1 Structures constituting the digestive tract.

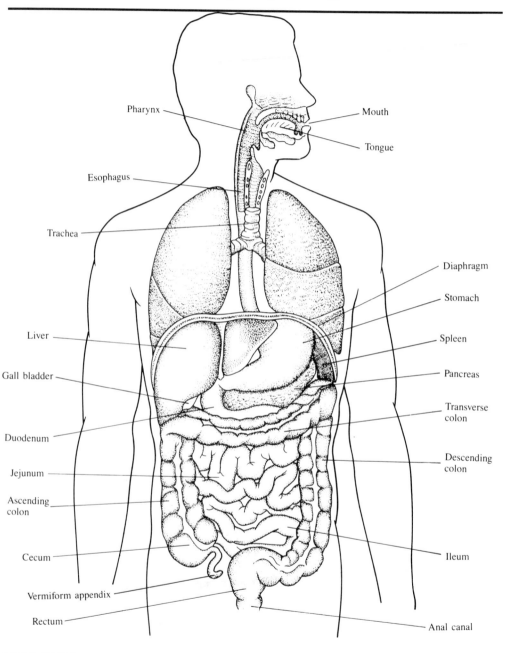

From Barrett J.M., et al.: Biology. *Englewood Cliffs: Prentice Hall, 1986, p. 266.*

Review of Structure and Function

We begin our consideration of the digestive system by briefly reviewing the normal structure and function of the various regions and organs of the system.

Mouth

Food is ingested into the digestive tract through the *mouth*, where it is mechanically reduced to smaller pieces by being crushed and ground between the teeth and mashed against the roof of the mouth by the tongue. At the same time, the food is thoroughly moistened by saliva secreted into the mouth from three pairs of large salivary glands located in the cheeks and beneath the tongue.

No food is absorbed in the mouth, and only limited chemical preparation of food occurs there, but carbohydrate digestion is begun by an enzyme (*salivary amylase*) contained within saliva. Most tastes buds are located in the mouth, so this region is important for stimulating the appetite with pleasant taste sensations.

Pharynx and Esophagus

Food that is swallowed passes from the mouth into the *pharynx* and then into the *esophagus*. From the esophagus to the anus the wall of the digestive tube is composed of four distinct layers called tunics. Although there are modifications in the structure of the gastrointestinal wall in various regions of the tract, the four basic layers are always present. From the lumen of the digestive tube outward the layers consist of (1) a mucous membrane lining (*tunica mucosa*); (2) a rather thick layer of connective tissue (*tunica submucosa*); (3) a muscular layer (*tunica muscularis*) that in most regions consists of a double layer of smooth muscle, with the inner layer arranged circularly and the outer layer oriented longitudinally along the long axis of the tube; and (4) an outer connective tissue layer (*tunica serosa*).

The esophagus travels through the chest behind the trachea and enters the abdominal cavity by means of an opening in the diaphragm called the *esophageal hiatus*, to empty into the stomach. When food is present, the muscles in the wall of the esophagus are stretched and undergo waves of contractions (*peristalsis*) which propel the food through the esophagus and into the stomach.

Absorption does not occur in the mouth, pharynx, or esophagus because the food within them is not reduced to a simple form that can be absorbed, and the mucous membrane lining these regions consists of several layers of flat cells, (i.e. *stratified squamous epithelium*), which hinders absorption.

Stomach

Beginning with the *stomach* and continuing throughout the intestines, the mucous membrane consists of a single layer of tall cells (i.e. *simple columnar epithelium*) and contains many gland cells. In the case of the stomach, these secretory cells are called *gastric glands*. The gastric secretions include *mucus*, which lubricates and protects the walls of the tract; *hydrochloric acid* (HCL), which facilitates protein digestion and kills many of the bacteria that enter the digestive tract with the food; and *pepsin*, an enzyme capable of digesting protein.

The muscular tunic of the stomach is especially well developed, containing an oblique layer in addition to the circular and longitudinal layers. Because of the additional layer of muscle, the stomach is capable of extrastrong contractions that aid in mashing the food, converting it into a semifluid form called *chyme* and mixing it with digestive juices. The movement of food from the stomach into the small intestine is restricted by a circular ring of smooth muscles called the *pyloric sphincter* at the lower end of the stomach.

Small Intestine

After passing through the pyloric sphincter food enters the *small intestine*. The small intestine is the longest portion of the digestive tract and is also the most important portion as far as digestion and absorption are concerned.

Food that reaches the small intestine has not been completely digested and is not yet adequately prepared to be absorbed. Some carbohydrate digestion is begun in the mouth by salivary amylase, and protein digestion begins in the stomach, but neither carbohydrate nor protein digestion is complete by the time food enters the small intestine. Lipid digestion has not even begun up to this point. Thus, most digestive activity occurs within the small intestine, and practically all of the absorption of the digested food into the blood occurs there.

Gland cells in the mucosa of the small intestine produce enzymes which complete carbohydrate and protein digestion—reducing the carbohydrates to simple sugars and the proteins to amino acids—and digest lipids into fatty acids and glycerol. Simple sugars, amino acids, fatty acids, and glycerol can all be absorbed through the wall of the digestive tract and enter the blood or lymph.

The small intestine also receives digestive enzymes from the pancreas and bile from the liver. The *pancreatic juice* contains enzymes that digest carbohydrates, proteins, and lipids. *Bile* emulsifies lipids, making them more easily digestible by the enzymes secreted by the intestine and the pancreas.

The small intestine, which is about 22 feet long, has three regions: the *duodenum*, the *jejunum*, and the *ileum*. The ducts transporting pancreatic juice and bile empty into the duodenum. The ileum empties into the large intestine through a ring of smooth muscles called the *ileocecal valve*. The surface area of the mucous membrane lining the small intestine, across which absorption occurs, is increased by many small projections of the lining called *villi* which extend into the lumen (Figure 12-2). Very tiny projections of the cell membrane called *microvilli* occur on the free surface of the absorptive cells and further increase the area of the absorptive surface in the small intestine.

Large Intestine

The *large intestine* extends from the ileocecal valve to the anus, a distance of about 4 ft. It is so named because it has a diameter in most regions that is greater than the diameter of the small intestine. From its junction with the small intestine, the large intestine travels upward on the right side of the abdominal cavity to the vicinity of the liver. It then passes across the abdominal cavity and descends along the left side of the cavity. Beyond the descending portion, the large intestine curves sharply toward the midline of the body and continues as the *rectum* and *anal canal*, which opens on the body surface as the *anus*.

Although it lacks villi, the large intestine, like the small intestine, is lined with a mucous membrane composed of simple columnar epithelium with microvilli on the free surfaces of the cells. Both absorptive cells and mucous cells are present in the lining, but very few, if any, enzymes are produced by the epithelial cells. Therefore, although no digestion is initiated in the large intestine, absorption does occur. The main substances absorbed in the large intestine are water, sodium, and chloride.

Many microorganisms inhabit this region of the digestive tract, and some of the bacteria present produce certain vitamins (e.g. vitamin K) which are also absorbed. Because of the absorption of water, the food substances in the digestive tract become a more solid consistency in the large intestine and are called *feces* when they are expelled through the anus.

The anal canal is surrounded by two rings of muscle called the *internal* and *external anal sphincters*. The internal sphincter is formed of smooth muscle and therefore is not under voluntary

Fig. 12-2　Diagram of villi in the small intestine showing the capillaries and lymphatic vessels within them.

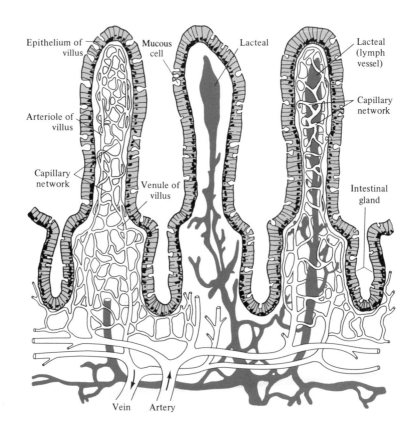

From Barrett, J.M., et al.: Biology. *Englewood Cliffs, N. J., Prentice Hall, 1986, p. 270.*

　　　　　　　　　　　　　　　Chapter 12　The Digestive System

control. The external sphincter is formed of skeletal muscle and is under voluntary control. Consequently, although the internal anal sphincter relaxes when fecal material is present in the rectum, a person can normally control his or her bowel movements by contracting or relaxing the external sphincter.

Pancreas

Secretions from the pancreas play important roles in digestion. The *pancreas* is located beneath the stomach, extending from the duodenum to the vicinity of the spleen. The gland consists of two groups of cells. One group (*acinar cells*) secrete *pancreatic juice*, which contains digestive enzymes that act on carbohydrates, proteins, and lipids. The pancreatic juice is transported to the duodenum through a duct. Because it is alkaline, pancreatic juice helps neutralize the acid contents of the stomach as they reach the small intestine.

The other group of pancreatic cells secrete hormones and are part of the endocrine system. We will discuss these cells in Chapter 15.

Liver

The *liver* is a large organ located in the upper right region of the abdominal cavity, just beneath the diaphragm. It is an extremely important organ, being responsible for a sizeable number of vital functions in addition to its role in digestion. Contributing to its ability to perform these functions is the fact that all of the venous blood from the digestive tract, pancreas, and spleen is carried directly to the liver (through the *hepatic portal vein*) before it is returned to the heart. Consequently, everything which enters the blood from the digestive tract passes through the liver before being transported to other regions in the body. As the venous blood from the digestive tract passes through the liver, substances that were absorbed into the blood from the tract diffuse out of the blood and enter liver cells, where they are metabolized or otherwise altered.

The liver produces several important blood proteins and other molecules, stores iron and certain vitamins, eliminates old hemoglobin, detoxifies many drugs and toxins, and is the major site for the metabolism of the products produced by the digestion of carbohydrates, proteins, and fats. The end products of this metabolism may be returned to the blood for use by other cells throughout the body or they may be stored in the liver. Thus, large amounts of glucose are stored in the liver in the form of glycogen, providing a readily available source of carbohydrates as they are needed anywhere in the body.

The liver is also an important protective organ, containing active phagocytes (*macrophages*) that remove bacteria and other foreign materials from the blood as it passes through the liver.

Of particular importance to digestion is the bile produced by the liver and stored in the *gall bladder*. The gall bladder is drained by a system of ducts which empty into the duodenum, at the same point as does the pancreatic duct. As was mentioned earlier, bile aids in the digestion of fats by reducing larger fat droplets into very small droplets that are more readily acted upon by digestive enzymes.

Age-Related Changes

With aging, the secretions of the digestive glands tend to diminish somewhat and the muscles in the walls of the tract become weaker, causing a decrease in the motility of the tract. In addition to these general changes, there are also specific age-related changes that occur in each region of the digestive tract. We will consider some of these regional changes.

Mouth

Loss of teeth is a major concern in older people. Almost one-half of those living in the United States have or need dentures by age 65, and it has been reported that three-fourths of those over 75 years of age have lost all of their teeth. Because of the improved dental care that is now available, it is hoped that those data will improve in the future as today's young become elderly.

The chief cause of tooth loss is gum (*periodontal*) disease, in which inflammation can destroy the periodontal membrane that lines the tooth socket and cause the tooth to become loose. A common cause of gum disease is the recession of the gum away from the tooth. This forms a pocket in which bacteria and food debris can lodge and cause an infection.

Lost teeth are often replaced with dentures, but these may not be comfortable, especially as people grow older and their gums atrophy and shrink. Fixed bridges, which have become popular in recent years, may prove more satisfactory in older persons. Missing teeth and unsatisfactory dentures make it difficult to chew efficiently, encouraging older persons to switch to softer foods. The consequence may be that they no longer eat a balanced diet and gradually develop malnutrition.

Chapter 12   The Digestive System

Because of a gradual atrophy of the salivary glands, production of saliva is reduced and the mouth tends to be drier than normal in older persons. The reduction in the volume of saliva diminishes taste sensations and provides less cleansing for the mouth and teeth. The amount of salivary amylase in the saliva also diminishes with age, but this is not thought to have a significant effect on carbohydrate digestion.

Dryness of the mouth may be caused in part by mouth breathing and the production of thicker mucus, both of which occur more commonly in older persons. A chronically dry mouth can lead a person to select softer foods which lack fiber or bulk and may thus contribute to chronic constipation. Dry mouth is such a common problem that a saliva substitute has been developed and is available in pharmacies.

A diminished sense of taste is a common complaint among the elderly. Although decreased secretion of saliva accounts for some loss of taste, atrophy of taste buds is thought to be the major cause. It has been estimated that there are 70% fewer taste buds present at age 70 than at age 30. As a result of this extensive atrophy, a large reduction in the ability to differentiate between various tastes has been reported in persons over 75 years of age. Although a diminished sense of taste may not seem to be a particularly serious consequence of aging, it can affect a person's appetite and thus eventually affect his or her nutritional status.

Esophagus
Difficulty in swallowing and esophageal pain are not uncommon in older persons. The swallowing problems can be a result of neurological disorders affecting the muscles in the wall of the esophagus, but most often they result from incomplete relaxation of the lower esophageal sphincter, which is located just above the entrance into the stomach and regulates the movement of food from the esophagus into the stomach. In other cases, the sphincter may become weakened with age, allowing food to enter the esophagus from the stomach. The acid from the stomach irritates the lining of the esophagus, producing discomfort referred to as "heartburn." In a similar manner, gas from the stomach may pass through the weakened sphincter into the esophagus, increasing the incidence of belching.

It has been reported that peristalsis in the esophagus tends to diminish in older persons. However, more recent data suggest that, although the intensity of peristalsis does decline, esophageal motility does not decrease significantly with age. Thus, in a healthy older person, food passes through the esophagus to the stomach as readily as it did when he or she was younger.

Stomach

The mucous membrane lining the stomach tends to thin with age, due in part to atrophy of the mucous glands and the gastric glands. As a result, secretions of mucus, hydrochloric acid, and digestive enzymes into the stomach are reduced. These reductions particularly hinder the digestion of proteins and may cause symptoms that are referred to as "chronic atrophic gastritis."

Because of the gradual atrophy of the digestive-tract lining, reduction of hydrochloric acid secretion becomes more common in both men and women with aging, occurring in about 20% of persons over age 70. If severe enough, the reduced secretion of hydrochloric acid may alter the acidity of the digestive juice and thereby affect bacterial growth in the large intestine. In a similar trend, the volume of gastric juice secreted has been reported to diminish by as much as 25% by 60 years of age.

There are indications that stomach motility is diminished in older persons. However, it has not been established that the reduction is actually age-related. Although the rate of emptying of solids from the stomach does not change with age, liquids tend to remain in the stomach longer than usual in elderly persons.

Small Intestine

Because of a general atrophy of the layers composing its wall, the weight of the small intestine decreases with age. Atrophy of the mucosa lining the small intestine alters the shape of the villi and reduces the surface area across which absorption occurs. However, although a slight reduction in the rate of fat absorption has been reported, absorption in general does not seem to be significantly affected by the age-related atrophy of the mucosa. This may be due to the rapid replenishment of the epithelial cells of the villi. It is estimated that these cells are completely replaced by new cells every three to five days, thereby reducing the cumulative effects of increased atrophy.

Accompanying the atrophy of the mucosa, the levels of digestive enzymes secreted into the small intestine gradually diminish, and there is reported to be a decrease in the extent and permeability of the capillary bed in the intestine wall. These changes would be expected to affect the rate of absorption of digested foods across the wall of the tract into the blood. However, as was previously mentioned, no general reduction in absorption has been reported. A decrease in absorption of calcium and vitamins B_6 and B_{12} does seem to occur in elderly persons.

Large Intestine

The wall of the large intestine becomes weaker due to gradual atrophy of all four basic layers. This weakening makes an older person more likely to have outpockets develop from the wall of the large intestine, a condition referred to as *diverticulosis*.

There is a change in the composition of the bacterial flora of the large intestine with aging, perhaps due in part to a reduction in the secretion of hydrochloric acid by the stomach. Diminished hydrochloric acid causes the gastrointestinal contents to shift from being strongly acid toward becoming alkaline. Because some activities and metabolic products (e.g. certain vitamins) of intestinal bacteria are beneficial to the person, alterations of bacterial growth may lead to nutritional deficiencies. For instance, some abnormal bacteria can bind vitamin B_{12} and reduce its availability to the person, and others are known to tie up bile salts, which may affect fat digestion.

Pancreas

The rate of replacement of secretory cells diminishes in the pancreas with age, and fat deposits in the gland increase. Consequently, there is some decrease in the amount of pancreatic enzymes released. However, except for some decline in fat digestion, the reduction in pancreatic enzymes does not noticeably hinder digestion. Moreover, the volume of pancreatic juice remains stable, thereby allowing for the continued neutralization of the acid stomach contents.

With aging, there is an increase in the incidence of obstruction of the pancreatic ducts, hindering the passage of pancreatic juice to the small intestine and causing it to accumulate within the pancreas. This is a major cause of inflammation of the pancreas (*pancreatitis*), which can lead to chronic disturbances of digestion and become quite debilitating.

Liver

Some studies report decreases of up to 20% in the weight of the liver with age, but others report no such decline. To explain these discrepancies, it has been suggested that a decrease in liver weight may be correlated with a decrease in total body weight, rather than indicating excess atrophy of liver cells.

Some moderate fibrosis has been reported, but there is little evidence for significant cell loss in the liver with age. However, there does seem to be an increase in atypical liver cells, and a decrease in the number of mitochondria per cell. As is the case in many tissues, lipofucsin is more common in the liver cells of elderly persons. The structural changes the liver undergoes with aging probably do not adversely affect its functioning, because new liver cells regenerate very quickly and the liver has a large measure of redundancy. As much as 80% of the organ can be removed and the remainder can still adequately provide for the body.

Although the liver usually does not show any appreciable reduction in the ability to perform its various functions in healthy elderly persons, there is a slightly reduced synthesis of proteins in the aging liver. More important, the ability of the liver to metabolize certain drugs declines with age. As a result, older persons may react differently to drugs than do younger persons, and dosages need to be determined with the patient's age in mind. This may even be true for drugs a person has taken for many years for a chronic condition.

The gall bladder does not seem to be affected much with aging; however, the incidence of most gall-bladder problems increases after age 65. These problems are largely due to reduced ability of the gall bladder to empty and the bile becoming more viscous and reduced in volume.

Age-Related Dysfunctions

The incidence of gastrointestinal symptoms generally increases with age, especially such non-life-threatening conditions as loss of appetite, dry mouth, belching, heartburn, difficulty in swallowing, and decreased acidity of digestive juices—all of which we have mentioned previously. We now want to consider a few more serious digestive dysfunctions that are more common in older persons.

Hiatal Hernia

A *hiatal hernia* occurs when the junction of the esophagus and the upper portion of the stomach protrudes from the abdominal cavity into the thoracic cavity through the opening in the diaphragm through which only the esophagus normally passes. The condition is most common in obese individuals over 50 years of age, and women are affected more than men.

Hiatal hernias cause severe discomfort when eating and may lead to inflammation, ulceration, and narrowing of the esophagus. Because surgical repair of the hiatus is not often successful, the condition is generally treated with medications, smaller and less frequent meals, and by programs leading to weight reduction. Although these treatments do not correct the hiatal defect, they do reduce the symptoms so that the condition is more tolerable.

Cancer

There is a steady rise in the incidence of tumorous cancers (*carcinomas*) of the esophagus, stomach, and intestines with age. In the esophagus, carcinomas may obstruct the lumen of the tube, causing difficulty in swallowing, pain beneath the sternum, and excessive belching. These are common and fairly innocuous symptoms that may be caused by a number of factors other than cancer. But such symptoms are cause for concern in older persons if they become persistent.

Stomach cancer is more common in men, especially those over 60 years of age. Symptoms of stomach cancer may include loss of appetite and weight, and a general feeling of bodily discomfort. Again, these are fairly innocuous symptoms, which makes diagnosis of cancer of the digestive tract difficult and may lead to self-medication for an extended period before a physician is consulted. As the stomach cancer progresses, the symptoms may become more severe and include nausea, vomiting of blood, and the presence of blood in the feces.

Cancer of the large intestine is the most common malignancy in those over 70 years of age and results in a significant number of deaths. Therefore, cancer should be considered a possible cause for any change in bowel habits in older persons. The incidence of cancer of the colon is greater in women, whereas men are more susceptible to rectal cancer.

Contributing to the high death rate of cancer of the large intestine is the fact that it is so often diagnosed only after it has reached an advanced stage of development. This is unfortunate, as a high percentage of cancers in the large intestine can be detected during a proctoscopic examination, and survival rates increase appreciably if they are removed surgically during their early stages. The value of regular complete physical examinations cannot be overemphasized.

Diverticulitis

Diverticula are tiny herniations in the wall of the intestines, producing pouches that protrude outward through the muscular layer. Fecal matter can collect in the diverticula, inflaming them and sometimes causing ulcerations of the mucosa. When the mucosa within the diverticula becomes infected, the condition is called *diverticulitis*. The incidence of diverticulitis increases steadily from age 40, especially in women. Diverticula occur in a fairly high percentage of the elderly but in most cases do not cause severe problems.

The symptoms of diverticulitis include abdominal pain accompanied by diarrhea or constipation, or alternating episodes of both. Blood may be present in the feces. Occasionally, diverticula will perforate, spreading the infection to other organs of the abdominal cavity. A perforated diverticulum requires immediate surgery, but in the absence of complications, diverticulitis is managed with a special diet and antibiotic therapy.

Diverticulitis is common in older persons only in developed countries. For this reason it is suggested that it is a result of a diet that does not include sufficient fiber. Diets high in fiber tend to move more quickly through the intestinal tract and produce large, soft stools. In populations whose diets have a high fiber content, food remains in the tract less than two days, compared with as long as seven days for those with diets low in fiber. It has been suggested that the harder stools associated with low-fiber diets require stronger peristaltic contractions to move them, and thus the pressure within the lumen of the intestine is increased. The increased pressure may force the mucosa lining the intestine out through any weak spots present in the muscle layer, thus forming diverticula.

Constipation

Constipation refers to infrequent or difficult evacuation of the feces from the bowel. It is often associated with large quantities of dry, hard feces in the descending colon. The hard feces are the result of abnormally slow movement of the digestive residues through the large intestine. The longer fecal materials remain within the colon, the more water is absorbed and the drier and harder they become. Although constipation is a common complaint in older persons, it is not considered to be an inevitable consequence of aging. In fact, a major cause of constipation in elderly persons is thought to be a long-term overreliance on laxatives.

In addition to overuse of laxatives, constipation may be caused by reduced fluid intake, lack of bulk in the diet, lack of exercise, irregular bowel habits, and some cases seem to have psychological causes. When they were younger, the elderly of today were taught that it was necessary to have a bowel movement every day in order to prevent autointoxication. As a consequence, they tend to be overly concerned if they do not have a daily bowel movement. It is hoped the younger generation does not share this fixation on regularity. They should be well enough informed to realize that although there are advantages to daily bowel movements, they are not absolutely necessary, and many people remain quite healthy with much less frequent bowel movements.

It is important, however, that a person not constantly upset the normal defecation reflex. Clinical evidence indicates that if defecation is not allowed to occur when the defecation reflexes are activated, or if one overuses laxatives and does not allow the normal defecation reflexes to occur, the reflexes themselves become progressively weaker over a period of time and the muscle tone of the colon is diminished. This can lead to chronic constipation. For this reason, a person who establishes regular bowel habits early in life is less likely to experience constipation as he or she grows old.

Fecal Incontinence

Diminished capability of regulating bowel movements is a problem in many older persons, particularly in long-term patients, where the incidence of *fecal incontinence* has been reported to be as high as 60%.

With prompt attention to personal hygiene, fecal incontinence need not cause additional health problems. However, its effect on one's self-esteem can be very important. Episodes of fecal incontinence are embarrassing and can be quite depressing—particularly when experienced by a person who is mentally alert.

Fecal incontinence can be caused by any condition which impairs a person's ability to control the external anal sphincter. This frequently results from cancer of the lower bowel or neurological problems that affect the nerve supply to the anal sphincter. It may also result from surgery to correct hemorrhoids, which can damage the anal sphincter so that it is no longer able to resist the movement of feces resulting from the defecation reflexes.

Hemorrhoids

Hemorrhoids, which are swollen or ruptured blood vessels located in the lower bowel, are present in most older people. They may occur internally, within the anal canal, or externally, around the anus. Hemorrhoids may not cause any discomfort, but often cause pain, itching, and bleeding.

Constipation is the most common cause of hemorrhoids in the elderly, as it makes excessive straining necessary in order to have a bowel movement, and this interferes with the flow of blood through the veins. Prolonged use of laxatives and repeated enemas may also contribute to the development of hemorrhoids.

Intestinal Obstruction

Intestinal obstruction is a fairly common problem in older persons. The obstruction may be due to a physical blockage of the lumen of the intestine, or to paralysis of the muscles in the wall of the intestine, which interferes with peristalsis. Physical obstructions may be caused by a variety of things, including carcinomas that enlarge enough to block the intestine, adhesions across the lumen of the intestine, diverticulitis, or intestinal hernias that become strangulated. Paralysis of a region of the intestine is generally a side effect of some other condition, such as pneumonia, pancreatitis, or kidney stones.

A person suffering from an intestinal obstruction experiences abdominal pain, vomiting, distension, and constipation. Physical obstructions are usually surgically corrected, whereas paralytic obstructions generally respond to medical treatment.

Nutrition in the Elderly

As we grow older and our growth rate gradually declines while normal cell death continues, or even increases, we eventually reach a point where the total number of cells in the body becomes progressively less. At the same time, there is generally a steady decline in energy requirements. This is due in part to the loss of body tissue, but reduced physical activity and lowered basal metabolic rate (BMR) also contribute to the declining energy requirements typical of older persons. The BMR is a measure of the kilocalories (kcal) of energy used per square meter of body surface area per hour by a person at rest under standard environmental conditions.

Since energy requirements are altered with aging, it is to be expected that the nutritional needs of older persons are also altered. The study of nutrition is a specialized field, and geriatric nutrition is among the newer subdivisions within the field. Although it is beyond the scope of this book to discuss nutrition in elderly persons in any depth, a brief consideration of the changing nutritional requirements during aging will help you to appreciate the importance of the digestive system in the aging process.

Basically, there are no major changes in nutritional needs with aging. Elderly persons, like young persons, require a diet consisting of carbohydrates, fats, proteins, vitamins, and minerals, along with ample water.

What does change is the amount of these substances that should be ingested. Generally, the amount of foods consumed should be reduced with aging. Although the energy reduction associated with aging varies in each individual, the National Research Council reported in 1980 that between the ages of 55 and 75 the average BMR declines 5% every ten years, and 7% every ten years after the age of 75. Thus, a person 75 years old has energy requirements that are about 10% lower than they were at age 55. To maintain nutritional balance, food consumption should be reduced accordingly.

However, while elderly persons require less energy, and thus fewer carbohydrates and fats, there are no large changes in their need for proteins, vitamins, or minerals. Minimal requirements for these substances have been fairly well established, but optimal requirements are not as well agreed upon by nutritionists. In the absence of known optimal dietary levels for proteins, vitamins, and minerals, tables of *Recommended Dietary Allowances* (RDA) are used (Table 12-1). The values given for the various nutrients on these tables are those which are currently felt to provide adequate, if not optimal, daily levels for each nutrient. The RDA values are periodically revised as more information concerning optimal levels is obtained. It should be kept in mind that the RDA values are only guidelines, and the nutritional requirements of an individual may vary from these standards because of age-related changes which may affect many functions, such as decreasing the rate of absorption of nutrients through the wall of the digestive tract, diminishing the production of enzymes, or altering kidney functioning. Various diseases, not necessarily related to aging, can also affect individual nutritional requirements, as can drugs used to treat the diseases.

Carbohydrate Requirements

Carbohydrates constitute a major portion of the diets of most people, and this trend continues into old age. They provide quick energy, and tend to be easy to eat. Because the calories in carbohydrates are readily available to the body, they may contribute to weight gain if excessive carbohydrates are ingested while energy requirements diminish. Carbohydrates are the main source of fiber, which is a complex molecule that the body cannot digest. Although dietary fiber does not provide any nutrients to the body, it does serve as an important source of roughage and thus helps prevent constipation. Other complex carbohydrates that are present in breads, cereals, vegetables, and fruits are digestible and are the preferred form in which carbohydrates should be consumed because, in addition to sugars,

Table 12-1   Recommended Dietary Allowances of Vitamins and Proteins for Persons 51 to 75 Years of Age

	MALES	FEMALES
Fat-Soluble Vitamins		
A	1,000 µg RE[*]	800 µg RE[*]
D	5 µg	5 µg
E	10 TE[†]	8 TE[†]
K	70–140 µg	70–140 µg
Water-Soluble Vitamins		
C	60 mg	60 mg
Thiamin	1.2 mg	1.0 mg
Riboflavin	1.4 mg	1.2 mg
Niacin	16 mg	13 mg
B_6	2.2 mg	2.0 mg
Folic Acid	400 µg	400 µg
B_{12}	3.0 µg	3.0 µg
Pantothenic Acid	4–7 mg	4–7 mg
Protein	56 grams	44 grams

[*]*RE = Retinol Equivalents*
[†]*TE = Tocopherol Equivalents*

Source: National Research Council, Food and Nutrition Board, 1980. Recommended Dietary Allowances, Revised 1980. *Washington, D.C., National Research Council, National Academy of Sciences.*

they contain other important molecules, such as vitamins and minerals. In contrast, refined carbohydrates typical of cookies, pastries, and candies, contain only sugars and thus serve only as a source of calories.

With aging, the body is often unable to handle glucose as efficiently as it used to. As a result, elderly persons are more likely to experience fluctuations of blood sugar, with its level becoming abnormally high shortly after a meal and then falling to unusually low levels several hours later. In order to control blood-sugar levels it seems to be beneficial for elderly persons to increase the complex carbohydrates and reduce the amount of refined carbohydrates in their diets. However, carbohydrates should continue to be an important component of the diets of elderly persons, and it is recommended that they make up 50% to 55% of the diets of persons over 50 years of age.

Protein Requirements

Although protein requirements are estimated to decline by as much as 30% by the age of 75, it is generally suggested that protein intake should remain fairly constant as a person ages. In persons over 50 years of age proteins should make up 12% to 15% of their diets, or about 56 grams per day in males and 44 grams per day in females (Table 12-1). Proteins are necessary for tissue growth and maintenance, activities which are diminished with aging. However, they also form enzymes, the need for which does not decline appreciably in elderly persons. Under normal conditions proteins are not utilized as energy sources by the body, but they may be when a person is suffering from a prolonged wasting disease. The continuing need for proteins in the diets of elderly persons may be difficult to meet, as they tend to be expensive and require extra preparation before they can be eaten—which many elderly, especially those living alone, may consider to be too much trouble. In addition, many proteins are difficult to chew if teeth are lacking.

Proteins are available in meat, fish, poultry, eggs, dairy products, and some plant foods, such as rice and beans. Animal proteins and dairy products supply essential as well as nonessential amino acids and therefore must be included in a balanced diet. Plant foods are deficient in one or more of the essential amino acids and thus cannot supply all of the amino acids necessary for normal growth and maintenance.

A decline in kidney functioning often occurs during aging. This may cause, among other things, a decrease in the elimination of proteins (serum albumin) from the blood. Increased serum albumin levels can upset fluid balance in the body, and thus kidney malfunction may require restriction of proteins in the diet.

Fat Requirements

Fats serve primarily as a reserve source of energy, being utilized when the availability of carbohydrates in the body becomes diminished. Fats provide twice as many calories as does a similar quantity of carbohydrates. Thus, a good way to reduce caloric intake is to reduce the amount of fat in the diet. Fats should not make up more than 25% to 35% of the diets of persons over 50 years of age. However, fats should not be completely excluded from one's diet because in addition to providing energy they also assist in the absorption of the fat-soluble vitamins (A,D,E, and K), which are vital to proper body functioning. Older persons often absorb fats more slowly than do younger persons, perhaps because of diminished secretion of fat-digesting enzymes by the pancreas and structural changes in the lining of the small intestine.

An important by-product of fat digestion is *cholesterol*, which is a precursor of several vital compounds in the body. However, cholesterol is best known to the general public because it is thought to contribute to the development of atherosclerosis and coronary heart disease. Unsaturated fatty acids seem to lower the level of cholesterol in the blood, whereas saturated fatty acids appear to increase the levels of cholesterol esters. Because atherosclerosis results from the deposition of cholesterol esters on the walls of the blood vessels, it is suggested that unsaturated fatty acids are the preferable form for dietary fats.

Vitamin Requirements

In addition to carbohydrates, proteins, and fats, very small amounts of vitamins are also required for normal body growth and development. Rather than providing energy or serving as structural components, most vitamins serve as *coenzymes* which activate enzymes and thus affect numerous chemical reactions within the body. With few exceptions, vitamins cannot be manufactured by the body. Rather, they must be included in one's diet. It has become common, especially in elderly persons, to supplement dietary vitamins with vitamin tablets. Although this may help prevent vitamin deficiency, it is also possible to produce toxic effects by ingesting excessively large dosages of vitamins. As is so often true, moderation is the wisest policy to follow when taking supplemental vitamins.

Some vitamins, known as *fat-soluble* vitamins, are absorbed from the digestive tract along with dietary fat and are eliminated from the body only after being used. Vitamins A,D,E, and K are fat soluble. Other vitamins are *water soluble* and are absorbed into the blood from the digestive tract dissolved in water. If taken in excess of daily needs, water-soluble vitamins are freely eliminated from the body through the urine and thus are not likely to accumulate in toxic quantities. The B-complex vitamins and vitamin C are water soluble. The recommended daily dietary allowances for various vitamins are listed in Table 12-1. The major dietary sources of the vitamins are listed in Table 12-2.

Fat-Soluble Vitamins. Vitamin A maintains the epithelial tissues forming the surface of the skin and lining the respiratory, digestive, and genitourinary tracts. It also forms the photopigments of the eye, making vision in dim light possible, and enhances the development of the teeth and the skeleton. If more than ample supplies of vitamin A are ingested,

Table 12-2   Major Dietary Sources of Vitamins

Fat-Soluble Vitamins

A	Milk, butter, cheese, liver, and fortified margarine (retinol)
	Green and yellow vegetables and fruits (carotene)
D	Cod liver oil, fortified milk and margarine, liver, fatty fish, eggs
E	Seeds, nuts, green leafy vegetables, corn oil margarines, oils such as corn, safflower
K	Green leafy vegetables, liver

Water-Soluble Vitamins

Thiamin	Pork, organ meats, whole grains, legumes
Riboflavin	Milk, eggs, cheese, meats, green vegetables, legumes
Niacin	Liver, lean meats, whole grains, legumes
B_6	Whole grains, meat, vegetables, bananas, legumes
Pantothenic Acid	Organ meats, eggs, legumes, whole grains
Folic Acid	Legumes, whole wheat, green vegetables
B_{12}[*]	Organ meats, muscle meats, eggs, shellfish, liver, dairy products
C	Citrus fruit, tomatoes, green peppers, cabbage, potatoes, other fruit (melon, strawberries), other dark green leafy vegetables

[*]*No known plant source*

Source: National Research Council, Food and Nutrition Board, 1980. Recommended Dietary Allowances, Revised 1980. *Washington, D.C., National Research Council, National Academy of Sciences.*

it may be stored for many months, primarily in the liver. Consequently, toxic symptoms may result from ingesting excessive amounts of supplemental vitamin A.

Vitamin D aids the absorption of calcium and phosphorous fro:.1 the digestive tract, and their deposition into bone tissue. Deficiency of vitamin D may lead to softening of the bones in adults (*osteomalacia*), and it has been suggested that such a deficiency may affect calcium metabolism and thus contribute to the development of *osteoporosis*. Because vitamin D may be stored in the body, excessive intake may be harmful.

Vitamin E helps maintain the integrity of the cell membrane by inhibiting the breakdown of certain fatty acids. It has also been claimed to improve male sexual activity, prevent heart disease, and, because of its antioxidant activity, to slow the aging process. None of these claims has been satisfactorily supported by sufficient data.

Vitamin K causes the liver to synthesize several factors that enhance blood clotting, thereby protecting against excessive hemorrhaging following injury. There are several forms of vitamin K, one of which is synthesized by bacteria that live in the intestine. Antibiotic therapy may destroy these bacteria, thus reducing the availability of the vitamin.

Water-Soluble Vitamins. B-complex vitamins include thiamine (B_1), riboflavin (B_2), niacin, vitamin B_6, vitamin B_{12}, pantothenic acid, and folic acid. Each of these vitamins has a different chemical structure, but their functions are interrelated.

Thiamine regulates the synthesis of a coenzyme that is involved in the release of energy from carbohydrates. Riboflavin is a coenzyme necessary for certain oxidation-reduction reactions of tissue metabolism. *Niacin* is involved in the synthesis of proteins and fats, as well as in the release of energy from carbohydrates, fats, and proteins. *Vitamin B_6* must be present for normal metabolism of amino acids and proteins. *Vitamin B_{12}* is necessary for the normal functioning of cells in the bone marrow, digestive tract, and central nervous system. An intrinsic factor produced by cells lining the digestive tract is necessary for vitamin B_{12} to be absorbed. Because absorption of vitamin B_{12} tends to decrease in elderly persons, it is thought that the amount of intrinsic factor secreted decreases with age. *Pantothenic acid* is a component of a coenzyme which helps release energy from fats and carbohydrates and is involved in the formation of certain hormones. *Folic acid* interacts with vitamin B_{12} in the maturation of red blood cells and is involved in the synthesis of several molecules needed for DNA formation.

Vitamin C is the final water-soluble vitamin. It is involved in many of the oxidation reactions of cellular metabolism and plays an important role in the formation of collagen, which provides the framework for connective tissues in organs, bones, teeth, muscle, and skin. Vitamin C also maintains the strength and elasticity of capillary walls and aids in wound healing. Since the body does not store the water-soluble vitamins and vitamin C is often destroyed during food processing, deficiencies of the vitamin do occur. Such deficiencies are especially prevalent in older persons, who find it difficult to shop regularly and thus use canned fruits and vegetables instead of fresh foods. It is estimated that about 10 percent of elderly persons ingest less than the recommended dietary allowances of the water-soluble vitamins.

Mineral Requirements

Carbohydrates, fats, proteins, and vitamins are all organic molecules. In addition to these, certain inorganic molecules, or *minerals*, are required for normal body functioning. Those minerals that are required in relatively large amounts are considered to be *macronutrients*. Calcium, magnesium, sodium, potassium, phosphorus, chlorine, and sulfur are macronutrients. Other minerals are called *micronutrients*, or trace elements, because they are needed in very minute quantities.

Minerals are necessary components of numerous body functions, and their actions are often interrelated. As a result, a deficiency of one mineral may affect the actions of others. Moreover, the absorption of some minerals, notably calcium and iron, decreases with age. Therefore, it is important that the diets of elderly persons contain adequate amounts of all the necessary minerals, and the intake of certain minerals may need to be increased as a person ages.

The recommended daily dietary allowances for minerals are listed in Table 12-3. Table 12-4 lists the major food sources for the more important minerals. Examples of the functions of certain minerals are listed in Table 12-5.

Water Requirements

A person may carefully monitor his or her intake of various foods, vitamins, and minerals and still experience dietary problems if adequate amounts of fluid are not included in the diet. Water is necessary in all of the metabolic reactions in the body, and a balance must be maintained between the fluids within cells, in the tissue spaces, and in the blood. Water also aids waste removal by increasing kidney functioning and preventing constipation.

Because their diets are not always balanced and they tend to drink less fluids, dehydration can be a problem in elderly persons. To maintain

Table 12-3   Recommended Dietary Allowances for Minerals

	MALES	FEMALES
Macronutrients		
Calcium	800 mg	800 mg
Magnesium	305 mg	300 mg
*Sodium	1,100–3,300 mg	1,100–3,300 mg
*Potassium	1,875–5,625 mg	1,875–5,625 mg
Phosphorus	800 mg	800 mg
*Chlorine	1,700–5,100 mg	1,700–5,100 mg
Sulfur	No RDAs at this time	
Micronutrients (trace elements)		
*Manganese	2.5–5 mg	2.5–5 mg
Iron	10 mg	10 mg
Copper	2–3 mg	2–3 mg
Iodine	150 μg	150 μg
Zinc	15 mg	15 mg
*Fluorine	1.5–4 mg	1.5–4 mg
*Molybdenum	.15–0.5 mg	.15–0.5 mg
*Selenium	.05–0.2 mg	.05–0.2 mg
*Chromium	.05–0.2 mg	.05–0.2 mg

Less information is available, so the ranges are less precise and not as well graded by age.

Source: National Research Council, Food and Nutrition Board, 1980, Recommended Dietary Allowances, Revised 1980. *Washington, D.C., National Research Council, National Academy of Sciences.*

adequate fluid levels in the body at least 2 liters of fluid should be ingested each day. The foods included in a balanced diet will provide approximately 1 liter of fluid. Therefore, drinking four to six glasses of water each day should insure adequate water intake.

Summary

Structural changes occur in all regions of the digestive tube with aging. In the mouth there is a tendency to lose teeth and develop gum disease.

Chapter 12   The Digestive System

Table 12-4   Major Food Sources for Selected Minerals

MINERAL	FOOD SOURCES
Calcium	Milk, cheese, legumes, green leafy vegetables
Chlorine	Salt
Copper	Water, meat
Fluorine	Water, tea, seafood
Iodine	Iodized salt, ocean foods
Iron	Eggs, meat, legumes, green leafy vegetables
Magnesium	Whole grains, green leafy vegetables
Phosphorus	Milk, cheese, meat, poultry, grains
Potassium	Potatoes, fruits, meat, milk
Sodium	Salt, meat, cheese, processed foods
Zinc	Meat, shellfish, nuts

Source: National Research Council, Food and Nutrition Board, 1980, Recommended Dietary Allowances, Revised 1980. *Washington, D.C.: National Research Council, National Academy of Sciences.*

The volume of saliva gradually diminishes, leading to a dry mouth, which affects the ability to taste and makes chewing and swallowing more difficult.

The mucous membrane lining the stomach and intestines becomes thinner, due to atrophy of gland cells. As a result, less hydrochloric acid is secreted in the stomach, and fewer digestive enzymes are secreted in both the stomach and the small intestine. Atrophy of the mucous membrane also affects the villi of the small intestine, reducing the surface area across which absorption occurs. However, in spite of these changes, digestion and absorption are not altered noticeably in healthy older persons.

Atrophy causes the wall of the large intestine to become weaker and more prone to diverticulosis. Because of the reduced hydrochloric acid secretion in the stomach, bacterial growth in the large intestine is affected, and this may have nutritional consequences.

The liver and gall bladder do not seem to be functionally affected to any great degree with age. There is some decline in the amount of digestive enzymes secreted by the pancreas, but the volume of pancreatic juice secreted remains the same.

Table 12-5 Representative Functions of Selected Minerals

MINERAL	FUNCTIONS
Calcium	Development of bones and teeth; assists blood clotting; normal nerve functioning
Cobalt	Component of vitamin B_{12}, thus aids development of red blood cells
Copper	Assists in manufacture of hemoglobin
Fluorine	Strengthens and hardens bones and teeth
Iodine	Formation of thyroid hormones
Iron	Formation of hemoglobin in red blood cells and muscle myoglobin
Magnesium	Development of bones and teeth; muscle and nerve functioning; activates several enzymes
Phosphorus	Development of bones and teeth; component of energy storage and transfer compounds (e.g. ATP); serves as a buffer to regulate acid–base changes
Potassium	Muscle and nerve functioning; acid–base balance
Sodium	Helps maintain water balance; muscle and nerve functioning; acid–base balance
Zinc	Component of several enzymes; involved in collagen formation

Source: National Research Council, Food and Nutrition Board, 1980. Recommended Dietary Allowances, Revised 1980. *(Washington, D.C.: National Research Council, National Academy of Sciences)*

As a result of loss of body mass, reduced physical activity, and a lowered basal metabolic rate, older persons expend less energy and thus require fewer calories. At the same time, nutritional needs do not change significantly with aging; therefore, no radical changes in dietary habits are necessary. Diets which maintain adequate levels of vitamins and minerals and consist of 50% to 55% carbohydrates, 12% to 15% proteins, and 25% to 35% fats are recommended for persons over the age of 50.

The Urinary System

13

$\mathbf{W}$hen we think of the urinary system excretion of urine comes to mind, but we generally do not give much thought as to what is included in the urine. In fact, urine serves as an extremely important means of removing from the body waste products and excessive concentrations of numerous substances that are potentially harmful.

If they are to function effectively, the cells of the body must be surrounded by a fluid environment (i.e. tissue fluid) whose composition remains relatively stable. And yet, the foods we eat and absorb in varying amounts are continually added to the tissue fluid, and cellular metabolism constantly consumes some substances (e.g. glucose and oxygen) and produces others (e.g. carbon dioxide and urea). These activities tend to upset the stability of the tissue fluid, as well as the blood and the intracellular fluid.

Several body systems are involved in eliminating unneeded substances from the body and thus help maintain a stable internal environment for the cells. For instance, the digestive system supplies nutrients that the cells must have in order to function properly and excretes waste products produced by various body activities. The respiratory system supplies oxygen to the body, which makes cellular metabolism possible, and eliminates carbon dioxide, which is a waste product of cellular metabolism. However, the *kidneys*, which are part of the urinary system, are the principal excretory organs. As such, they are critically important in maintaining optimal levels of inorganic and organic substances within the body, thereby maintaining the internal environment within narrow limits. The kidneys accomplish this by regulating how much water is retained in the body and selectively excreting varying amounts of numerous substances.

The selectivity of the kidneys allows them to retain the total amounts of some substances in the blood, like glucose, while excreting other substances in the amounts required to maintain optimal levels of each substance. If the kidneys did not function in this manner, it would be necessary to determine how much of each substance was needed by the body and regulate the amount of each substance ingested to meet these needs. Since the needs of the body are constantly changing, it is obvious that this method of maintaining internal homeostatis would not be effective.

Review of Structure and Function

The urinary system consists of two *kidneys*, which produce urine; the *ureters*, which carry urine from each kidney to be temporarily stored in the *urinary bladder*; and the *urethra*, which transports urine from the urinary bladder to the outside of the body (Figure 13-1).

Kidneys

The *kidneys* are bean-shaped organs situated on the posterior wall of the abdominal cavity, just below the diaphragm. They are about five inches long and extend downward from the level of the twelfth thoracic vertebra. Each kidney is covered with a layer of connective tissue called the *renal capsule*.

There are two distinct regions in each kidney. The outer region is the *cortex*, and the deeper region is the *medulla* (Figure 13-2). The medulla consists of several triangular masses called *renal pyramids*. The tip of each pyramid, from which urine is released, projects toward the center of the kidney into a funnel-shaped chamber called a *calyx*. The various calyces join with one another to form a single tube-shaped chamber called the *renal pelvis*, which is the expanded upper end of the ureter. Urine, which is formed primarily in the medulla of the kidney, passes as droplets from tiny pores in the tips of the pyramids into the calyces. From here it enters the renal pelvis and flows into the ureter, which carries the urine to the urinary bladder.

Fig. 13-1   The human urinary system.

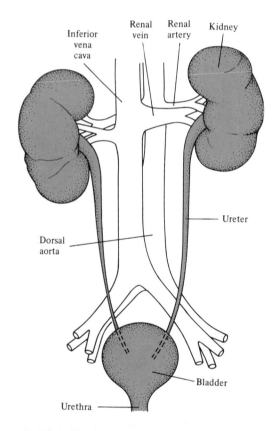

Adapted from Barrett, J.M., et al.: Biology. *Englewood Cliffs, N.J., Prentice Hall, 1986, p. 362.*

Fig. 13-2   **Longitudinal section showing the internal structure of a human kidney.**

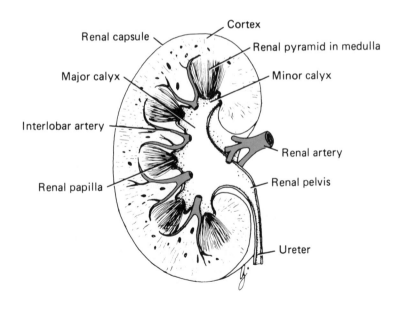

Adapted from Snell, R.S.: Student's Aid to Gross Anatomy. *Norwalk, Ct., Appleton and Lange, 1986, p. 418.*

The functional units of the kidneys, where urine is formed, are called *renal tubules*. Each renal tubule consists of a *nephron* and a *collecting tubule* (Figure 13-3). There are estimated to be over 1 million nephrons in each kidney. Each nephron consists of a network of parallel capillaries called a *glomerulus*, which receives blood from the renal artery, and a *tubule*. Various regions of the tubule differ from one another structurally and functionally.

The proximal end of the tubule, which is located in the cortical region of the kidney, is closed and forms a double-walled cup known as the *glomerular capsule* (Bowman's capsule) that surrounds the capillaries of the glomerulus (Figure 13-4). The inner (visceral) layer of the capsule, which is tight against the glomerular capillaries, is formed of specialized cells called *podocytes* which have small clefts between them. The clefts allow rather free passage of substances between the capillaries and the capsule. Thus, most substances in the blood plasma filter out of the glomerular capillaries and enter the space between the inner and outer layers of the glomerular capsule. The plasma is then referred to as *glomerular filtrate*.

Beyond the glomerular capsule each nephron forms a tightly looping tubule called the *proximal convoluted tubule*. The lumen of the proximal convoluted tubule is continuous with the capsular space; therefore, the glomerular filtrate enters this portion of the tubule. Beyond the proximal convoluted tubule each nephron straightens out and descends into the medullary region of the kidney, where it enters a pyramid and curves sharply back upon itself, forming a *loop of Henle*. The ascending limb of the loop of Henle passes out of the medulla and back into the cortex, where the tubule again becomes highly coiled, forming a *distal convoluted tubule*. The distal convoluted tubules of all the nephrons empty into *collecting tubules*, which transport urine back into the renal pyramids of the medulla and release it into the calyces from the tips of the pyramids.

All regions of the tubules are surrounded by a network of capillaries called *peritubular capillaries*, which are formed from vessels (*efferent arterioles*) that leave the glomeruli. Consequently, each nephron is closely associated with two capillary beds: the glomerulus and the peritubular capillaries. This anatomical oddity is vital to effective kidney functioning.

As blood flows through the kidneys, the blood pressure within the glomerular capillaries forces some of the plasma to filter out of the capillaries and into the glomerular capsules of the tubules. The glomerular filtrate contains everything that was within the blood except for those molecules which are too large to pass through the clefts between podocytes. Thus, the filtrate contains minerals and digested foods, as well

Fig. 13-3   A nephron and its blood supply.

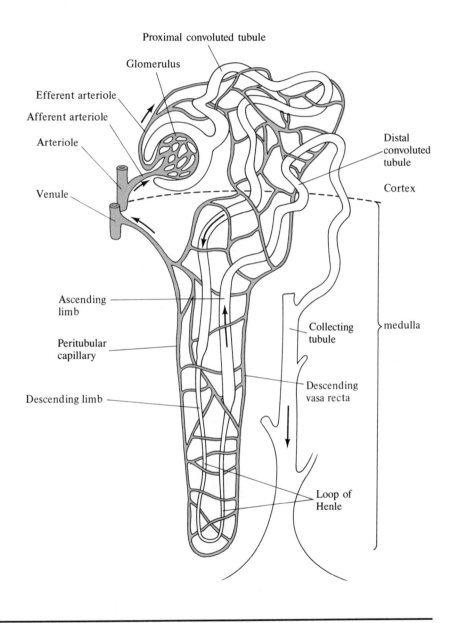

Proximal convoluted tubule

Glomerulus

Efferent arteriole

Afferent arteriole

Arteriole

Distal convoluted tubule

Cortex

Venule

Ascending limb

Peritubular capillary

Descending limb

Collecting tubule

medulla

Descending vasa recta

Loop of Henle

Adapted from Barrett, J.M., et al. Biology. *Englewood Cliffs, N.J., Prentice Hall, 1986, p. 363.*

Review of Structure and Function

Fig. 13-4 A glomerular capsule, showing the podocytes forming the inner layer of the capsule tight against the glomerular capillaries.

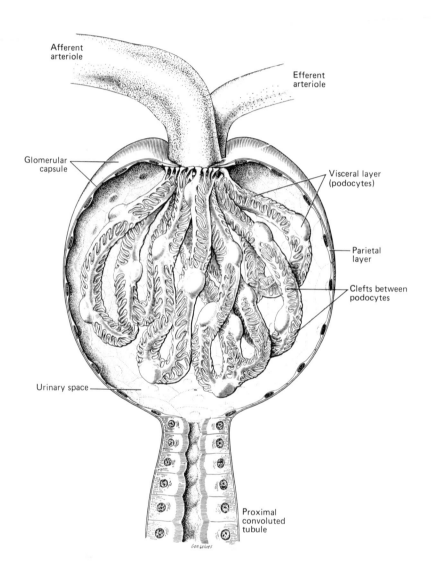

Afferent arteriole

Efferent arteriole

Glomerular capsule

Visceral layer (podocytes)

Parietal layer

Clefts between podocytes

Urinary space

Proximal convoluted tubule

Adapted from Junqueira, L.C., J. Carneiro, and J.A. Long: Basic Histology, *5th Ed. Copyright Appleton and Lange, 1986, p. 415.*

Chapter 13 The Urinary System

as waste products, but normally does not contain blood cells or large protein molecules.

From the capsules, the filtrate flows along the remaining portions of the tubules, where specific quantities of water, glucose, chloride, sodium, and other substances as required by the body are resorbed from the tubules into the peritubular capillaries and thus are returned to the blood. Some materials that are unable to leave the blood through the glomerular capillaries can leave the peritubular capillaries and enter other portions of the tubules.

When the reabsorption process is completed and the glomerular filtrate reaches the collecting tubules, it is transported out of the kidney to be excreted as urine. Thus, urine consists of water and other materials that were filtered from the blood into the renal tubules but were not entirely resorbed back into the blood. About 20% of the blood plasma that enters the kidneys by way of the renal arteries is filtered from the glomerular capillaries into the capsules of the nephrons and forms the glomerular filtrate. Under normal circumstances, the kidneys produce about 180 liters of glomerular filtrate each day. However, approximately 99% of the fluid portion of the filtrate is resorbed from the renal tubules, and only about 1 to 2 liters of urine is formed each day.

The final concentration of urine, and thus the volume of urine excreted, is determined largely by the *antidiuretic hormone*. This hormone, which is manufactured in the brain and secreted by the pituitary gland, increases the permeability of the walls of the collecting tubules to water. When the levels of body fluids become low, monitoring cells in the brain manufacture and release antidiuretic hormone into the blood stream. The hormone causes more water to be resorbed through the collecting tubules than normally would be. As a result, body fluid levels increase, while the volume of urine decreases and it becomes more concentrated. Conversely, if the body contains more than ample amounts of fluids, secretion of antidiuretic hormone diminishes, causing less water to be resorbed from the collecting tubules. This increases the volume of dilute urine which must be excreted, a condition referred to as *diuresis*.

Ureters

The *ureters* are hollow tubes which leave the medial concave borders of the kidneys and travel downward to empty into the urinary bladder. They serve to transport urine from the kidneys to the bladder. The walls of the ureters are composed of several layers of tissue, including a layer of smooth muscle capable of undergoing peristaltic contractions which propel urine to the bladder.

Urinary Bladder

Urine is temporarily stored in the *urinary bladder*, which is a hollow muscular organ that rests on the floor of the pelvic cavity, just behind the pubic symphysis. The bladder is lined with a mucous membrane and has three distinct layers of smooth muscle in its wall. It can hold about 600 ml of urine, but the pressure within the bladder increases as it fills, stimulating receptors that cause the muscles in its wall to contract. Generally, by the time about 300 ml of urine has collected the pressure is great enough to cause the muscles to contract, emptying the bladder through the urethra.

Urethra

The *urethra* carries urine from the bladder to the exterior of the body. It is a mucous-membrane–lined muscular tube that leaves the urinary bladder through its lower surface. Just after leaving the bladder the urethra is surrounded by a ring of smooth muscle called the *internal urethral sphincter*. A short distance beyond this point, as it passes through the pelvis floor, the urethra is surrounded by a ring of skeletal muscle called the *external urethral sphincter*. Because the internal sphincter is composed of smooth muscles, and thus cannot be controlled voluntarily, it relaxes automatically when the urinary bladder contracts. The external sphincter, which is formed of skeletal muscle, is under voluntary control. Therefore, by controlling the contraction and relaxation of the external sphincter, a person can regulate when he or she urinates.

The urethra is short (4 cm) in females, and opens to the exterior between the labia minora. In males, the urethra is about 20 cm long, opening at the tip of the penis. The male urethra passes through the prostate gland, which is located just beneath the urinary bladder. This relationship commonly causes problems in older men, which we will discuss later in this chapter. Within the prostate gland the male urethra receives the ejaculatory ducts of the reproductive system. Therefore, the male urethra is used for reproduction as well as urine transport.

Age-Related Changes

Kidneys

With aging, a number of structural changes occur within the kidneys, including a thickening of the connective tissue capsule surrounding the organ, a decrease in the thickness of the cortical region, and a general atrophy of cells within the organ. The loss of cells is reflected in a gradual decrease in kidney weight after age 40. By 80 years of age the kidneys may have lost about 30% of their earlier adult weight.

Loss of mass from the cortex is thought to be due largely to a decrease in the number of glomeruli. Atrophy of glomeruli reduces the total glomerular surface across which filtration occurs by about one-third by the age of 80, and thus kidney functioning is diminished in older persons. Accompanying the decrease in the number of glomeruli, there is an increase in the incidence of abnormal glomeruli, which may represent over 30% of all glomeruli by age 80. The presence of large numbers of abnormal glomeruli is thought to adversely affect filtration rate. Degenerated glomeruli are often replaced by fibrous connective tissue or hyaline, neither of which is permeable, and this further reduces the filtration rate of substances from the blood into the glomerular capsules. Glomerular filtration begins to decline gradually at about 40 years of age. The decline becomes more noticeable after age 60, and by 75 years of age glomerular filtration rate may be only 50% of that in a young adult (i.e. 60 ml per minute at age 75 versus 120 ml per minute at age 30).

There are also increased abnormalities and degeneration of renal tubules with age. Most commonly seen are thickening of the tubular walls, due in part to the deposition of fat. Shortening of the tubules and the development of small pouches extending off the tubules are also more common with aging. Consequently, the ability of kidneys to concentrate urine is somewhat reduced and the specific gravity of urine decreases slightly with age. The ability of the tubules to resorb glucose and sodium is also diminished in older persons. Impaired tubular functioning may affect the removal of drugs administered for medical treatments from the body and cause higher than optimal levels to accumulate in the blood. For this reason, the dosages for certain drugs need to be adjusted as a person becomes older.

The blood vessels that supply the kidneys—and thus the glomeruli—undergo aging changes typical of many blood vessels, including a thickening of their walls, a loss of muscular tissue, and the presence of atherosclerotic deposits in their walls. The aging changes of these vessels tend to diminish blood flow through the kidneys, reducing the volume of blood per unit of time that may be cleansed. Blood flow is especially reduced in the cortical region of the organ, where most of the glomeruli are located. The decline in blood flow reaching the kidneys parallels the decline in glomerular filtration rate. At 20 years of age approximately one-fourth (1100 ml) of the cardiac output circulates through the kidneys each minute; by age 80 this volume is reduced to about one-eighth (475 ml per minute).

It has been suggested that a decrease in blood supply is a major cause of the loss of nephrons and other aging changes in the kidneys. Although this would seem to be a logical relationship, a correlation between reduced blood supply and degeneration of nephrons has not been demonstrated. In fact, one study reported a loss of nephrons without reduced blood supply in certain nonhuman species.

With aging, the kidneys' ability to handle large changes in either acid or base levels in the blood declines. This is due in part to a reduction in the secretion of buffers (e.g. bicarbonates) and weak organic acids by the tubular cells into the glomerular filtrate. If ample levels of buffers are available they are able to moderate changes in the body fluids as needed in either the acidic or the basic direction. Organic acids are continually being formed by various metabolic reactions, and a decrease in their excretion by the kidneys will affect the acid–base balance of the body. The kidneys of elderly persons can usually maintain acid–base equilibrium when subjected to normal metabolic loads; therefore, the maintenance of an acid–base balance generally becomes a problem only in the presence of sudden, large changes in body chemistry.

Bladder and Urethra

The muscles in the walls of the bladder and urethra tend to become weakened and less elastic with age. Because of the muscle weakness and age-related changes in connective tissue, the bladder is less able to expand or contract in older persons than in younger persons. Consequently, the bladder of an elderly person has a capacity of about 250 ml, which is less than half that of a young adult (600 ml). In addition, as a result of the muscular weakness, the bladder of an elderly person may retain as much as 100 ml of residual urine following urination.

Becoming aware of the need to urinate, which normally is signaled when the bladder is about one-half full, may be delayed in persons over age 65—often until the bladder is almost completely full. Thus, in older persons the need to urinate may be very urgent, and because of weakness of the external urethral sphincter, they may be unable to reach the lavatory in time.

In older women weakness of the muscles forming the floor of the pelvic cavity may reduce the effectiveness of the external urethral sphincter. The pelvic floor muscles help restrict the outlet of the bladder, and their weakness can contribute to leakage of urine from the bladder. Such leakage, which is known as stress incontinence, is generally caused by a sudden rise in pressure within the bladder, such as occurs in coughing or sneezing. Although younger women may experience stress incontinence, it is more common in older women whose pelvic floor muscles have become weakened.

Age-Related Dysfunctions

Urinary Incontinence

Urinary incontinence is the involuntary passing of urine through the urethra. Incontinence is generally due to an inability to maintain the voluntary contraction of the muscles of the external urethral sphincters. It can be a significant problem in older persons, often resulting in urination at inappropriate times, such as during sleep or when riding in an automobile. In fact, incontinence is so common in older persons that the marketing of diaperlike undergarments for adults has become a profitable enterprise.

Contributing to the increased incidence of urinary incontinence in older persons is the reduction in the volume of the bladder and the delayed sensation indicating the need to urinate until the bladder is almost full. However, muscle atrophy is also thought to play a primary role in the condition. As a result, incontinence is more common in bedridden persons and is not as prevalent in persons who are physically active and still able to care for themselves.

Involuntary passage of urine may be the result of a number of mechanical conditions which elevate the pressure within the bladder, including a sudden increase in pressure due to a cough or a sneeze, overactivity of the muscles in the wall of the bladder, or incomplete emptying of the bladder, causing it to be constantly distended. The latter condition may result in a fairly continuous leakage of urine through the urethra. In all cases, weakness of the external urethral sphincter and the muscles of the pelvic floor are thought to be contributing factors. Emotional factors also seem to be involved in some instances of incontinence.

Dysfunctions Caused by the Prostate Gland

Although the prostate gland is an organ of the reproductive system, it frequently interferes with the functioning of the urinary system of older men.

Benign hyperplasia of the prostate, in which the gland enlarges and develops nodules within it, is very common after age 50, and becomes most prevalent in men in their 60s. There seems to be a decline in incidence in men over 70 years of age. As the gland enlarges, it compresses the urethra, which passes through it. In time the urethra may be squeezed to the extent that urination becomes difficult, and the bladder is never completely emptied.

As urine accumulates within the bladder, it causes the pressure in the bladder to increase. If the bladder pressure increases enough, it may cause the urine to back up into the ureters. This, in turn, dilates the renal pelvis and calyces, and may increase the pressure within the glomerular capsules. Increased capsular pressure hinders filtration from the glomerular capillaries into the capsules and thus interferes with kidney functioning.

Men with benign hyperplasia of the prostate gland experience reduced force behind their stream of urine, urinate frequently, are unable to completely empty their bladders, and dribble following urination. Enlargement of the prostate may be surgically corrected by a procedure called transurethral resection, in which an instrument is passed up the urethra and the portion of the gland compressing the urethra is removed.

Carcinoma of the prostate is the most frequent tumor of old men. In the early stages a prostatic tumor may produce little or no urethral obstruction. But when it enlarges to the extent that it does restrict the flow of urine, the tumor may be too far advanced to be treated effectively. For this reason, all older men should have their prostate glands examined regularly. This is a simple procedure in which the physician inserts a finger into the patient's rectum and palpates the gland. If not detected early, the cancer may spread from the prostate gland to other organs of the body. Although drug therapy may produce lengthy remissions, carcinoma of the prostate is often best treated by surgical removal.

Pyelonephritis
Pyelonephritis is an inflammation of the kidney. The condition is not restricted to old persons, but most cases occur in people over 60 years of age. Acute pyelonephritis is a bacterial infection that generally affects the renal pelvis and adjacent tissues of the kidney. The bacteria usually travel to the kidneys in the blood or lymph from other sites of infection. In some cases the infection reaches the kidneys by spreading up the ureters from the bladder.

Pyelonephritis causes the kidney to become swollen as fluid builds up within it. In severe cases abscesses may develop on the surface of the kidney and the renal pelvis may become inflamed and filled with pus. As a result of recurrent bacterial infections of the kidney, the condition may become a chronic problem and cause extensive formation of scar tissue in the kidney. This affects kidney functioning and may cause kidney failure. Pyelonephritis generally responds well to treatment with antibiotics. However, it is a serious condition and can cause fatal complications, such as uremia.

Renal Calculi

Renal calculi, or kidney stones, are not a problem only in the elderly. In fact, they are most common in middle-aged men younger then 60. However, the presence of stones in the urinary bladder does become progressively more common with aging.

Most stones do not cause problems severe enough to produce symptoms. However, the passage of a stone from a kidney through the ureter or from the bladder through the urethra can cause strong contractions of the muscles in the walls of the ureter or urethra, producing episodes of severe pain. If a stone becomes lodged within the ureter it may obstruct the flow of urine to the bladder, causing it to build up within the renal pelvis and eventually damaging the kidney. The passage of kidney stones can cause ulcerations in the lining of the urinary tract, making the tract more prone to infections. Kidney stones are particularly serious in older persons because they have more difficulty passing them than do younger persons. Consequently, the possibility of urinary obstructions is more likely in elderly persons.

The cause of kidney stones is not fully known. It has been suggested that their formation may be related to various kidney infections, an excessive concentration of salts in the urine, a deficiency of vitamin A, or a tumor of the parathyroid glands.

Summary

Under normal conditions the kidneys of elderly persons are capable of maintaining relatively stable balances in the blood and body fluids. However, they have undergone a number of age-related changes that reduce their efficiency and may make them less able to respond to abnormally large alterations in body chemistry, such as variations in the acid–base balance.

With aging, there is a decrease in the number of glomeruli and an increase in the number of abnormal glomeruli. Both of these changes reduce the total glomerular surface across which filtration occurs. As a result, glomerular filtration rate declines with age and may be only one-half of the rate typical of young persons.

The renal tubules also undergo some degenerative changes, resulting in a reduced ability to resorb some substances, including water, sodium, and glucose. Thus, aging diminishes the ability of the kidney to concentrate the urine. Resorption of drugs is also affected, possibly requiring modification of dosages in elderly persons.

Reduction in the volume of blood flowing through the kidneys per unit of time further affects their functioning in elderly persons.

The Reproductive System

$\mathbf{A}$lthough reproduction is an activity that is perhaps best suited for young people, the reproductive system remains important in elderly persons because it is such an integral part of maintaining one's self-esteem and expressing love for another person. Consequently, aging changes that occur in this system generally affect older persons more emotionally and psychologically than physically. For this reason, it is important for those who care for elderly persons to realize that many are concerned about their sexuality and may still feel the need for sexual relationships. These needs are often difficult to satisfy if a person's spouse has died, or if he or she is institutionalized and lacks adequate privacy to allow for sexual activity. Changes that affect sexual functioning may cause a person to become conscious of his or her age more than do the aging changes that occur in most other bodily systems.

Many of the age-related changes in the reproductive system are associated with changes that occur in the endocrine system, which we will discuss in Chapter 15.

Review of Structure and Function

Aside from their auxiliary role in the expression of love and affection, the primary function of the organs of the male and female reproductive systems is to provide for the continuance of the human species. They achieve this by producing cells called *gametes (eggs* or *sperm*), and by providing means by which the gametes of the male can be introduced into the reproductive system of the female, where fertilization occurs. The female reproductive system provides an environment which supports the development of a fertilized egg until it eventually reaches a stage at which it is capable of surviving outside the mother's body.

The gametes are produced by organs referred to as *gonads*, which include the *testes* in the male and the *ovaries* in the female. Other structures of the reproductive tracts transport and nourish the gametes after they leave the gonads. In addition to producing gametes, the gonads also produce hormones that influence one's bodily development in either a male or a female direction and regulate the reproductive cycle. In the male, specialized cells in the testes produce a group of hormones called *androgens*, of which *testosterone* is the most active. In the female, the ovaries produce two hormones: *progesterone*, and several compounds referred to collectively as *estrogens*.

Male Reproductive System

The male reproductive system includes two testes, which produce sperm; a system of ducts that store and transport sperm; several accessory glands whose secretions contribute to the formation of semen; and the penis, which conveys semen to the exterior of the body (Figure 14-1).

The testes are located in a skin-covered pouch called the *scrotum*, which hangs from the body, just behind the base of the penis. It is necessary for the testes to be within the scrotum, rather than within the abdominopelvic cavity, because a temperature lower than body-core temperature is required for the normal development of sperm. The scrotum provides for this lower temperature by, in effect, air-cooling the testes. In fact, because the testes are suspended in the scrotum by a cremaster muscle, their temperature is automatically regulated to some extent. When the environmental temperature is high, relaxation of the cremaster muscle allows the testes to move farther from the body and thus lowers their temperature. When the environmental temperature is low, contraction of the cremaster muscle draws the testes closer to the body and thus raises their temperature.

The testes are divided into compartments, each of which contains several *seminiferous tubules*, in which sperm are produced. Between the seminiferous tubules are clusters of cells called *interstitial endocrinocytes* (Leydig cells), which secrete the hormone *testosterone* into the bloodstream. The seminiferous tubules join together and leave the testes,

Fig. 14-1   Sagittal section of the male reproductive system.

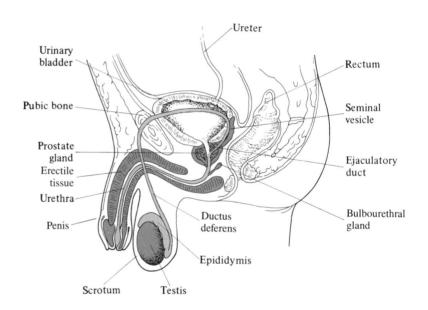

Ureter

Urinary
bladder

Rectum

Pubic bone

Seminal
vesicle

Prostate
gland

Ejaculatory
duct

Erectile
tissue

Urethra

Bulbourethral
gland

Penis

Ductus
deferens

Epididymis

Scrotum   Testis

Adapted from Barrett, J.M., et al: Biology. Englewood Cliffs, N.J. Prentice Hall, 1986, p. 578.

emptying into a highly coiled tube called the *epididymis*. In the epididymis, which is nestled tightly against the testis, sperm mature and are stored.

Each epididymis empties into a tube called the *ductus deferens*, which transports sperm through the abdominal wall by way of an opening called the inguinal canal. Inside the abdominopelvic cavity the ductus deferens passes along the top of the urinary bladder and travels downward behind the bladder to empty into the urethra, shortly after it leaves the bladder. Just before emptying into the urethra, each ductus deferens is joined by the duct of a *seminal vesicle*. The joining of the two ducts forms a short, muscular *ejaculatory duct* that passes through the *prostate gland* before entering the urethra. The prostate gland and the seminal vesicles produce secretions that contribute to semen formation.

The urethra carries semen out of the abdominopelvic cavity and through the penis to the exterior of the body. Just before it enters the penis, the urethra receives ducts from another pair of glands called the *bulbourethral glands*. Secretions of the bulbourethral glands neutralize the urethra, which tends to be acidic as a result of transporting urine. Thus, *semen* is a mixture of sperm from the testes and secretions from the seminal vesicles and the prostate and bulbourethral glands.

The *penis* contains three cylindrical bodies which are composed of highly vascular connective tissue called *erectile tissue*. During sexual arousal blood fills the spongelike spaces within the erectile tissue, causing the penis to enlarge and become firm—a phenomenon referred to as an *erection*.

Adequate levels of testosterone must be maintained in the blood, as the development of male secondary sex characteristics is dependent largely upon its presence. Testosterone also influences the production of sperm by the testes. However, gonadal activity is regulated by two hormones released from the pituitary gland. The amount of testosterone secreted by the interstitial cells of the testes is controlled by secretion of *luteinizing hormone* (LH) by the pituitary, and the formation of sperm by the seminiferous tubules is dependent upon the presence of *follicle-stimulating hormone* (FSH).

Female Reproductive System

The female reproductive system includes two ovaries, which produce eggs (ova); uterine tubes, which transport eggs from the ovaries and furnish nourishment to them; the uterus, which provides an environment that is conducive for the development of an embryo; and the vagina, which receives sperm from the male penis and serves as the birth canal (Figure 14-2).

Eggs develop in the ovary within small spheres of cells called *follicles*. When the egg reaches a certain stage of development, the follicle ruptures and releases it—a process called *ovulation*. Beginning at puberty and continuing throughout the 30 or 40 years during which a female is capable of reproduction, one or more follicles mature and rupture each month (28 to 30 days). In addition to producing eggs, the ovaries also secrete *estrogens* and *progesterone*. These hormones influence the general development of the female body as well as the reproductive organs.

Following ovulation, the egg released from the ovary is carried to the uterus by a *uterine (fallopian) tube*. Transportation of the egg is dependent upon a fluid current produced by the rhythmical beating of cilia lining the tube, aided by peristaltic contractions of the smooth muscles in the wall of the tube. Fertilization generally occurs within the upper portion of the uterine tube.

The uterine tubes empty into the upper lateral angles of the uterus. The *uterus* is a hollow, muscular organ, capable of strong contractions. The epithelial lining of the uterus, which plays an important role in the reproductive cycle of the female, is called the *endometrium*. The lower end of the uterus narrows into a cylindrical outlet called the *cervix*, which leads to the vagina. The *vagina* extends from the cervix to the exterior of the body, opening between two pair of lips, or *labia*. At the anterior junction of the labia is a small elongated structure called the *clitoris*. The clitoris is composed of erectile tissue, much like the penis, and when stimulated contributes to sexual arousal.

Reproduction in females is more cyclical than it is in males. We are made aware of this by the menstrual cycle, but it is actually the ovarian cycle that drives the menstrual cycle. The *ovarian cycle* consists of a series of events that recur regularly in an ovary. The cycle begins with the development of follicles in the ovary, followed by the release of an ovum from a mature follicle and the transformation of the ruptured follicle into a structure called a *corpus luteum*.

It takes from 10 to 14 days for a follicle to mature and release its egg. During this time, the cells of the follicle secrete rather high levels of estrogens. Following ovulation, the cells of the ruptured follicle undergo changes which transform it into a corpus luteum, whose cells secrete progesterone and smaller amounts of estrogens. The corpus luteum reaches its maximum development about 8 to 10 days after ovulation and then gradually degenerates if the released egg has not been fertilized.

Fig. 14-2   Sagittal section of the female reproductive system.

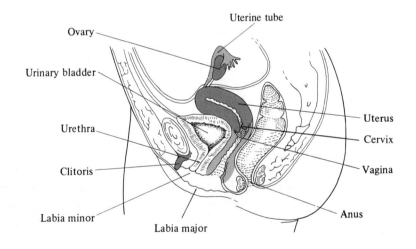

Adapted from Barrett, J.M., et al. Biology. *Englewood Cliffs, N.J. Prentice Hall, 1986, p. 580.*

Review of Structure and Function   **227**

The ovarian cycle is regulated by blood levels of follicle-stimulating hormone (FSH) and luteinizing hormone (LH) from the pituitary gland. As the name implies, FSH stimulates the development of follicles and thus raises the level of estrogens. Just before ovulation, LH levels in the blood increase significantly. This elevation stimulates ovulation and transforms the follicle into a corpus luteum, thereby increasing progesterone secretion.

The *menstrual cycle* consists of a series of changes that occur each month in the endometrium lining the uterus. The cycle is closely associated with the ovarian cycle in that the estrogens and progesterone produced during the ovarian cycle control the events of the menstrual cycle. The estrogens produced during the first portion of the ovarian cycle stimulate the endometrium, causing it to proliferate and become thicker, more glandular, and more vascular. Following ovulation, the cells of the corpus luteum produce progesterone as well as estrogens. The combination of these two hormones causes the endometrium to develop even more, thereby preparing it to receive the embryo should fertilization occur.

If fertilization does not occur, the corpus luteum degenerates and the levels of estrogens and progesterone decline. Since these are the hormones which stimulated the endometrium to develop, their decline causes it to degenerate and be sloughed off as the *menstrual flow*. As a new ovarian cycle begins, the levels of estrogens rise, causing the endometrium to undergo repair and a new menstrual cycle to commence.

Age-Related Changes

Changes in the Male

Although the weight of the testes does not change greatly, they decrease in size and firmness with age. It is uncertain whether these changes may be in part due to a decline in the number of interstitial cells in the testes with age, but this possibility is raised by a gradual age-related decline in the secretion of testosterone. Although this decline could result from atrophy of interstitial cells, it may also be caused by a reduced capability of functioning cells to produce sufficient testosterone. The decline in testosterone levels in the blood is generally not severe, but may reduce muscle strength and contribute to a general wasting appearance in older men, as well as affecting sperm production.

Whether reduced sexual desires in elderly men are also due to falling testosterone levels has not been established. Although that would seem to be a logical relationship, some data suggest it happens the other way. That is, reduced opportunities to engage in sexual activity, which is often the case in older men, may cause the interstitial cells to degenerate and thus provoke the reduced testosterone levels.

Although sperm production continues into old age, there is a decline in the number of sperm and in their motility after about 50 years of age. One study reported a 30% reduction in sperm count in men in their 60s. However, even in quite elderly men, there may be adequate numbers of viable sperm in the semen to make fertilization possible. The age-related reduction in sperm count is thought to be due to degeneration of some seminferous tubules and the narrowing of the lumina of others with connective tissue, causing the walls of the tubules to thicken. Fibrous connective tissue formation also increases between the tubules, which tends to diminish their blood supply and could contribute to their atrophy.

The prostate gland begins to atrophy by about 50 years of age, especially in its posterior regions. Atrophy may be extensive enough to reduce the secretory capacity of the gland noticeably in persons over 60 years of age. Hard masses may also appear in the gland, and during this time muscle fibers in the wall of the gland are gradually replaced with connective tissue, diminishing its ability to expand or contract. Consequently, the volume of fluid contributed to semen by the prostate and the force behind its contraction during orgasm are both reduced. At the same time, the portions of the prostate gland surrounding the urethra often enlarge with age, and the gland may double in weight by age 70. As was mentioned in Chapter 13, this hypertrophy may constrict the urethra and make urination difficult.

The seminal vesicles decrease in weight and storage capacity after age 60. These reductions are thought to be correlated with several structural changes the glands undergo, including the replacement of muscle fibers in their wall with connective tissue. Age-related changes in the bulbourethral glands have not been described, but a decrease in their secretory activities has been reported.

The penis undergoes some atrophy with age, and tends to become smaller. The walls of the blood vessels and the erectile tissue in the penis become somewhat rigid and less elastic after about 55 years. Since an erection is dependent upon the accumulation of blood within the penis, causing the erectile tissue to expand, the loss of elasticity hinders the attainment of an erection.

Changes in the Female

Age-related changes in the female reproductive system occur first in the ovaries and result in reduced amounts of estrogens and progesterone being secreted by them. The declining hormonal levels, in turn, are responsible for degenerative changes in the vagina and uterus, as well as in the external genitalia. The level of estrogens in the blood remains fairly constant until about 40 years of age, after which there is a steady decline that finally stabilizes in women over 60 years of age.

One result of the low levels of estrogens is the cessation of the menstrual cycle, which signals the beginning of *menopause*. Menopause is thought to result from changes in the follicle cells in the ovaries that make them unable to respond to FSH and LH from the pituitary gland. This generally occurs in women in their 40s or 50s, but it actually is the conclusion of insensible hormonal changes that have been occurring for several years. During this time, menstrual flow gradually declines, and the interval between menstrual periods increases. Following the onset of menopause, hormonal secretion by the ovaries is reduced to the extent that the adrenal glands serve as the primary source of estrogens in postmenopausal women.

A variety of symptoms have been associated with the onset of menopause. Some women experience hot flashes, sweating, and red patches on the face and chest as a result of irregular dilation and constriction of blood vessels. Episodes of depression or irritability, headache, and insomnia have also been reported. It should be emphasized, however, that a large number of women experience few of the subjective symptoms of menopause.

Structural changes that have been reported in postmenopausal women include a decline in the weight of the ovaries due to progressive atrophy and increased formation of fibrous tissue. There is also a tendency for follicles to degenerate and follicular cysts to develop. Because of the decline in hormone levels associated with menopause, the reproductive tracts no longer undergo cyclic changes and therefore become relatively stable. However, as they stabilize, the reproductive organs tend to decrease in size and their linings undergo atrophic changes.

By age 50 the uterus may have lost as much as one-half of its weight due to the replacement of muscles in its walls with fibrous connective tissue. The diameter of the cervical canal becomes less, and as the endometrium atrophies there is a decline in the number of active endometrial glands. The uterine tubes become thin and undergo weaker peristaltic contractions. The vagina becomes narrower and shorter, and its walls become thin and lose much of their elasticity. Glands which normally lubricate the vagina undergo atrophy, and do not secrete as copiously as in younger women. Consequently, the vagina becomes dry, and sexual intercourse may be painful. The vaginal secretions that do continue are less acidic than the secretions in women who have not undergone menopause. This allows bacteria and yeasts that were unable to flourish in the vagina when its secretions were more acid to do so in postmenopausal women. As a result, vaginal infections are more common in older women.

The body and external genitalia of females also undergo atrophic changes in response to the hormonal decline of menopause. Postmenopausal women tend to accumulate fat beneath the skin in numerous places, especially in the waist, thighs, and buttocks. Wrinkles develop and the skin becomes thinner and sags. The hair on the head and in the pubic region becomes thinner and coarser. Fat and elastic tissue are lost from the genital labia, causing them to become thinner, wrinkled, and less prominent. Glandular tissue in the breasts is gradually replaced with fat, causing them to become less firm and to sag. The nipples decrease in size and become less responsive to stimulation.

Age-Related Dysfunctions

There are few dysfunctions of the reproductive system that are specifically related to age. Most age-related conditions that are typical of the organs of this system tend to be problems with declining sexual functioning, rather than actual disorders.

Cancer

One dysfunction of the reproductive system that is age-related is *cancer*. Cancer of the prostate is more prevalent in older men, and the incidence of cancer of the uterus, ovary, and breast increases in postmenopausal women. In contrast, cervical cancer is more common in younger women.

The increase in cancer with age points to the need for older persons to have regular examinations and to watch for symptoms that may indicate cancer development. Men should have their prostate gland palpated each year, as part of a general physical examination. Similarly, women should undergo pelvic examinations, including cervical smears, at least once a year, have regular mammograms, and routinely perform self-examination of their breasts. Any occurrence of vaginal bleeding or spotting, or the presence of a lump in the breast, should be brought promptly to the attention of a physician.

About 1 of every 11 women in the United States will develop breast cancer, accounting for over 100,000 new cases being diagnosed each year. There are a number of risk factors that are important in predicting which women are more likely to develop the disease. One such factor is age. More than 80% of the women who develop breast cancer are over 40 years old, and about 60% are over 50 years of age.

The stage of the cancer when it is first detected provides the best prognosis for survival. For instance, early detection of a breast tumor while it is still small and localized increases a person's chances of surviving longer than 5 years to about 90%. Thus, early detection is the best protection against breast cancer. Yet, in spite of the fact that mammography is capable of detecting a breast tumor while it is still too minute to be noticeable by self-examination, only a small percentage of women have regular mammographic examinations.

Atrophic Vaginitis

The reduced levels of hormones—particularly the estrogens—typical of menopause cause atrophic changes in the lining of the female reproductive tract which make inflammation of the vagina more prevalent in older women. When the inflammation is due in part to degenerative changes, it is referred to as *atrophic vaginitis.*

Because the walls of the vagina are thinner and less moist in postmenopausal women, they are more fragile and susceptible to damage. In some instances adhesions may occur between damaged areas on apposed surfaces, obliterating the vaginal canal. A lessening of the acidity of the vaginal secretions, which often occurs in older women, may allow certain bacteria, yeasts, and protozoans to multiply rapidly in the vagina and cause an inflammatory reaction.

Symptoms of vaginitis include vaginal itching and burning, generally accompanied by a discharge that differs in color and odor from a normal vaginal discharge. In severe cases, the external genitalia may be reddened and swollen.

Prolapse of the Uterus

One of the more common dysfunctions of the reproductive system in elderly women is *prolapse of the uterus.* In this condition, which is a result of weakness of the ligaments supporting the organ, the uterus drops through the cervical canal and protrudes into the vagina. The supporting ligaments tend to become progressively weaker with age, and damage that occurred years before when the woman was giving birth may also contribute to the weakness.

Impotence

Probably the most disturbing, and most common, dysfunction of the male reproductive system is *impotence*, in which a man is unable to attain an erection of the penis or to retain an erection long enough to complete sexual intercourse.

Impotence can result from physical disorders of the vascular or nervous systems, diabetes, prostate surgery, and some medications—such as those taken to lower blood pressure. A large percentage of the cases of impotence are thought to be at least in part psychological; therefore, counseling is often helpful. Impotence may respond to treatment with medications that dilate the blood vessels, and penile implants are becoming increasingly popular. In this procedure, either a flexible rod or an inflatable cylinder is surgically implanted in the penis and provides the rigidity necessary for sexual intercourse.

Diminished Sexual Functioning

Most complaints of older persons, especially elderly men, concerning their reproductive systems involve a diminished ability to function sexually.

There is a growing awareness that elderly persons have sexual needs and can enjoy sexual relations. Previously, sexual activity in elderly persons was not studied or discussed in any depth because it was not considered to be an especially important topic. This is changing as more studies demonstrate that sexuality remains important to many older persons.

There are, of course, age-related physical and hormonal changes that may alter one's sexual functioning as well as his or her sexual needs. Furthermore, elderly persons are frequently without a sexual partner, due to the death of their husband or wife. In other cases, disease or disability may make sexual activity difficult or impossible. In one study involving men between the ages of 64 and 91, 75% indicated a continued interest in sex, but only about one-half reported continued sexual activity. Other studies report continued sexual intercourse in 20% to 50% of men over 75 years of age. Although sexual activity can continue in elderly persons, its frequency declines. Married couples over 50 report engaging in sexual intercourse less than twice each week, compared with about four times each week in young married couples.

Interest in sexual activity may increase in women following menopause, as the fear of pregnancy is no longer a factor. However, the availability of a sexual partner is a greater problem in older women than it is in men, as husbands, who are generally older than their wives, die or become incapacitated. The problem of having a suitable sexual partner is even greater in unmarried women, and one study reported 95% of unmarried women over 60 years of age do not engage in sexual activity.

Detailed studies have been carried out on the physiological decline in sexual function with age in both males and females. Generally, it may take several minutes for an older man to attain an erection, whereas only a few seconds is required in younger men. And the erection may not be as full or firm as in younger males. The time required to reach the level of stimulation where ejaculation occurs can be quite prolonged in older males, and the amount of ejaculate is reduced. Furthermore, ejaculation is not as forceful and the sensations associated with orgasm are less intense and of a shorter duration. Following orgasm, the erection subsides more rapidly in an older man and several hours may be required before he can achieve another erection. In young men, this is often possible within a few minutes.

Older women may require several minutes for lubrication of the vagina to occur in response to sexual stimuli. In younger women this is generally achieved within 30 seconds. If the atrophic changes in the vaginal lining are advanced, adequate lubrication may not be possible and it may be necessary for an older woman to apply lubricating gels in order to prevent intercourse from being painful. During sexual stimulation, the labia do not become as engorged with blood as they do in younger women; consequently, they do not press as tightly against the penis during intercourse. Orgasms in older women are generally less intense because they involve fewer contractions of the uterus and vagina, and painful muscle spasms may accompany the uterine contractions. Following orgasm, older women return to the prearousal stare more rapidly than do younger women.

Summary

While sexual interest and activity may continue well into old age, changes occur within the organs of the reproductive system which affect sexual functioning.

In males there is a gradual decline in testosterone levels in the blood, which may result from atrophy of interstitial cells in the testes. Atrophy of the seminiferous tubules, prostate gland, and seminal vesicles reduces the number of sperm and the volume of semen ejaculated by older men. Loss of elasticity in the blood vessels and erectile tissue of the penis, as

Chapter 14 The Reproductive System

well as psychological factors, may interfere with the attainment of erections.

The ovaries are the first reproductive organs to show age-related changes in females, and the atrophy of follical cells results in lower blood levels of estrogens and progesterone. The decline of these hormones leads to atrophic changes in the vagina and uterus, culminating in menopause by 40 or 50 years of age. In postmenopausal women the ovaries and uterus decline in weight, and the walls of the vagina become thin and dry. Diminished hormonal levels also cause the general bodily changes characteristic of older women.

The Endocrine System

15

The endocrine system consists of a number of glands that work closely with the nervous system to maintain relatively stable conditions within the body. The glands regulate many body processes through their release of chemical messengers called *hormones*. Most hormones are composed either of various length chains of amino acids or complex rings of carbon atoms. The chain-like hormones are polypeptides or proteins, depending on the length of the chain, while those composed of carbon rings are steroids.

The main endocrine glands are the *pituitary*, the *thyroid*, the *parathyroids*, the *adrenals*, and the *gonads* (Figure 15-1). Hormones are also secreted by the thymus gland and by cells within the digestive tract. In addition, the *hypothalamus* region of the brain is involved in endocrine functioning as it releases several factors or hormones which stimulate or inhibit the release of hormones by the pituitary gland. In fact, it has been suggested that the hypothalamus may be the site of an "aging clock" responsible for the entire endocrine control of metabolism and thus may serve to control the aging process. It is proposed that if such a clock exists it may regulate changes in metabolic activity according to the age of the individual and thereby control age-related changes in body functions.

In a similar manner, with the hormone-mediated aging changes that occur in the female reproductive tract as an example, it has long been

Fig. 15-1   Locations of the principal endocrine glands.

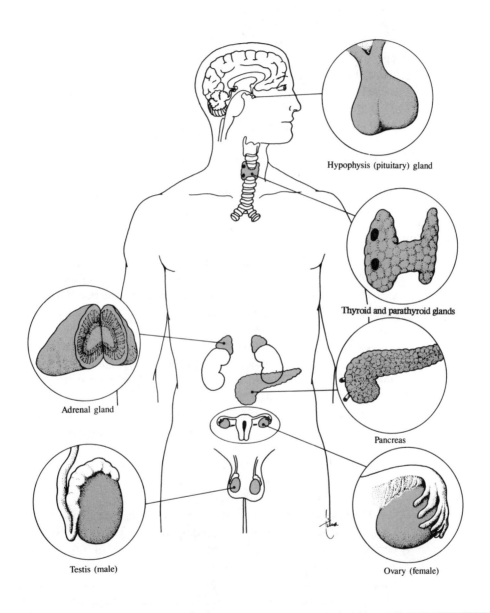

Hypophysis (pituitary) gland

Thyroid and parathyroid glands

Adrenal gland

Pancreas

Testis (male)

Ovary (female)

From Rice, J.: Medical Terminology with Human Anatomy. *Norwalk, Ct., Appleton and Lange, 1986, p. 188; adapted from Evans, W.F.; Anatomy and Physiology, 3rd Ed. Englewood Cliffs, N.J., Prentice Hall, 1983, p. 229.*

proposed that the general aging process may be, at least in part, due to a programmed deficiency of one or more hormones. This prospect has generated much interest in aging changes in the endocrine system and has lead to attempts to delay the aging process by supplementation of hormones and hormone-secreting cells. Significant success in the treatment or prevention of aging by such means has not been adequately substantiated. However, data does indicate that changes in hormonal levels or in the cells that react to the hormones may be important in the aging process. Thus, the effects of aging on the various components of the endocrine system need to continue to be thoroughly researched.

Endocrine glands are ductless glands and thus lack a means of conveying their secretions directly to a specific location. Rather, their hormones are released into the bloodstream and transported in that manner throughout the body. This would seem to be an inefficient method of getting a message from one region of the body to another, and, indeed, endocrine responses are slower than responses to messages conveyed by the nervous system. However, the use of chemical messengers is more efficient than it might seem because although the hormones are transported throughout the body, each hormone does not affect all of the body cells. Only specific cells, called *target cells*, respond to any one hormone. The specificity of the target cells is dependent upon the presence of receptors with which only one hormone can interact.

Receptors for the polypeptide and protein hormones are located on the cell membrane of the target cells, whereas receptors for the steroid hormones are located within the target cells. When a hormone attaches to a receptor on the cell membrane a second messenger is released into the cell from the membrane and affects various cellular functions, including the activity of enzymes and the synthesis of secretory molecules. In contrast, the steroid hormones pass through the target cell membrane and combine with receptor molecules in the cytoplasm. The combination of hormone and receptor then enters the cell nucleus and activates certain genes, resulting in the synthesis of specific enzymes.

The release of hormones from various endocrine glands may be controlled by a number of factors, including nerve impulses and the levels of certain chemical substances in the blood. However, in most glands hormonal secretion is dependent upon the concentration in the blood of those substances which the hormones cause to be produced. This type of regulation is known as *feedback control*. The pituitary gland provides an example of this type of control. Among the hormones released by the pituitary is one which stimulates the thyroid gland, causing it to release its hormones. In turn, increasing levels of the thyroid hormones in the blood inhibit the hypothalamus and the pituitary gland, and the release of the thyroid-stimulating hormone by the pituitary diminishes.

Review of Structure and Function

Pituitary Gland

The *pituitary gland* (hypophysis) is located in a deep bony depression on the floor of the skull. The gland is connected to the hypothalamus region of the brain by a slender hollow stalk called the *infundibulum*. The hormones released by the pituitary gland regulate the functioning of several other endocrine glands and have wide-ranging effects on various body activities (Figure 15-2). For this reason it is sometimes referred to as the "master gland" of the body.

The pituitary gland has two lobes, which develop from cells derived from different regions in the embryo. The differences in development of the lobes are reflected in the diverse functions of the hormones released from each lobe. The *neurohypophysis* (posterior lobe) is derived from nervous tissue, developing as an outgrowth from the floor of the brain in the region of the hypothalamus. It remains connected to the hypothalamus by the infundibulum. In contrast, the *adenohypophysis* (anterior lobe) develops from tissue that forms the roof of the mouth.

The neurohypophysis releases two hormones; the *antidiuretic hormone* (ADH or vasopressin) and *oxytocin*.

Antidiuretic hormone promotes the resorption of water by the kidneys, thereby retaining fluid within the body. When present in relatively high concentrations it also causes arterioles to constrict, thus the name vasopressin.

Oxytocin is secreted in higher amounts toward the end of pregnancy and causes the smooth muscles of the uterus to contract, expelling the baby. It also stimulates contraction of cells in the mammary glands, assisting in lactation. The function of oxytocin the males is uncertain.

Although ADH and oxytocin are released from the neurohypophysis, both are manufactured in the hypothalamus of the brain and reach the pituitary by traveling along specialized cells within the infundibulum.

The adenohypophysis releases six hormones; *growth hormone* (GH or somatotropin), *thyroid-stimulating hormone* (TSH or thyrotropin), *adrenocorticotropic hormone* (ACTH), *follicle-stimulating hormone* (FSH), *luteinizing hormone* (LH), and *prolactin*.

Fig. 15-2 **Major functions of the pituitary hormones and their target organs and tissues.**

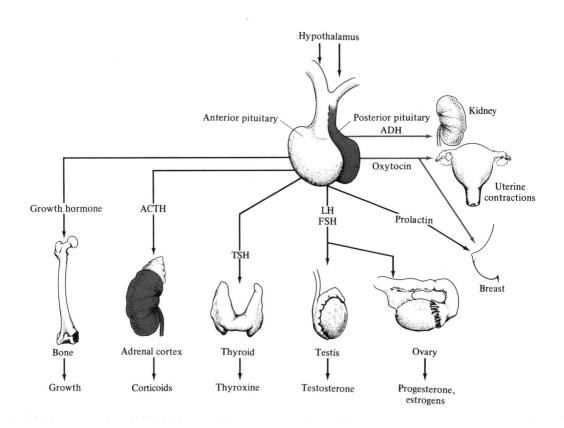

Adapted from Barrett, J.M., et al. Biology. Englewood Cliffs, N.J. Prentice Hall, 1986, p. 385.

Chapter 15 The Endocrine System

Growth hormone stimulates growth in many tissues and is especially active in promoting the development of bone. It also increases the rate of protein synthesis and the breakdown of fat and carbohydrates. GH is released from the pituitary in response to a substance called growth-hormone-releasing hormone produced by the hypothalamus.

Thyroid-stimulating hormone causes the cells of the thyroid gland to synthesize and release the thyroid hormones. TSH is released from the pituitary in response to thyrotropin-releasing hormone from the hypothalamus.

Adrenocorticotropic hormone stimulates the release of hormones from the outer, or cortical, regions of the adrenal glands. ACTH is released from the pituitary in response to corticotropin-releasing hormone from the hypothalamus.

Follicle-stimulating hormone initiates the development of follicles in the ovary and induces the secretion of estrogens. In males, FSH enhances the development of sperm.

Luteinizing hormone, together with FSH, is responsible for ovulation and the formation of a corpus luteum in the female. In males it stimulates the synthesis of testosterone by the interstitial cells of the testes, and thus is referred to as *interstitial-cell-stimulating hormone* (ICSH). Both FSH and LH are released from the pituitary in response to gonadotropin-releasing hormone from the hypothalamus.

Prolactin is involved in milk production in females. Its function in males is uncertain. The release of prolactin from the pituitary is controlled by prolactin-inhibiting factor from the hypothalamus.

Thyroid Gland

The *thyroid gland* is located anterior to the upper portion of the trachea, near its junction with the larynx. The gland contains hollow spheres of cells called *follicles*, in which the thyroid hormones are stored prior to their release. The thyroid is the only endocrine gland that stores its hormones outside of the gland cells.

The thyroid gland releases three hormones, two of which contain iodine. The iodine-containing hormones are tetraiodothyronine (T_4 or thyroxine) and *triiodothyronine* (T_3). These hormones affect metabolism in most body tissues, generally increasing oxygen consumption and heat production. Both of these hormones are released from the thyroid in response to TSH from the pituitary, which, in turn, is regulated by thyrotropin-releasing hormone from the hypothalamus.

The thyroid also releases the hormone *calcitonin*, which lowers the levels of calcium and phosphate in the blood by increasing their deposition into bones. Thus, calcitonin contributes to bone formation. Release of calcitonin from the thyroid is stimulated by high levels of calcium in the blood.

Parathyroid Glands

The four small *parathyroid glands* are embedded on the posterior surface of the thyroid gland. The glands secrete *parathyroid hormone* (PTH or parathormone), which, like calcitonin from the thyroid gland, controls calcium and phosphate metabolism. Thus, both hormones are involved in the remodeling of bone. However, the actions of the parathyroid hormone on calcium and phosphate metabolism are the opposite of those of calcitonin.

Parathyroid hormone is released when blood calcium level is low. The hormone increases the blood calcium level by reducing the excretion of calcium by the kidneys and increasing its resorption into the blood from bone. At the same time, the hormone increases phosphate excretion by the kidneys, thus lowering the blood phosphate level.

Because of its role in maintaining blood calcium levels, parathyroid hormone is also important in muscle contraction and the generation of nerve impulses.

Adrenal glands

There are two *adrenal glands*, one lying against the top border of each kidney. Each gland consists of an inner region called the *medulla* and an outer region called the *cortex*. The actions of the hormones secreted by the two regions differ considerably; thus, each adrenal gland essentially functions as two distinct endocrine organs. As is the case in the pituitary gland, the reason for this lies in the embryonic development of the glands. During embryonic development the cells that form the adrenal medulla separate from a population of cells which eventually form postganglionic sympathetic neurons, whereas those of the cortex separate from future gonadal cells. The hormones produced by each region of the adrenal gland reflect these diverse embryonic origins.

The cells of the adrenal medulla produce two closely related hormones; *epinephrine* and *norepinephrine*. These hormones cause widespread functional changes that are advantageous under emergency or stressful conditions. For instance, release of epinephrine and norepinephrine increases the heart rate, dilates the bronchioles of the lungs, and causes the vessels supplying most organs to constrict, while dilating the vessels supplying skeletal muscle.

The responses initiated by the hormones of the adrenal medulla are similar to those resulting from stimulation by the sympathetic division of the autonomic nervous system. Recall that norepinephrine is released by neurons of this division. As might be expected, the release of epinephrine and norepinephrine from the adrenal medulla is controlled by preganglionic neurons of the sympathetic nervous system.

The cells of the adrenal cortex produce several hormones, all of which are steroids. Most of these hormones, which are referred to collectively as *adrenal corticoids*, can be separated into two rather distinct groups on the basis of their actions. One group of hormones, called *mineralocorticoids*, promote the resorption of sodium and the excretion of potassium by the kidneys. *Aldosterone* is a mineralocorticoid hormone. The second group of hormones are the *glucocorticoids*. Hormones included in this group increase the glucose level in the blood by converting fats and proteins into glucose. *Cortisone* and *cortisol* are glucocorticoid hormones.

In addition to the corticoids, the adrenal cortex also produces some *androgens* and small amounts of *estrogens*. In males the adrenal androgens supplement those produced by the testes. In females they are thought to cause the tendency for masculinization that occurs in postmenopausal women, in whom the adrenal androgens are no longer masked by estrogens from the nonfunctioning ovaries.

Release of the mineralocorticoid hormones from the adrenal cortex is controlled by the elevation of potassium and the decrease of sodium concentrations in the tissue fluid and by an enzyme called renin that is secreted by the kidneys. Release of the glucocorticoids is under control of ACTH from the pituitary, which, in turn, is regulated by the corticotropin-releasing hormone (CRH) from the hypothalamus. Therefore, under conditions of stress the hypothalamus secretes CRH, triggering the release of ACTH from the pituitary and causing the adrenal cortex to release glucocorticoid hormones.

Pancreas

The *pancreas* is located behind the stomach and extends between the spleen and the duodenum of the small intestine. In addition to secreting hormones, it also produces several digestive enzymes.

The pancreas secretes two hormones: insulin and glucagon. *Insulin* lowers the blood glucose level by facilitating the movement of glucose into body cells and its metabolism within the cells. In contrast, *glucagon* decreases glucose utilization, thereby increasing the blood glucose level. By their antagonistic actions, insulin and glucagon maintain blood glucose within normal levels.

Release of the pancreatic hormones is mainly controlled by the blood glucose levels. Elevated levels of glucose in the blood stimulate the release of insulin, whereas lowered blood glucose levels increase glucagon release.

Gonads

The endocrine functions of the androgens from the testes and estrogens and progesterone from the ovaries were discussed in Chapter 14 with the reproductive system.

Age-Related Changes

During aging, the ability of endocrine glands to synthesize hormones appears to remain within normal limits, and the synthesis of releasing factors by the hypothalamus does not change significantly. What does seem to occur with age in many tissues is a reduction in the number of receptors for certain hormones. Histological changes have been reported in various glands, but they do not noticeably affect their functions.

Pituitary Gland

After about age 50 there is a decrease in the blood supply to the pituitary gland and an increase in connective tissue within the gland. At the same time, its cells become more tightly packed and contain more vesicles. A slight decrease in the weight of the gland with aging has also been reported by some, but not all, researchers.

These structural changes do not seem to be correlated with any significant changes in the ability of the pituitary gland to respond to stimulation and release its hormones. The blood levels of TSH, ACTH, and GH remain constant after age 60, at least under basal conditions.

Because of its role in regulating growth, it has been suggested that maintaining high levels of growth hormone may slow the rate of aging. However, this has not proven to be the case. In fact, excessive GH levels in adults has been implicated in premature death. The role of GH is actually more complex than simply affecting body growth. It is also involved in various metabolic activities, which may explain why one study reported that older men who were in excellent physical condition showed greater GH responsiveness. This may indicate that physical training can help maintain the sensitivity of tissue receptors to GH or enhance the ability of the hypothalamus to cause the release of GH by the pituitary gland.

The levels of FSH and LH in the blood are regulated by feedback inhibition of the hypothalamus and pituitary gland by estrogens. Following menopause the ovary ceases to produce estrogens and the inhibition is no longer effective. Consequently, the release of FSH and LH by the pituitary proceeds without interference and the blood levels of both hormones rise significantly in postmenopausal women. The elevated levels may last for 15 to 20 years before slowly declining.

There is little information concerning the effects of aging on the posterior pituitary gland. Circulating levels of antidiuretic hormone have been reported to be somewhat elevated in elderly persons, but this may be due to reduced elimination of the hormone by the kidneys and the liver rather than to its increased secretion.

Thyroid Gland

Because of similarities between functional changes typical of thyroid deficiency and aging, it has been suggested that normal aging may be the result of inadequate levels of thyroid hormone. However, the blood levels of thyroid hormones do not decrease significantly with age, and therefore hypofunction of the thyroid does not appear to be a major cause of normal aging.

Atrophy causes the thyroid gland to decrease in mass with age, and there is increased deposition of fibrous tissue between the follicles as well as a reduction in the size of the follicles. However, as was previously indicated, these structural changes apparently do not affect thyroid functioning, as the thyroids of elderly persons are still capable of responding normally to TSH from the pituitary by releasing T_3 and T_4. Since the level of TSH remains essentially unchanged with age, thyroid functioning does not change significantly.

Reductions in secetion of the thyroid hormones—particularly T_4—have been reported, but these are thought to result from slower degradation of the hormone in the tissues because of the declining oxygen consumption typical of old age. As physical activity and basal metabolic rate decline, lower levels of thyroid hormones are required to meet the metabolic needs of the body, and they may accumulate in the blood. As blood levels of the thyroid hormones increase, feedback stimulation of the thyroid gland diminishes, and secretion of hormones by the gland declines.

Parathyroid Glands

The major structural change in the parathyroid glands with aging is an increase in fat deposition between its cells. The glands do not appear to experience significant atrophy, and while secretion of parathormone shows some sex-related differences, it remains relatively constant during aging.

In men, the levels of parathormone increase steadily, reaching a peak at about 50 years of age. The level then declines gradually. Young women have higher levels of parathormone than do men. These levels decline until about 40 years of age, after which they gradually increase.

Adrenal Glands

Structural changes that have been reported to occur with aging in the adrenal glands include increased formation of fibrous tissue to replace degenerating cells, increased pigment accumulation, and in the cortex, increasing numbers of abnormal cells.

Although the adrenal glands do not appear to lose functional capacity with age, there is an age-related decline in the secretion of hormones by the glands. In the case of the glucocorticoid hormones, the diminished secretion rates seem to result from slower disposal rates of the hormones, since cortical cells continue to be responsive to ACTH in elderly persons. After about 50 years of age a relatively large decline in the secretion of aldosterone may occur. However, this decline does not usually affect salt and water balance to any great degree in healthy persons. The diminished secretion of aldosterone is thought to be due to decreased release of renin by the kidney, rather than to aging changes in the adrenal glands.

Pancreas

Unlike the other endocrine glands we have discussed, the pancreas is not under control of the hypothalamus. Rather, the levels of glucose in the blood regulate the amounts of insulin and glucagon that are released by the gland.

Some atrophy of the pancreatic cells that synthesize insulin, and declining levels of insulin the blood with aging, have been reported. However, not all studies support these findings, and it is generally felt that any reduction of insulin activity in elderly persons is more likely to be due to declining sensitivity of body cells to insulin than to diminished secretion by the pancreas. The lessened sensitivity to insulin may result from increased resistance by the cell membranes to its movement across them, causing insulin to accumulate in the blood and inhibiting secretory activity by the pancreas. At the same time, reduced physical activity or a decrease in the amount of actively metabolizing tissues may reduce the amount of glucose needed within the tissue cells and thereby reduce insulin secretion.

However, although pancreatic functioning is not thought to be affected greatly with age, many elderly persons show reduced responses to a glucose tolerance test. To test for glucose tolerance, a measured amount of glucose is administered, and residual blood glucose levels are determined 1 to 3 hours afterwards. A reduced response indicates that less than normal amounts of glucose have moved from the blood into the tissue cells. As was indicated above, there may be a number of explanations for this decline that do not implicate the pancreas. At any rate, because of the insulin imbalance there is a substantial increase in the incidence of diabetes mellitus in persons over 65 years of age.

Age-Related Dysfunctions

Disorders of the endocrine system are not frequent in old age, and when they do occur they are most often the result of pathological changes rather than being age-related. Because functioning of the endocrine glands is so interrelated, with the activities of most glands often affecting the activities of others, and because of the close relationship between the nervous and endocrine systems, it is difficult to isolate specific factors that cause endocrine dysfunctions. The most common age-related condition that is often due to endocrine dysfunction is diabetes mellitus.

Diabetes Mellitus
In *diabetes mellitus* inadequate amounts of glucose to support metabolic activities enter the tissue cells. The decline in glucose entering the cells may be the result of deficient secretion of insulin by the pancreas or a decreased sensitivity of target cells to insulin.

There are two types of diabetes. *Juvenile-onset* (Type I or insulin-dependent) *diabetes* can occur at any age but is more common in young people. This type of diabetes is due to a reduction of insulin production because of pathological changes in the pancreas. *Maturity-onset* (Type II or non-insulin-dependent) *diabetes* is the most prevalent endocrine dysfunction in older persons. This type of diabetes develops more slowly than juvenile-onset diabetes and occurs mainly in overweight people—especially those who are middle-aged or older. About 1% of persons under 65 develop diabetes, as compared to 7% of those between age 65 and 74—and most of these are, or have been, overweight.

In maturity-onset diabetes the production of insulin remains within normal limits. The reduced amounts of glucose entering the cells are usually caused by a diminished sensitivity to insulin by the target cells. As a consequence, the pancreas generally produces extra insulin in an attempt to compensate for the insensitivity, and persons suffering with this condition may have elevated insulin levels.

Maturity-onset diabetes often responds to medication, but diet modification and weight loss are important adjuncts to its control. It has been shown that exercise decreases the concentration of glucose in the blood by promoting its entry into the tissue cells and enhances the use of glucose by the cells. Data also suggest that exercise increases the number of insulin receptors on tissue cells.

Because inadequate amounts of glucose enter body cells and the ability of cells to use glucose is impaired, person suffering from diabetes mellitus use fats as their main source of energy. The oxidation of fatty acids, which is a necessary step in obtaining the energy stored in them, produces ketone bodies. If present in excessive amounts, ketone bodies give off a characteristic odor and cause the body fluids to become more acid. If severe enough, this may lead to generalized acidosis, coma, and death.

Chronic diabetes can cause skin ulcers, loss of weight as fats and proteins are used as energy sources, glaucoma, cataract, and may interfere with peripheral circulation—causing gangrene of the limbs and ultimately requiring amputation of the affected parts.

Summary

Numerous structural changes occur with age in the various endocrine glands, including some atrophy, increased fibrous tissue, and deposition of fat. However, the blood levels of most hormones remain within normal limits into old age, and the glands continue to be responsive to stimulating hormones from the hypothalamus or other endocrine glands. The gonads are the only exceptions, with age-related declines occurring in testosterone, progesterone, and estrogens.

At the same time, the demand for the various hormones by tissue cells changes, and there may be reduction in the number or sensitivity of hormonal receptors. These peripheral changes can affect the rate of secretion of the hormones and alter their blood levels as the glands respond to the changing conditions.

There is no convincing evidence that age-related changes in the functioning of endocrine glands contribute significantly to the normal aging process.

Bibliography

General References

Behnke, J., Finch, C., & Moment, G. (Eds.) (1978). *The biology of aging.* New York: Plenum Press.

Bergsma, D., & Harrison, D.E. (Eds.) (1978). *Genetic effects on aging.* New York: Alan R. Liss, Inc.

Berscheid, E., Walster, E., & Bohrnstedt, G. (1973). Body image. The happy American body: A survey report. *Psychology Today,* 7(6): 119–131.

Birren, J.E., & Schaie, K.W. (eds.) (1977). *Handbook of the psychology of aging.* New York: Van Nostrand Reinhold.

Bittles, A.H., & Collins, K.J. (Eds.) (1986). *The biology of human aging.* New York: Cambridge University Press.

Borkan, G.A. & Norris, A.H. (1980). Assessment of biological age using a profile of physical parameters. *Journal of Gerontology,* 25: 177–184.

Bortz, W.M. II. (1982). Disuse and aging. *Journal of the American Medical Association,* 248: 1203–1208.

Botwinick, J. (1973). *Aging and behavior: A comprehensive integration of research findings.* New York: Springer.

Comfort, A. (1979). *The biology of senescence*, 3rd ed. Edinburgh: Churchill Livingstone.

Cristofalo, V.J., Roberts, J., & Adelman, R.C. (Eds.) (1975). *Explorations in aging.* New York: Plenum Press.

Curtis, H.J. (1966). *Biological mechanisms of aging.* Springfield, IL: Charles C. Thomas.

Damon, A. (1972). Predicting age from body measurements and observations. *Aging and Human Development*, 3: 169–174.

Danon, D., Shock, N.W., & Marois, M. (Eds.) (1981). *Aging: A challenge to science and society.* Oxford: Unviersity Press.

Davis, B.B., & Wood, W.G. (Eds.) (1985). *Homeostatic function and aging.* New York: Raven Press.

Dilman, V.M. (1981). *Diseases of aging.* Boston: John Wright Publishing/PSG, Inc.

The Framingham Study (1968). An epidemiological investigation of cardiovascular disease. Sect. 19, Washington, D.C., U.S. Government Printing Office.

Finch, C., & Schneider, E. (Eds.) (1985). *Handbook of the biology of aging.* New York: Van Nostrand Reinhold.

Geokas, M. (Ed.) (1985). *The aging process—Clinics in geriatric medicine* (Vol. 1, No. 1). Philadelphia: W.B. Saunders.

Goldman, R., & Rockstein, M. (Eds.) (1975). *The physiology and pathology of aging.* New York: Academic Press.

Hall, D. (1984). *The biomedical basis of gerontology.* Littleton, MA: John Wright/PSG Publishing, Inc.

Jarvick, L.F., Greenblatt, M.D., & Harman, D. (1981). *Clinical pharmacology and the aging patient.* New York: Raven Press.

Kanungo, M.S. (1980). *The biochemistry of ageing.* London: Academic Press.

Kenney, R.A. (1982). *Physiology of aging: A synopsis*. Chicago: Yearbook Medical.

McGaugh, J.L. & Kiesler, S.B. (Eds.) (1981). *Aging: Biology and behavior*. New York: Academic Press.

O Hara-Devereaus, M., Andrus, L., & Scott, C. (Eds.) (1981). *Eldercare: A practical guide to clinical geriatrics*. New York: Grune & Stratton.

Palmore, E. (Ed.) (1974). *Normal aging II*. Durham, N.C.: Duke University Press.

Reichel, W. (Ed.) (1983). *Clinical aspects of aging* (3rd ed.). Baltimore: Williams & Wilkins.

Ries, W. (1974). Problems associated with biological age. *Experimental Gerontology*, 9: 145.

Rossman, I. (Ed.) (1979). *Clinical geriatrics*. Philadelphia: Lippincott.

Rowe, J.W., & Besdine, R.W. (Eds.) (1982). *Health and disease in old age*. Boston: Little, Brown.

Schaie, K.W., & Willis, S.L. (1986). *Adult development and aging,* 2nd ed. Boston: Little, Brown.

Shephard, R.J. (1978). *Physical activity and aging*. Chicago: Yearbook Medical.

Smith, E., & Serfass, R. (Eds.) (1981). *Exercise and aging: The scientific bases*. Hillside, N.J.: Enslow.

Sonstroem, R.J. (1984). Exercise and self-esteem. *Exercise and Sports Sciences Reviews*, 12: 123–155.

Stein, D.G. (Ed.) (1980). *The psychobiology of aging: Problems and perspectives*. New York: Elsevier.

Villaverde, M.M., & MacMillan, C.W. (1980) *Ailments of aging*. New York: Van Nostrand Reinhold.

Wantz, M.S., & Gay, J.E. (1981). *The aging process: A health perspective*. Cambridge, MA: Winthrop.

Whitbourne, S. (1985). *The aging body: Physiological changes and psychological consequences*. New York: Springer-Verlag.

Chapter 1   Introduction to Aging

Allen, C., & Brotman, H. (1981). *Chartbook on aging*. Washington DC: White House Conference on Aging.

Bier, W.C. (Ed.) (1974). *Aging: Its challenge to the individual and to society*. Bronx, N.Y.: Fordham University Press.

Bogue, D.J. (1969). *Principles of demography*. New York: John Wiley.

Durin, J.V.G.A., & Womersley, J. (1974). Body fat assessed from total body density and its estimation from skinfold thickness: Measurements on 481 men and women aged from 16 to 72 years. *British Journal of Nutrition*, 32: 77–97.

Forbes, G.B., & Reina, J.C. (1970). Adult lean body mass declines with age: Some longitudinal observations. *Metabolism*, 19: 653–663.

Fries, J.F. (1980). Aging, natural death and the compression of morbidity. *New England Journal of Medicine*, 303: 130–135.

Hall, D.A., Blackett, A.D., Zajec, A.R. et al. (1981). Changes in skinfold thickness with increasing age. *Age and Aging*, 10: 19.

Harris, C.S. (1978). *Fact book on aging: A profile of America's older population*. Washington D.C.: National Council on the Aging.

Kart, C., & Manard, B. (Eds.) (1976). *Aging in America*. Port Washington, N.Y.: Alfred Publishing.

Kent, S. (1980). The evolution of longevity. *Geriatrics*, 35 (1): 98–104.

Kimmel, D. (1974). *Adulthood and aging*. New York: John Wiley.

Ludwig, F., & Smoke, M.E. (1980). The measurement of biological age. *Experimental Aging Research*, 6: 497–522.

Matras, J. (1973). *Populations and societies*. Englewood Cliffs, N.J.: Prentice-Hall Inc.

Ostfeld, A.M., & Gibson, D.C. (1972). *Epidemiology of aging*. Bethesda, Md.: U.S. Department of Health, Education and Welfare.

Rose, C.L., & Cohen, M.L. (1977). Relative importance of physical activity of longevity. *Annals of the New York Academy of Sciences*, 301: 671–697.

Siegel, J., (1979). *Demographic Aspects of aging and the older population in the United States.* CPS, Special Studies, Series P-23, No. 78, Washington, D.C.: Bureau of the Census.

Soldo, B. (1980). America's elderly in the 1980s. *Population Bulletin,* 35 (4): 1–48.

U.S. Bureau of the Census (1976). Demographic aspects of aging and the older population in the U.S. *Current Population Reports,* Series P-23, no. 59. Washington D.C.: U.S. Government Printing Office.

Chapter 2   Theories of Aging

Curtis, H.J. (1963). Biological mechanisms underlying the ageing process. *Science,* 141: 686.

Hall, D.A. (1978). The ageing process—two theories explained. *Modern Geriatrics,* 8: 60.

Hall, D.A. (1981). The ageing of collagenous tissues: Genetic and random effects. *Journal of Clinical Experimental Gerontology,* 3: 201.

Harman, D. (1968). Free radical theory of aging: Effect of free radical reaction inhibitors on the mortality rate of male LAF mice. *Journal of Gerontology,* 23: 476.

Kohn, R.R. (1971). Effect of antioxidants on life-span of C57BL mice. *Journal of Gerontology,* 26: 378.

Lewis, C.M., & Tarrant, G.M. (1972). Error theory and ageing in human diploid fibroblasts. *Nature,* 239: 316.

Morrow, J., & Garner, C. (1979). An evaluation of some theories of the mechanism of aging. *Gerontology,* 25: 136–144.

Pantelouris, E.M.M. (1972). Thymic involution and aging: a hypothesis. *Experimental Gerontology,* 7: 73.

Rockstein, M., Sussman, M.L., & Chesdy, J. (Eds.) (1974). *Theoretical aspects of aging.* New York: Academic Press.

Salser, J.S., & Balis, ME (1972). Alterations in DNA bound amino acids with age and sex. *Journal of Gerontology,* 27: 1.

Schofield, J.D., & Davies, I. (1978). Theories of ageing. In Brocklehurst, J.C. *Textbook of Geriatric Medicine and Gerontology*, Edinburgh: Churchill Livingstone.

Slater, T.F., (1972). *Free radical mechanisms of tissue injury*. London: Pion Ltd.

Smith, K.C. (Ed.) (1976). *Aging, carcinogenesis, and radiation biology*, New York: Plenum Press.

Steffl, B.M. (Ed.) (1984). *Handbook of gerontological nursing*. New York: Van Nostrand Reinhold.

Walford, R.L. (1974). The immunologic theory of aging: current status. *Federation Proceedings, Federation of American Society of Experimental Biology*, 33: 2020.

Chapter 3   Cellular Aging

Cristofalo, V.J. (1972). Animal cell cultures as a model system for the study of aging. *Advances in Gerontological Research*, 4: 45–79.

Davies, I., & Fotheringham, A.P. (1981). Lipofuscin—does it affect cellular performance? *Experimental Gerontology*, 16: 119–125.

Hayflick, L. (1965). The limited *in vitro* lifetime of human diploid cell strains. *Experimental Cell Research*, 37: 614–636.

Hayflick, L. (1968). Human cells and aging. *Scientific American* (Mar) 218: 32–37.

Hayflick, L. (1979). The cell biology of aging. *Journal of Investigative Dermatology*, 73(1): 8–14.

Martin, G.M., Sprague, C., & Epstein, C.J. (1970). Replicative lifespan of cultivated human cells. *Laboratory Investigation*, 23: 86–92.

Reff, M.E., & Schneider, E.L., (Eds.) (1982). *Biological markers of aging*. NIH Publication No. 82–2221.

Schneider, E.L., & Mitsui, Y. (1976). The relationship between *in vitro* cellular aging and *in vivo* human age. *Proceedings of the National Academy of Sciences of the USA*, 73: 3584–3588.

Strehler, B.L. (1977). *Time, cells, and aging*. 2nd ed. New York: Academic Press.

Chapter 4   The Integument

Carnevali, D.L., & Patrick, M. (Eds.) (1986). *Nursing management for the elderly*, 2nd ed. Philadelphia: J.B. Lippincott.

Daly, C.H., & Odland, G.F. (1979). Age-related changes in the mechanical properties of human skin. *Journal of Investigative Dermatology*, 73: 84–87.

Dotz, W., & German, B. (1983). The facts about treatment of dry skin. *Geriatrics*, 38: 93.

Gilchrest, B.A. (1982). Age-associated changes in the skin. *Journal of the American Geriatrics Society*, 30: 139.

Lavker, R.M., Kwong, F., & Kligman, A.M. (1980). Changes in skin surface patterns with age. *Journal of Gerontology*, 35: 348–354.

Montagna, W. (Ed.) (1965). *Aging: Vol. 6. Advances in biology of skin*. New York: Pergamon Press.

Montagna, W., & Carlise, K. (1979). Structural changes in aging human skin. *Journal of Investigative Dermatology*, 73: 47–53.

Parker, F. (1983). Skin Tumors: Malignant and premalignant. *Geriatrics*, 38: 79.

Ridge, M.D., & Wright, W. (1966). The ageing of skin. *Gerontologia*, 12: 174.

Robinson, J.K. (1983). Skin problems of aging. *Geriatrics*, 38: 57–65.

Spencer, S., & Kierland, R. (1970). The aging skin problems and their causes. *Geriatrics*, 24: 81–89.

Thorne, N. (1981). The aging of the skin. *Practitioner*, 225: 793–800.

Verbov, N.J., (1974). *Skin diseases in the elderly*. London: Wm. Heinemann Medical Books.

Walther, R.R., & Harber, L.C. (1984). Expected skin complaints of the geriatric patient. *Geriatrics*, 39: 67.

Chapter 5 The Skeletal System

Adams, P., Davies, G.T., & Sweetname, P. (1970). Osteoporosis and the effect of aging on bone mass in elderly men and women. *Quarterly Journal of Medicine*, 39: 601–615.

Aloia, J.F., Cohn, S.H., Ostuni, J.A., Cane, R., & Ellis, K. (1978) Prevention of involutional bone loss by exercise. *Annals of Internal Medicine*, 89: 356–358.

Burstein, A.H., Reilly, D.T., & Martens, M. (1976). Aging of bone tissue: Mechanical properties. *Journal of Bone and Joint Surgery* (A), 58: 82–86.

Chapman, E.A., deVries, H.A., & Swezey, R. (1972). Joint stiffness: Effects of exercise on old and young men. *Journal of Gerontology*, 27: 218–221.

Fujii, K,. Kaboki, Y., & Sasaki, S. (1976). Ageing of human bone and articular cartilage collagen: Changes in the reducible cross-links and their precursors. *Gerontology*, 22: 363.

Hall, D.A. (1976). *Aging of connective tissue*. London: Academic Press.

Mazess, R.B. (1982). On aging bone loss. *Clinical Orthopaedics and Related Research*, 165: 239–252.

Pizer, H. (Ed.) (1983). *Over fifty-five, healthy and alive*. New York: Van Nostrand Reinhold.

Pogrund, H., Bloom, R.A., & Menczel, J. (1986). Preventing osteoporosis: Current practices and problems. *Geriatrics*, 41: 55.

Quinet, R. (1986). Osteoarthritis: Increasing mobility and reducing disability. *Geriatrics*, 41: 36.

Raisz, L.G. (1982). Osteoporosis. *Journal of the American Geriatrics Society*, 30: 127.

Smith, R., (1976). Bone disease in the elderly. *Proceedings of the Royal Society of Medicine*, 69: 925.

Stevens, M.B. (1983). Rheumatic disease: An overview of geriatric problems. *Geriatrics*, 38: 67.

Twomey, L,., Taylor, J., & Furiss, B. (1983). Age changes in the bone density and structure of the lumbar vertebral column. *Journal of Anatomy*, 136: 15–25.

Chapter 6   The Muscular System

Aniansson, A., Grimby, G., Nygaard, E., & Saltin, B. (1980). Muscle fiber composition and fiber area in various age groups. *Muscle and Nerve*, 2: 217–272.

Bassey, E.J. (1978). Age, inactivity, and some physiological responses to exercise. *Gerontology*, 24: 66–77.

Campbell, M.J., McComas, A.J., & Petito, F. (1973). Physiological changes in aging muscles. *Journal of Neurology, Neurosurgery and Psychiatry*, 36: 174–182.

Grimby, G., & Saltin, B. (1983). The aging muscle. *Clinical Physiology*, 3: 209–218.

Kasch, F.W. (1976). The effects of exercise on the aging process. *The Physician and Sportsmedicine*, 4: 64–68.

Kavanagh, T., & Shepard, R.J. (1977). The effects of continued training on the aging process. *Annals of New York Academy of Science*, 301: 656–667.

Moritani, T., & deVries, H.A. (1980). Potential for gross muscle hypertrophy in older men. *Journal of Gerontology*, 35: 673–682.

Orlander, J., & Aniansson, A. (1980). Effects of physical training on skeletal muscle metabolism and ultrastructure in 70–75-year-old men. *Acta Physiologica Scandinavica*, 109: 149–154.

Ringel, S.P., & Simon D.B. (1983). Practical management of neuromuscular diseases in the elderly. *Geriatrics*, 38: 86.

Sidney, K.H., & Shephard, R.J. (1978). Frequency and intensity of exercise training for elderly subjects. *Medicine and Science in Sports and Exercise*, 10: 125–131.

Chapter 7   The Nervous System

Ball, M.J. (1977). Neuronal loss, neurofibrillary tangles and granuovacuolar degeneration in the hippocampus with ageing and dementia. *Acta Neuropathologica*, 37: 111–118.

Brody, H. (1970). Structural changes in the aging nervous system. *Interdisciplinary Topics in Gerontology*, 7: 9.

Caird, F.I. (Ed.) (1982). *Neurological disorders in the elderly*. Bristol: John Wright & Sons.

Fields, W.S., (Ed.) (1975). *Neurological and sensory disorders in the elderly*. New York: Stratton.

Giacobini, E., Filogamo, G., Giocobini, G., et al. (Eds.) (1982). *The aging brain: Cellular and molecular mechanisms of aging in the nervous system*, Vol. 20. New York: Raven Press.

Gilmore, R. (1984). Movement disorders in the elderly. *Geriatrics*, 39: 65.

Greer, M. (1985). Recent developments in the treatment of Parkinson's disease. *Geriatrics*, 40: 34.

Mankovsky, N.B., Mints, A.Y., & Lisenyuk, V.P. (1982). Age peculiarities of human motor control in aging. *Gerontology*, 28: 314–322.

Mortimer, J.A., Pirozzola, F.J., & Maletta, G.I. (Eds.) (1982) *Advances in neurogerontology: The aging motor system*. New York: Praeger.

Ordy, J.M., & Brizzee, K.R. (Eds.) (1975). *Neurology of Aging*, New York: Plenum.

Ross, V., & Robinson, B. (1984). Dizziness: Causes, prevention, and management. *Geriatric Nursing*, Sept./Oct.: 290.

Rowe, T.W., & Troen, B.R. (1980). Sympathetic nervous system and aging in man. *Endocrinological Review.*, 1: 167–179.

Scheibel, A.B. (1982). Age-related changes in the human forebrain. *Neurosciences Research Progress Bulletin*, 20: 577–583.

Schneider, E.L., & Emr, M. (1985). Alzheimer's disease research highlights. *Geriatric Nursing*, 6: 136.

Severson, J.A. (1984). Neurotransmitter receptors and aging. *Journal of the American Geriatrics Society*, 32: 24.

Stein, D. (Ed.) (1981). *The psychobiology of aging: Problems and perspectives*. Amsterdam: Elsevier North Holland.

Terry, R.D., & Gershon, S. (Eds.) (1976). *Aging: Vol. 3, Neurobiology of aging*. New York: Raven Press.

Tyler, K.L., & Tyler, H.R. (1984). Differentiating organic dementia. *Geriatrics*, 39: 38.

Williams, L. (1986). Alzheimer's: The need for caring. *Journal of Gerontological Nursing*, 12: 21.

Yamaura, H., Ito, M., Kubota, K., & Matsuzawa, T. (1980). Brain atrophy during aging: A quantitative study with computed tomography. *Journal of Gerontology*, 35: 492–498.

Chapter 8   The Special Senses

Anderson, R.G., Simpson, K., & Roeser, R. (1983). Auditory dysfunction and rehabilitation. *Geriatrics*, 38: 101.

Babin, R.W., & Harker, L.A. (1982). The vestibular system in the elderly. *Otolaryngologic Clinics of North America,* 15: 387–393.

Balogh, K., & Lelkes, K. (1961). The tongue in old age. *Gerontologia Clinica*, 3: 38–54.

Bell, B., Wolf, E., & Bernholtz, C.D. (1972). Depth perception as a function of age. *Aging and Human Devleopment*, 3: 77–81.

Bergman, M. (1971). Hearing and aging. *Audiology*, 10: 164–171.

Corso, J.F. (1977). Presbycusis, hearing aids, and aging. *Audiology*, 16: 146–163.

Devaney, K.O., & Johnson, H.A. (1980). Neuron loss in the aging visual cortex of man. *Journal of Gerontology*, 35: 836–841.

Eifrig, D.E., & Simons, K.B. (1983). An overview of common geriatric opthalomologic disorders. *Geriatrics*, 38: 55.

Eisdorfer, C., & Wilkie, R. (1972). Auditory changes in the aged: A follow-up study. *Journal of the American Geriatrics Society*, 15: 188–190.

Grzegorczyk, P.B., Jones, S.W., & Mistretta, C.M. (1979). Age-related differences in salt taste acuity. *Journal of Gerontology*, 34: 834–840.

Hay, S.S., & Coons, D.H. (Eds.) (1979). *Special senses in aging: A current biological assessment.* Ann Arbor: Univ. of Michigan Press.

Hermel, J., Schonwetter, S., & Samueloff, S. (1970). Taste sensation and age in man. *Journal of Oral Medicine*, 25: 39–42.

Jerger, J. (1973). Audiological findings in aging. *Advances in Oto-Rhino-Laryngology*, 20: 115–124.

Kimbrell, G. McA., & Furchgott, E. (1963). The effect of aging on olfactory threshold. *Journal of Gerontology*, 18: 364–365.

Kornzweig, A.L. (1980). New ideas for old eyes. *Journal of the American Geriatrics Society*, 28: 145.

Mader, S. (1984). Hearing impairment in elderly persons. *Journal of the American Geriatrics Society* 32: 548.

Marshall, L. (1981). Auditory processing in aging listeners. *Journal of Speech and Hearing Disorders*, 46: 226–240.

Northern, J.L. (Ed.) (1976). *Hearing disorders.* Boston: Little, Brown.

Ordy, J.M., & Brizzee, K. (Eds.) (1979). *Aging: Vol. 10. Sensory systems and communciation in the elderly.* New York: Raven Press.

Sekuler, R., Hutman, L.P., & Owsley C. (Eds.) (1982) *Aging and human visual function.* New York: Alan R. Liss.

Weale, R.A. (1978). The eye and aging. *Interdisciplinary topics in gerontology*, 13: 1–13.

Chapter 9   The Circulatory System

Burch, G. (1977). The special problems of heart disease in old people. *Geriatrics*, 32: 51–54.

deVries, H.A., & Adams, G.M. (1977). Effect of the type of exercise upon the work of the heart in older men. *Journal of Sports Medicine and Physical Fitness*, 17: 41–48.

Harris, R. (1970). *The management of geriatric cardiovascular disease.* Philadelphia: Lippincott.

Hodgson, J.L., & Buskirk, E.R. (1977). Physical fitness and age, with emphasis on cardiovascular function in the elderly. *Journal of the American Geriatrics Society*, 25: 385–392.

Hossack, K.F., & Bruce, R.A. (1982). Maximal cardiac function in sedentary normal men and women: comparison of age-related changes. *Journal of Applied Physiology*, 53: 799–804.

Kolatata, G. (1977). The aging heart: changes in function and response to drugs. *Science*, 195: 166–167.

Pulliam, J.P., & McCarron, D.A. (1984). Hypertension: Special concerns in geriatric patients. *Geriatrics*, 39: 34.

Renlund, D.G., & Gerstenblith, G. (1986). Angina: Current approaches to diagnosis, drug therapy, and surgical referral. *Geriatrics*, 41: 35.

Robbins, A.S., & Rubenstein, L.Z. (1984). Postural hypotension in the elderly. *Journal of the American Geriatrics Society*, 32: 769.

Sleight, P. (1979). The effect of aging on the circulation. *Age and Aging*, 8: 98.

Weisfeldt, M.L. (Ed.) (1980). *Aging: Vol. 12. The aging heart: Its function and response to stress*. New York: Raven.

Chapter 10   The Immune System

Harrison, E.E., & Doubleday, J.W. (1975). Normal function of immunologic stem cells from aged mice. *Journal of Immunology*, 114: 1314–1317.

Harrison, D.E., Astle, C.M., & Doubleday, J.W. (1977). Stem cells from old immunodeficient donors give normal responses in young recipients. *Journal of Immunology*, 118: 1223–1227.

Kay, M.M.B. (1978) The effect of age on T-cell differentiation. *Federation Proceedings*, 37: 1241.

Makinodan, T., & Alder, W.H. (1975). The effects of aging on the differentiation and proliferation potentials of cells of the immune system. *Federation Proceedings*, 34: 153.

Makinodan, T., & Yunis, E. (Eds.) (1977). *Immunology and aging*. New York: Plenum Press.

Singal, S.K., Sinclair, N.R., & Stiller, C.R. (1979). *Aging and immunity*. New York: Elsevier.

Thompson, R.A. (Eds.) (1977). *Recent advances in clinical immunology*. New York: Churchill Livingstone.

Walford, R.L. (1970). Antibody diversity, histocompatibility systems, disease states and aging. *Lancet*, 2: 1126.

Walford, R.L. (1974). The immulogic theory of aging: Current status. *Federation Proceedings*, 33: 2020.

Chapter 11   The Respiratory System

Astrand, I., Astrand, P.O., Hallback, I., & Kilbom, A. (1973). Reduction in maximal oxygen uptake with age. *Journal of Applied Physiology*, 35: 649–654.

Brandstetter, R.D., & Kazemi, H. (1983). Aging and the respiratory system. *Medical Clinics of North America*, 67: 419–431.

Campbell, E.J., & Lefrak, S.S. (1978). How aging affects the structure and function of the respiratory system. *Geriatrics*, 33(6): 68–78.

Davies, C.T.M. (1973). The oxygen transporting system in relation to age. *Clinical Science*, 42: 1–13.

deVries, H.A., & Adams, G.M. (1972b). Comparison of exercise responses in old and young men: II. Ventilatory mechanics. *Journal of Gerontology*, 27: 349–352.

Gibson, G.J., Pride, N.B., O'Cain, C., & Quagliato, R. (1976). Sex and age differences in pulmonary mechanics in normal nonsmoking subjects. *Journal of Applied Physiology*, 41: 20–25.

Levitzky, M.G. (1984). Effects of aging on the respiratory system. *Physiologist*, 2: 102.

Lynne-Davies, P. (1977). Influence of age on the respiratory system. Geriatrics, 32: 57–62.

Chapter 12   The Digestive System

Albanese, A.A., (1980). *Nutrition for the elderly*. New York: Alan R. Liss.

Alford, B.B., & Bogle, M.L. (1982). *Nutritition during the life cycle.* Englewood Cliffs, N.J.: Prentice-Hall.

Bowman, B.B., & Rosenberg, I.H. (1983). Digestive function and aging. *Human Nutrition: Clinical Nutrition,* 37C: 75–89.

Brin, M., & Bauernfeind, J.C. (1978). Vitamin needs of the elderly. *Postgraduate Medicine,* 63(3): 155–163.

Dawson, J. (1986). Tips on nutrition. *Journal of Gerontological Nutrition,* 12: 37.

Driezen, S. (1974). Clinical manifestations of malnutrition, *Gerontology,* 29: 97–103.

Dychtwald, K., & MacLean, J. (Eds.) (1985). *Wellness and health promotion of the elderly.* Rockville, Md.: Aspen.

Eastwood, G.L. (1984). GI problems in the elderly. *Geriatrics,* 39: 59.

Evans, M.A., Triggs, E.J., Cheung, M., Broe, G.A., & Creasey, H. (1981). Gastric emptying rate in the elderly: Implications for drug therapy. *Journal of the American Geriatrics Society,* 29: 201–205.

Exton-Smith, A.N. & Caird, F.I. (Eds.) (1980). *Metabolic and nutritional disorders in the elderly.* Chicago: Year Book Medical Publishers.

Franz, M. (1981). Nutritional requirements of the elderly. *Journal of Nutrition for the Elderly,* 1: 39.

Freedmen, M.L., & Ahronheim, J.C. (1985). Nutritional needs of the elderly: Debate and recommendations. *Geriatrics,* 40: 45.

Geokas, M.C., & Haverback, B.J. (1969). The aging gastrointestinal tract. *American Journal of Surgery,* 117: 881–892.

Goodhart, R.S., & Shils, M.E. (Eds.) (1973). *Modern nutrition in health and disease.* Philadelphia: Lea and Febiger.

Harper, A.E. (1978). Recommended dietary allowances for the elderly. *Geriatrics,* 33: 73–80.

Karkeck, J.W. (1984). Assessment of the nutritional status of the elderly. *Nutritional Support Services,* 4: 23–33.

Kart, C.S., & Metress, S.P. (1984). *Nutrition, the aged, and society.* Englewood Cliffs, N.J.: Prentice-Hall.

Khan, A.H. (1984). Colorectal carcinoma: Risk factors, screening, and early detection. *Geriatrics*, 39: 42.

Kohrs, M.B. (1983). New perspectives on nutritional counseling for the elderly. *Contemporary Nutrition*, (8): 1.

Lamy, P.P. (1980). Drug interactions and the elderly—a new perspective. *Drug Intelligence and Clinical Pharmacy*, 14: 513–515.

Lamy, P.P. (1981). Nutrition and the elderly. *Drug Intelligence and Clinical Pharmacy*, 15: 887–891.

Metress, S.P. (1980) Food fads and the elderly. *Journal of Nursing Care*, 13: 10–13.

Miller, D.C. & Payne, P.R. (1968). Longevity and protein intake. *Experimental Gerontology*, 3: 231.

National Research Council. (1980). *Recommended dietary allowances, Revised 1980.* Washington D.C.: National Academy of Sciences.

Nelson, R.A. (1984). Clinical nutrition in the elderly: Its time has come. *Geriatrics*, 39(8): 15.

Nutrition and Your Health: Dietary Guidelines for Americans, 2nd ed. (1985) U.S. Department of Agriculture, U.S. Department of Health and Human Services. Hyattsville, MD

O'Hanlon, P., & Kohrs, M.B. (1978). Dietary studies of older Americans. *American Journal of Clinical Nutrition*, 31: 1257–1269.

O'Sullivan, J.B., Mahan, C.M., Freedlender, A.E., & Williams, R.G. (1971). Effect of age on carbohydrate metabolism. *Journal of Clinical Endocrinology and Metabolism*, 33: 619–623.

Poe, W.D., & Holloway, D.A. (1980). *Drugs and the aged.* New York: McGraw-Hill.

Posner, B.M. (1979). *Nutrition and the elderly.* Lexington, MA: Lexington Books.

Rao, D.A. (1983). *Geriatric Nutrition.* Englewood Cliffs, N.J.: Prentice-Hall.

Rockstein, M., & Sussman, M.L. (1976). *Nutrition, longevity and aging.* New York: Academic Press.

Roe, D.A. (1981). Drug interference with the assessment of nutritional status. *Clinical Laboratories of Medicine*, 1: 647–664.

Schiffman, S. (1977). Food recognition by the elderly. *Journal of Gerontology*, 32: 586–592.

Todhunter, E.N. (1980). Nutritional care of the elderly. *Food and Nutrition News*, 52: 1.

Watkins, D.M. (1983). *Handbook of nutrition, health, and aging*, Park Ridge, N.J.: Noyes Publications.

Weg, R. (1978). *Nutrition and later years.* Los Angeles: Univ. of Southern California Press.

Whanger, A.D., (1973). Vitamins and vigor at sixty-five plus. *Postgraduate Medicine*, 53(2): 167–172.

Winic, M. (1981). *Nutrition in health and disease.* New York: John Wiley.

Chapter 13   The Urinary System

Bell, D.P., & Frentz, G.D. (1983). Urinary tract infections in the elderly. *Geriatrics*, 38: 42.

Burton, J.R. (1984). Managing urinary incontinence—a common geriatric problem. *Geriatrics*, 39: 46.

Darmady, E.M., Offer, J., & Woodhouse, M.A. (1973). The parameters of the aging kidney. *Journal of Pathology*, 109: 195–207.

Epstein, M. (1979). Effects of aging on the kidney. *Federation Proceedings*, 38: 168–172.

Goyal, V.K. (1982). Changes with age in the human kidney. *Experimental Gerontology*, 17: 321–331.

McLachlan, M.S.F. (1978). The aging kidney. *Lancet*, 2: 143–146.

Paper, S. (1973). The effects of age in reducing renal function. *Geriatrics*, 28(5): 83-98.

Parsons, V. (1977). What decreasing renal function means to aging patients. *Geriatrics*, 32: 93.

Rosen, H. (1976). Renal disease in the elderly. *Medical Clinics of North America*, 60: 1105–1119.

Chapter 14   The Reproductive System

Burnside, I.M. (Ed.) (1975). *Sexuality and aging.* Los Angeles: University of Southern California Press.

Costello, M.K. (1975). Sex, intimacy and aging. *American Journal of Nursing*, 38: 1330.

Croft, L.H. (1982). *Sexuality in later life: A counseling guide for physicians.* Boston, Mass: John Wright.

Davidson, J.M., Chen, J.J., Crapo, L., Gray, G.D., Greenleaf, W.J., & Catania, J.A. (1983). Hormonal changes and sexual function in aging men. *Journal of Clinical Endocrinology and Metabolism*, 57: 71–77.

Davis, R.H. (Ed.) (1978). *Sexuality and aging.* Los Angeles: Univ. of Southern California Press.

Dean, S.R. (1974). Geriatric sexuality: Normal, needed and neglected. *Geriatrics*, 29: 134.

Edwards, A.E., & Husted, J.R. (1976). Penile sensitivity, age, and sexual behavior. *Journal of Clinical Psychology*, 32: 697–700.

Ellis, A., & Abarbenal, A. (Eds.) (1977). *The encyclopedia of sexual behavior.* New York: Jason Aronson.

Freeman, J.T. (1961) Sexual capacities in the aging male. *Geriatrics* 16: 37–43.

Hafez, E.S.E. (1976). *Aging and reproductive physiology.* Ann Arbor, Mich.: Ann Arbor Science Publishers, Inc.

Money, J., & Mousafh, H. (Eds.) (1977). *Handbook of sexology.* Amsterdam: ASP Biological and Medical Press.

Rubin, I. (1965). *Sexual life after sixty.* New York: Basic Books.

Schneider, E.L. (Ed.), (1978) *Aging: Vol. 4. The aging reproductive system.* New York: Raven Press.

Solnick, R.L., & Birren, J.E. (1977). Age and male erectile responsiveness. *Archives of Sexual Behavior*, 6: 1–9.

Yen, S.S.C. (1977). The biology of the menopause. *Journal of Reproductive Medicine*, 18: 287–296.

Chapter 15   The Endocrine System

Andres, R. (1971). Aging and diabetes. *Medical Clincis of North America*, 55: 835–845.

Andres, R., & Tobin, J.D. (1977). Endocrine systems. In C.E. Finch & L. Hayflick (Eds.), *Handbook of the biology of aging*. New York: Van Nostrand Reinhold.

Bennett, P.H. (1984). Diabetes in the elderly: Diagnosis and epidemiology. *Geriatrics*, 39: 37.

Dudl, R.J., & Ensinck, J.W. (1977). Insulin and glucagon relationships during aging in man. *Metabolism*, 26: 33–41.

Everitt, A.V., & Burgess, J.A. (Eds.) (1976a). *Hypothalamus, pituitary, and aging*. Springfield, Ill.: Charles C Thomas.

Gitman, L. (1967). *Endocrines and aging*. Springfield, Ill.: Charles C Thomas.

Green, M. (Ed.) (1981). *Clinics in endocrinology and metabolism: Endocrinology and ageing*. London: Saunders.

Greenblatt, R.B. (1978). *Geriatric endocrinology*. New York: Raven Press.

Gregerman, R.I., & Bierman, E.L. (1974). Aging and hormones, In R.H. Williams (Ed.), *Textbook of endocrinology* (5th ed.). Philadelphia: W.B. Saunders.

Korenman, S.G. (Ed.), (1982) *Endocrine aspects of aging*. New York: Elsevier Biomedical.

Root, A.W., & Oski, F.A. (1969). Effects of human growth hormone in elderly males. *Journal of Gerontology*, 24: 97–104.

Vernandakis, A. (Ed.) (1982). *Hormones in development and aging*. New York: Spectrum.

Index

age-related changes of, 229
Bypass surgery in coronary artery disease, 140

C
Calcitonin
  therapy in osteoporosis, 71
  thyroid secretion of, 243-244
    and bone formation, 61, 64
Calcium
  in bones, 59, 61
    loss in aging, 63
  in diet
    food sources of, 203
    and osteoporosis, 70, 71
    requirements for, 202
  functions of, 204
Calculi, renal, 219
Caloric requirements of elderly, 194
Calyx, renal, 207
Canaliculi of bones, 59
Cancer
  of bone, 71
  of breast, 231, 232
  of esophagus, 191
  of large intestine, 191
  of prostate, 218, 231
  of reproductive system, 231-232
  of skin, 44-45, 52-54
  of stomach, 191
Capillaries, 132
  age-related changes of, 21
  peritubular, 210
Carbohydrates, dietary, 178-179
  digestion of, 182
  requirements for, 195-197
Carcinoma
  of digestive system, 191
  of prostate, 218
  of skin, 53
Cardiac conditions. *See* Heart
Cardiovascular system, 126, 127-132, 133-145
  age-related changes of, 133-139
  age related dysfunctions of, 139-145
Cartilage, 56, 61-63
  age-related changes of, 64-66
  articular, 64
    in osteoarthritis, 67
Cataracts, 114
Cell(s), 27-42
  age-related changes of, 7, 10, 15, 16, 28,
    35-42

in aging by program theory, 18-19
cell-culture studies of, 18, 35-37, 41
in free radical theory, 22
in garbage accumulation theory, 22-23
in number of divisions, 18-19, 36, 37
in rate of division, 37
in blood, 127, 149
  age-related changes of, 133, 135
components of, 28-35
and intercellular substances, 15, 16
lipofuscin accumulation in, 22-23, 39, 41
of nervous system, 86, 87-89
  age-related changes of, 95-99
postmitotic, 15, 39, 86
renewal, in reserve, 18-19
types of, 15
Cell-mediated immune response, 151, 154
Cellular garbage theory of aging, 22-23
Central nervous system, 90-92
  age-related changes of, 95-98
  age-related dysfunctions of, 100-103
Centrioles, 35
Cerebellum, 91
  age-related changes of, 95
Cerebrospinal fluid, 90
Cerebrovascular accident, 102-103
Cerebrum, 90, 91
  age-related changes of, 95, 98
  cortex of, 90, 98
  functional areas of, 90
Cervix of uterus, 226
  cancer of, 231
Chicken pox, and herpes zoster, 52
Chlorine
  dietary requirements for, 202
  food sources of, 203
Cholesterol blood levels, 198
Chondrin, in cartilage, 61
Choroid, 107
  age-related changes of, 111, 112
Chromatin condensation in aging, 38-39
Chromatophilic substance, 98
Chromium, dietary requirements for, 202
Chyme, 182
Ciliary body, 107
  age-related changes of, 11
Ciliary muscles, 107
Circulatory system, 125-146
  age-related changes of, 133-139
    in cross-linkage theory, 21
    in eye, 112

age-related changes of, 178, 186-190
age-related dysfunctions of, 178, 190-194
and nutrition, 178-179, 194-202
smooth muscle of, 77
  age-related changes of, 81
structure and function of, 178-179, 180,
  181-186
Discs
intercalated, of cardiac muscle, 77-78, 79
intervertebral, age-related changes of, 65-66
optic, 109
Diuresis, 213
Diverticula of digestive tract, 81
Diverticulitis, 81, 191-192
Diverticulosis, 189
Division of cells, age-related changes of, 18-19
in number of divisions, 18-19, 36, 37
in rate of division, 37
validity of cell-culture findings on, 36, 37
Dizziness, 120-121
DNA, nuclear, 29-34
age-related changes of, 37, 38-39
in cross-linkage theory of aging, 21
in gene mutation theory of aging, 20
Dopamine levels in Parkinson's disease,
  100-101
Drug metabolism in aging
kidney changes affecting, 215
liver changes affecting, 190
Dryness
of mouth, 187
of skin, 49, 51
Ductus deferens, 225
Duodenum, 183

E
Ear, 115-121
age-related changes of, 118-119
age-related dysfunctions of, 119-121
external region of, 115, 116, 118
inner region of, 116, 117, 118, 119, 121
middle region of, 116, 117, 118
ringing noise in, 120
structure and function of, 115-118
Earwax, 117, 118, 120
Efferent (motor) division of peripheral nervous
  system, 92
Ejaculation, age-related changes in, 234
Ejaculatory duct, 225
Elastic cartilage, 61, 62
Elastic recoil of lungs, 168

age-related changes of, 170
Elderly persons, definition of, 8
Embolism
in coronary artery disease, 140
pulmonary, 175
Emphysema, 172-173
Endocardium, age-related changes of, 135
Endocrine system, 237-250
age-related changes of, 238-240, 246-249
  in aging by program theory, 17
age-related dysfunctions of, 249-250
antidiuretic hormone in, 213, 241, 247
and bone development, 61
  in osteoporosis, 70-71
hormones of reproductive system in, 223,
  225, 226, 246
  age-related changes of, 228, 229, 230
receptors for homones in, 240
secretion of hormones in, 240-241
structure and function of, 238-246
Endocrinocytes, interstitial, 223
Endolymph, 117, 118
Endometrium of uterus, 226, 228
age-related changes of, 230
Endoplasmic reticulum, 34
Energy requirements of elderly, 194, 195
Environmental factors in respiratory
  dysfunctions, 172
Enzymes
in accumulation-of-errors theory of aging, 23
cellular production of, 32
in cross-linkage theory of aging, 20
digestive, 182, 188
  from pancreas, 183, 185, 189
and vitamins as coenzymes, 198
Epidermis, 45, 47
age-related changes of, 48
Epididymis, 225
Epinephrine, adrenal secretion of, 244-245
Epiphyses of bones, 57
Epithelium of digestive system, 182
Equilibrium and balance
age-related changes of, 119
and dizziness, 120-121
role of ear in, 117
Erection of penis, 225
age-related changes of, 229, 234
Esophagus, 181-182
age-related changes of, 187
carcinoma of, 191
in hiatal hernia, 190-191

Mucus (*cont.*)
    in respiratory system, 161
        in bronchitis, 173-174
        in emphysema, 173
Multi-infarction dementia, 103
Muscular system, 73-83
    age-related changes of, 10, 78-81
        respiratory function in, 171
    age-related dysfunctions of, 82
    bladder and urethral muscles in, 214
        age-related changes of, 216
    cardiac muscle in 77-78, 79, 81, 128
        age-related changes of, 81, 135
        lipofuscin granules in, 40, 81, 135
    in eye movements, 110
    in myasthenia gravis, 82
    in Parkinson's disease, 82, 100, 101
    skeletal muscle in, 75-77, 78-81, 82
    smooth muscle in, 77, 81
    structure and function of, 74, 75-78
Mutation of genes in aging, 19-20
Myasthenia gravis, 82
Myelinated neurons, 89
Myocardium, 128
    infarction of, 141
Myofibrils of skeletal muscle, 75
    age-related changes of, 80
Myofilaments of skeletal muscle, 75

N
Nails, finger and toe, age-related changes of, 49
Nasal cavity, 161
Nearsightedness, 110
Nephrons, 210, 211
    age-related changes of, 216
Nerve(s), 87
    cranial, 92
    optic, 109
    spinal, 92, 93
    vestibulocochlear, age-related changes of, 119
Nerve cells, 87. *See also* Neurons
Nerve impulses, 89
    age-related changes of, 97
    in heart, 128-130
Nervous system, 85-104
    age-related changes of, 8, 17, 86-87, 95-99
    age-related dysfunctions of, 82, 99-103
    in Parkinson's disease, 82, 100-101
    structure and function of, 86, 87-95

Neuritic plaques, development in aging, 98, 102
Neurofibrillary tangles, development in aging, 98, 102
Neuroglia, 89
    age-related changes of, 98
Neurohypophysis, 241
Neurolemmocytes, 89
Neuromusclar junctions, 75
    age-related changes of, 81
    in myasthenia gravis, 82
Neurons, 87, 88
    age-related changes of, 95-99
    association, 87
    lipofuscin accumulation in, 97
    motor, 87, 88, 92
        age-related changes of, 80-81
    myelinated, 89
    postsynaptic, 89, 94
    presynaptic, 89, 94
    sensory, 87, 88, 92
    unmyelinated, 89
Neurotransmitters, 89
    age-related changes of, 99
    in Parkinson's disease, 100
Niacin, 200
Nissl bodies, 98
Norepinephrine
    adrenal secretion of, 244-245
    as neurotransmitter, 89
        age-related changes of, 99
Nose, runny, 161
Nucleus of cells, 29-34
    age-related changes of, 38-39, 80
Nucleus pulposus, 66
Nutrition, 178-179, 194-202
    antioxidants in, 22, 41, 200
    and bone development, 61
    carbohydrates in, 178-179, 182, 195-197
    and diverticulitis, 192
    fats in, 179, 182, 195, 197-198
    and gouty arthritis, 69
    and hypertension, 145
    loss of teeth affecting, 186
    minerals in, *See* Minerals, dietary
    and organic brain syndrome, 101
    and osteoporosis, 70, 71
    proteins in. *See* Proteins, dietary
    recommended dietary allowances in, 195, 196

and sense of taste, 121-123
vitamins in. *See* Vitamins
water in, 201-202

O
Obstruction, intestinal, 194
Obstructive pulmonary disease, 172
chronic, 174
Occupation, and aging of skin, 45
Old and very old persons, definition of, 8
Optic disc, 109
Optic nerve, 109
Organ of Corti, 117
Organelles of cells, 28-29, 30, 34-35
Organic brain syndrome, 101-102
Ossicles, 117
Osteoarthritis, 67
Osteocoytes, 59
Osteomalacia, 200
Osteoporosis, 69-71, 200
Oval window of ear, 117, 118
Ovarian cycle, 226-228
Ovary, 223, 225, 226
age-related changes of, 230
Ovulation, 226
Oxygen
blood levels, age-related changes, 169, 170
maximum consumption of, 136
age-related changes of, 136, 137
Oxytocin, 241

P
Pacemaker of heart, 130
Pain
in angina pectoris, 141-142
in back, 66
esophageal, 187
in herpes zoster, 52
in osteoarthritis, 67
receptors in dermis for, 48
age-related changes of, 49
Pancreas
age-related changes of, 189, 248-249
in diabetes mellitus, 249-250
digestive functions of, 183, 185, 189
endocrine functions of, 185, 245-246,
248-250
hormones of, 245-246
Pancreatitis, 189
Pannus formation in rheumatoid arthritis, 68
Pantothenic acid, 196, 199, 200

Paranasal sinuses, 161
Parasympathetic nervous system, 92, 94, 95
age-related changes of, 99
Parathyroid gland, 238, 244
age-related changes of, 247-248
hormones of, 244, 247-248
and bone development, 61, 64
Parkinson's disease, 82, 98, 100-101
Pelvic floor muscles in urinary incontinence,
216-217
Pelvis, renal, 207
Penis, 225
age-related changes of, 229
Pepsin, 182
Perilymph, 117, 118
Periodontal disease, 186
Peripheral nervous system, 92-95
age-related changes of, 95
Peristalsis, 181
age-related changes of, 187
Pharynx, structure and function of, 161-163,
181-182
Phosphorus
dietary requirements for, 202
food sources of, 203
functions of, 204
Photoreceptors in retina, 107-109
age-related changes of, 111, 112
Pigments
in hair, in aging, 49
lipofuscin. *See* Lipofuscin
melanin, 47, 48, 50
Pituitary gland, 238, 241-243
age-related changes of, 246-247
hormones of, 241-243, 246-247
Plaque formation
in arteries, 144
coronary, 139-140
on heart valves, 135
neuritic, 98, 102
Plasma, 127
age-related changes of, 133
Plasma cells, 150
Plasma membrane of cells, 29, 31
age-related changes of, 38
Platelets, 127
Pleura, 165
Pleural cavity, 165
Pleural fluid, 165
Pneumonia, 174
Podocytes, 210, 212

Population of elderly persons, 4-7
  and mortality rate in younger age groups, 5, 14
  ratio to total population, 4
  sex ratio in, 5
  trends in, 4-5
Postmitotic cells, 15
  mitochondria in, 39
  in nervous system, 86
Postsynaptic neurons, 89, 94
Potassium
  dietary requirements for, 202
  food sources of, 203
  functions of, 204
Presbycusis, 119
Presbyopia, 110, 112-113
Pressure sores, 50, 52
Presynaptic neurons, 89, 94
Progeria, 36-37
Progesterone secretion, 223, 226
  age-related changes of, 230
Programmed aging theory, 17-19
Prolactin, 241, 243
Prolapse of uterus, 232
Prostate gland, 214, 217-218, 225
  age-related changes of, 229
  cancer of, 218, 231
  hyperplasia of benign, 217-218
Proteins
  in accumulaltion-of-errors theory of aging, 23
  cellular production of, 29-34
    age-related changes of, 38
  in cross-linkage theory of aging, 20-21
  dietary, 179, 195, 196, 197
    digestion of, 182
    in kidney disorders, 197
    requirements for, 195, 196, 197
    sources of, 197
Pruritis
  in herpes zoster, 52
  senile, 51
Pulmonary trunk, 128
Pulmonary valve, 128
Pulmonary veins, 128
Pupil of eye, 107
  age-related changes of, 111
Pyelonephritis, 218-219
Pyloric sphincter, 182
Pyramids, renal, 207

R
Rate of aging, individual differences in, 9-10
Receptors
  photoreceptors in retina, 107-109
    age-related changes of, 111, 112
  sensory, in dermis, 47-48
    age-related changes of, 49
Recreational activities, and aging of skin, 45
Rectum, 183
  cancer of, 191
Red blood cells, 127, 149
  age-related changes of, 133
Red bone marrow, 57, 127, 135, 149
  age-related changes of, 155
Reflexes, 92
  age-related dysfunctions of, 99-100
Reproductive system, 221-234
  age-related changes of, 222, 228-231
  age-related dysfunctions of, 231-234
  female, 225-228, 230-231, 232, 238
  male, 223-225, 228-229, 231, 233
  structure and function of, 222-228
Research methods
  animal studies in, 3-4
  cell-culture studies in, 35-37, 41
  longitudinal and cross-sectional studies in, 3
Respiratory system, 159-176
  age-related changes of, 8, 11, 160, 168-172
  age-related dysfunctions of, 172-175
    structure and function of, 160, 161-168
Reticulum, endoplasmic, 34
Retina, 107-109
  age-related changes of, 111, 112
  age-related dysfunctions of, 114-115
  detachment of, 115
  senile degeneration of macular area, 114
Rheumatoid arthritis, 67-69, 157
Riboflavin, 196, 199, 200
Robosomes, 32, 33, 34
Ringing of ears, 120
RNA
  in aging by program theory, 18
  in protein synthesis, 32-34
Rods and cones, 107, 109
Round window of ear, 117

S
Saccule, 117
  age-related changes of, 119
Saliva, 181

284

Tunica of digestive system, 181
Tunnel vision in glaucoma, 114
Twin studies in age at death, 19
Tympanic membrane, 117
  age-related changes of, 118

U
Ulcers, decubitus, 50, 52
Ureters, 207, 213
Urethra, 207, 214
  age-related changes of, 216-217
  sphincters of, 214
    age-related changes of, 216
Uric acid levels in gouty arthritis, 69
Urinary system, 205-220
  age-related changes of, 214-217
  age-related dysfunctions of, 217-219
  in prostate gland disorders, 217-218, 229
  structure and function of, 206, 207-214
Urination, 214
  awareness of need for, in elderly, 216
  incontinence of, 216-217
  in prostate disorders, 217-218, 229
Urine, 206, 213
  age-related changes of, 215
  retention of, in elderly, 216
Uterine tube, 226
  age-related changes of, 230
Uterus, 226, 228
  age-related changes of, 230
  cervical cancer of, 231
  prolapse of, 232
Utricle, 117
  age-related changes of, 119

V
Vagina, 226
  age-related changes of, 230-231
    and sexual functioning, 234
  atrophic vaginitis of, 232
Vaginitis, atrophic, 232
Valves of heart, 128
  age-related changes of, 135
Vasoconstriction, 132
Vasodilation, 132
Veins, 131, 132
  age-related changes of, 138
Venae cavae, superior and inferior, 128
Ventricles
  of brain, 90
    age-related changes of, 95
  of heart, 128

Venules, 132
Verbal ability, age-related changes in, 96
Vertebral column
  age-related changes of, 64-66
  in osteoporosis, 70, 71
Vestibule of ear, 117
Vestibulocochlear nerve, age-related changes
    of, 119
Villi of small intestine, 183, 184
Viral infections, herpes zoster in, 51-52
Visceral neurons, motor and sensory, 92
Vision
  age-related changes of, 110-112
  age-related dysfunctions of, 112-115
  role of eye in, 107-110
Vitamin A, 196, 198-199
Vitamin B_6, 196, 199, 200
Vitamin B_{12}, 196, 199, 200
Vitamin C, 196, 199, 200-201
  as antioxidant, 22
Vitamin D, 196, 199, 200
  and bone development, 61, 200
Vitamin E, 196, 199, 200
  as an antioxidant, 22, 200
Vitamin K, 196, 199, 200
Vitamins
  fat-soluble, 196, 198-200
  requirements for, 195, 196, 198-201
  sources of, 199
  water-soluble, 196, 198, 199, 200-201
Vitreous humor, 109
  age-related changes of, 111
  in detachment of retina, 115

W
Water. *See* Fluids
Wear-and-tear theory of aging, 24, 67
Weight changes in aging, 11
White blood cells, 127, 149
White matter, 90, 92
  age-related changes of, 95
Wrinkles of skin, 49, 231

Y
Yellow bone marrow, 57, 135, 149

Z
Zinc
  dietary requirements for, 202
  food sources of, 203
  functions of, 204